ASIA'S ROLE IN GLOBAL POLITICS

ASIA'S ROLE IN GLOBAL POLITICS

Edited by
Dr M D Dharamdasani

2007

CENTRE FOR ASIAN & EUROPEAN STUDIES,
JAIPUR

SBS PUBLISHERS & DISTRIBUTORS PVT. LTD.
NEW DELHI

ISBN : 81-89741-40-3

INDIAN PRICE - RS 795

FIRST PUBLISHED IN INDIA IN 2007

Published by:
SBS PUBLISHERS & DISTRIBUTORS PVT. LTD.
2/9, Ground Floor, Ansari Road, Darya Ganj,
New Delhi - 110002, INDIA
Tel: 23289119, 41563911
Email: mail@sbspublishers.com

Preface

The twenty first century is now widely considered to be the Asian Century. Since Asia constitute one of the most important region and civilization of the world cherishing the values of democracy, pluralism and liberalism, it is therefore appropriate to have an objective analysis of these values. Further, the political and economic changes currently sweeping the world have given added importance to the region of Asia. There has been resurgence of public level opinion at the popular and governmental level that efforts should be made to create cooperation and understanding among the Asian country to resolve the problems created due to the wave of globalization. Furthermore in order to face the problems created due to unipolar world dominated by the United States, the Asian Countries like European Union should come closer politically and economically. In this respect we can think of Japan's initiative to reorient its foreign policy to come closer to India. India on its part is also rethinking to revive its concept of Asianization and Asian values to have better relations with both China and Japan.

Keeping in view the above analysis, the Centre for Asian and European Studies is presenting the volume which broadly covers papers on Asia's Role in Global Politics.

The first paper is written by Prof. Farooq Hassan which deals with the impart of post 9/11 international developments on the peace process underway between India and Pakistan. Dr. Maharjan in his paper on Japan's Role in South Asia has described Japan's ODA role in Nepal's economic developments. Prof. M.D. Dharamdasani has critically examined India's security concerns in South Asia with special reference to India's interests and objectives in Nepal.

Prof. Y. Yagama Reddy deals with the geographical importance of the region. He believes that ASEAN cannot ignore the negative aspects of region's geography. Prof. Murthy in his paper on capital inflows in ASEAN deals with advanced countries capital contribution to ASEAN Nations. Dr. T. Nirmala Devi in his paper on Economic Cooperation deals with India-ASEAN experience. Dr. J.D. Khand in his paper on East Timor's independence describes how UN and people of East Timor had played significant role in Timor's independence. Prof. Furuoka and Mikio Oishi in their joint paper has described Japan's relations with the ASEAN countries. Dr. Bama Dev Sigdel in his paper has analyzed experiences of Economic reforms in China with special reference to Privatization and FDI. Dr. Aparajita Biswas deals with Japan's relations with African nations especially Japan's aid relations.

Dr. Ashwini Mohapatra has analyzed in his paper the causes and factors of religious terrorism. Prof. Satyanarayan in his paper has analyzed trends in Trading Patterns of Asia-Pacific countries. Shri A.K. Sahoo in his paper on Transnational Networks of Indian Diaspora has dealt with Indian migration with particular reference to Australia. Ms. Yachana in her paper on Security concerns and refugees in South Asia has co-related the problems of refugees with the national security of a given country.

The editor of the volume wishes to express his gratitude towards the authors for their scholarly papers. We do hope that this volume will be of great help to the scholars and students working in this area. Last but not least, I wish to express my thanks to family members especially wife Smt. Vimla, sons Ashok and Dinesh for their untiring support for this project.

Dr. M.D. Dharamdasani

Contents

Contributors

Biswas, Aparajita, Director, Centre for African Studies, Bombay University, Mumbai.

Devi, T. Nirmala, Centre for SAARC Studies, Andhra University, Vishakapatnam.

Dharamdasani, M.D., Director, Centre for the Study of Nepal, Benaras Hindu University, Varanasi.

Furuoka, Fumitaka, University Malaysia Sabah.

Hassan, Farooq, Professor of Laws & Foreign Affairs, Presently President of the Boston based American Institute of South Asian Strategic Studies.

Khand, Jitendra Dhoj, Central Department of Political Science, Tribhuvan University, Kathmandu.

Maharjan, Pancha N., Centre for Nepal and Asian Studies, Tribhuvan University, Kathmandu.

Mohapatra, Ashwini, School of International Studies, Jawahar Lal Nehru University, New Delhi.

Murthy, Gautam, Centre for Indian Ocean Studies, Osmania University, Hyderabad

Oishi, Mikio, Department of Political Science, University of Canterbury, New Zealand.

Reddy, Y. Yagama, Centre for Studies on Indo-China & South Pacific, Sri Venkateshwar University, Tirupati.

Sahoo, Ajaya Kumar, Centre for Study of Indian Diaspora University of Hyderabad.

Satyanaranyan, B., Emeritus Professor of Economics, Osmania University, Hyderabad.

Sigdel, Bama Dev, Deputy Director, Research Department, Nepal Rashtra Bank, Kathmandu.

Yachana, Ms., Department of Sociology, CCS University, Meerut (U.P.).

1

India-Pakistan Peace Initiatives
Strategic Implications

*Farooq Hassan**

One of the most significant post 9/11 international developments of far reaching transnational significance is the current Peace process underway between India and Pakistan. In many fundamental ways the current initiative from India and Pakistan emanated from the wider regional ramifications that occurred in this region after October 2001 when Afghanistan was invaded by the U.S. troops.

Amongst the major effects of this war was the displacement of the Taliban regime, otherwise until that time strongly and solely supported by Islamabad. However, that change of regime led to a series of connected implications involving regional as well as international repercussions. The presently visible détente between India and Pakistan, I believe, is one monumental though

* The author is a Senior Advocate Supreme Court of Pakistan, Barrister at law of England & an Attorney at Law of the U.S.; also David M. Kennedy Visiting Scholar & Professor of International Studies, Kennedy Center BYU & Visiting Professor, Fellow, Center for International Affairs, Harvard University. The author has been Advisor to four Pakistani Prime Ministers on Foreign Affairs & Law, Member & Delegate to the UN Human Rights Commission, and the UN Sub Commission on Human Rights, Geneva. He is also the current President of the Boston based American Institute of South Asian Strategic Studies.

unanticipated result of this strategic change in the geo-political situation in the South Asia.

It is the purpose of this work to briefly examine the extent of the prospects these fundamental changes in Sub-Continental politics. This transformation has infinite possibilities of ushering in an era of progress and prosperity for the over a billion plus population of these two countries. The strategic, political, economic and intellectual implications arising from this phenomenon are diverse and difficult to predict with precision at the present time. An attempt, however, is made in this analysis to foresee the probable practical eventualities of the prospects of continued peace by keeping in view, the known and perceived policies of the two countries.

But before adverting to this prognosis, it would be helpful, even necessary, to have in our focus, the policies of the U.S. in this region generally and with regard to the current détente, if any. As the solitary global super power, and after 9/11 visibly in pursuit of pro-active foreign policies and priorities, its approach to a fundamental transformation in the Sub-Continental politics deserves to be evaluated.

U.S. Interests in Sub-continent: Historical Background

After the creation of the new Dominions of India and Pakistan in 1947, in contrast to India's growing involvement with many major powers, Pakistan's links were almost entirely with Washington. But domestic changes in Pakistan and the Sino-Indian border disputes of the early sixties altered all that.

Initial Indian reaction, which I might call as the "traditional" approach of Delhi towards coups in general, Prime Minister Nehru rebuked the Pakistan government under General Ayub Khan as "naked military dictatorship".[1] Although India did not do anything rash, it soon got militarily embroiled with China in border disputes along its northern frontiers.[2] However, because of Anglo-American pressures on Ayub Khan, Pakistan did nothing to add to India troubles at that time.

Pakistan while keeping itself unconnected with these occurrences, yet realized that both India and China were formidable military powers and that the armed conflicts between them were too close to her frontiers to give her any comfort.[3] While being not unhappy at the ease with which China prevailed in these borders tussles, Islamabad realized that it too had to carefully weigh its options in territorial disputes with India.[4]

Yet such awareness not withstanding, armed conflict between Pakistan and India erupted in 1965. From Washington's perspective, it signaled a failure of an important element of its foreign policy in the Sub-Continent. Since the early sixties, Washington had attempted to keep a balance between both states by connecting all aid, particularly to Islamabad by conditioning it to an absence of armed hostilities between them.[5] Since the Vietnam War the U.S. foreign policy has largely been predicated by a priority to keep Washington aloof from international involvements generally unless its vital "security" was threatened.[6]

With this over-riding policy priority in view, we have to now see just how important is to the United States the Sub-Continent? Is it vital, as a national security matter that the Sub-Continent, or countries thereof are not hostile toward Washington? Or is it that the answer lies somewhere in between, that is that the area is important in at last some respects, but as a geographical region that has little of immediate impact on U.S. vital interests? Further, in light of the declared nuclear position of the two major Sub-Continental powers, India and Pakistan, does the Sub-Continent acquire automatically a status of permanent vigilance for the U.S.? If so does it require a similarity of treatment for both these countries from the U.S.? Or is that it is Pakistan that must be monitored more anxiously?[7] Lastly what is the significance of the element of so-called "Islamic fundamentalism" in Pakistan's domestic and external policies and does this issue *per se* qualitatively tantamount to a "security interest" of Washington? An allied inquiry would be clearly with regard to Pakistan role in the current U.S. war against terrorism and whether such a role makes the region of "vital strategic interests" to the US?[8]

I must admit that there is no easy way to answer all such questions with great precision. This partly due to the nature of the area. It is also not easy, furthermore, to do so since a number of political developments underlying these concerns are still in process of evolving. This is particularly evident in respect of the last three questions posed above. It is not within the purview of this work to go into the diverse facets of the war against terrorism alluded to in these questions; however it is safe to submit that a least until the U.S. war against terrorism is perceived to be still on by Washington, Islamabad's present importance to the U.S. is bound to remain in tact. However, with armed hostilities in Afghanistan assuming a secondary position since the U.S. invaded Iraq in March 2003, it is legitimately arguable that Pakistan's erstwhile priority niche in the Pentagon's planning has decreased and will continue to do so.[9]

Former Defense Secretary Robert McNamara as far back as 1966 described the essential *historical foundational ingredients* of the importance of the Sub-Continent to Washington when he said:

> *"South Asia has become, through a combination of circumstances and geography, a vital strategic area in the present context between the expansionist and non-expansionist power centers. In friendlier hands or as non-aligned states, South Asia can be a bridge between Europe and the Far East and a major physical barrier to the Southward expansion of Red China and the USSR; in hostile hands, it would seal the long term hope of building a free Asian Coalition able to provide counterweight to an expansionist China."*[10]

True some important practical and ground realities underscored in this statement have changed since 1966 and are no longer relevant. It is also clear that this view manifestly overstated the importance of this region to the U.S. by giving it an expansive base of significance that never reflected the actual situation to impress upon the Congress the Administration's needs of that time. Similarly the perceived threat from the north was also an exaggeration made out for political needs of that Administration. Admittedly absent also is the presence of any known and substantial natural resources of this region to qualify it *per se* as a "vital" interest of Washington.

But two most important postulates emphasized in this policy statement are still apparently valid as they were in historical terms over thirty years ago.[11] These essential elements in my view being:

1. The significance of South Asia regional politics in the global geo-political priorities of the U.S.[12]
2. The clear intent of the U.S. that this region does not fall under wrong or "hostile hands."[13]

These present basic postulates of the American foreign policy vis-à-vis South Asia are truly reflected in the post 9/11period. The preservation of the *status quo* remains, in my submission, a paramount objective of the U.S. policies in South Asia. The avoidance of chaos and anarchy in this region are manifestly evident in numerous U.S. declarations made in the last two years. In 2002 and early 2003 when India and Pakistan were looking to conceivably be at war soon, the U.S. duly led the international efforts to prevent such a catastrophe from occurring.

The chaos that the U.S. has tried to prevent from erupting can possibly emanate from two divergent causes. First is the threat, now clearly receded, of a nuclear confrontation between the countries. Such a horrible scenario can in theory arise out of just plane mishandling of ongoing political differences. Secondly is the theory that Islamabad's possible actions against the "fundamentalists" could conceivably result in unpredictable domestic and regional upheavals.[14]

Whether such causation criteria would stay and maintain its present form is difficult to predict since it is linked with the sustenance of such a phenomenon.[15] The U.S. has come to recognize that through elections it is difficult to completely prevent such possibilities. The political rise of religious elements from emerging cannot be easily prevented by elements that would rather see the retention of secular forces staying to continue to be in command. Elections in Turkey and Pakistan since 9/11 have amply proved this thesis. Indeed, already evidence is coming to light that after the initial ousting of the Taliban, U.S. has "lost" some of its zeal.[16]

Such noticeable vicissitudes notwithstanding, however, it is high on American priorities that this region can be kept as clam as possible. However, to prevent such chaos from occurring, can the U.S. go as far as it did in Afghanistan? With the most recent developments in Iraq, it is doubtful if this is a serious possibility. Short of actual involvement, though, Washington would do much to prevent such eventualities.

In the current phase of initiatives for peace both India and Pakistan have been intelligently cognizant of the international realities that exit since 9/11. Both countries are manifestly aware that in an highly charged international atmosphere, it was only prudent that, at least for the time being, the erstwhile attitudes towards each other be put aside for more active peace oriented policies. There are many cogent reasons for this awareness, but the most obvious is to keep the area free of direct involvement of outsiders. India's immediate strategic gain has been to satisfy an old need that Pakistan stop its help to cross border attacks on its people in Kashmir. Publicly admitted to by Pakistan is the fact that behind the scenes the U.S. has been actively assisting this process.[17]

The Current Détente

Having examined briefly the U.S. traditional and possibly current interests in South Asia, we can examine the salient characteristics of the on going bettering of relations between the two countries.

Since April 2003 when Premier Vajpayee made his opening diplomatic overture of friendship to Pakistan, clearly matters between the two nuclear armed neighbours have steadily improved. On most public related matters of interest, art, sports, or say journalism, there has been tremendous improvement, even high level of cordiality witnessed between the peoples of the two countries. So much so that in the recently concluded Cricket matches, which India convincingly won, there was much talk of describing them as "friendship series".

Considering that barely two years ago the armies of the two nations stood eyeball to eye to eyeball along hundreds of miles of their frontiers, this is surely a most welcome state of affairs. There is no gainsaying the fact that were the present dynamics, both at the public and governmental level, to stay the course, it would add to the happiness and prosperity of the teeming millions of peoples of both countries.

However, the question, which we must face as an intellectual matter as social scientists, is to see how far all that is now in evidence is for real and expected to endure the vicissitudes of time and political dynamics of both international and domestic proportions.

I have advisedly used the words "public" and at the "governmental" levels. There is no doubt in my mind that the people to people contact now being strengthened will grow. The more difficult, even uncertain matter is to correctly evaluate or predict the quality and extent of progress at the "governmental" levels. An allied and important inquiry would be to identify which of the two governments fundamentally wants substantial and a real détente. If both want a state of real friendship to emerge then no problem should theoretically arise, as bilateralism is the key to the success of any genuine betterment of relations.

Although I have been to nearly 130 countries in the world, only recently I had my first chance to visit India for the first time when I went to address an international conference at the JNU. I must confess at realizing, happily I might add, that in the fields that fundamentally matter to states, Constitutional governance, education and national policies towards intellectual pursuits, Indian attitudes and philosophy is at par with the highest levels for such activities anywhere. Indeed in acknowledgement of these facets of Indian life, I publicly wrote in one of my op e d pieces[18] recently that it is not the possession of nuclear weapons that make and count towards the strength of a country but its adherence to the rule of law that does so.[19] In particular I observed:

> *"While those in Islamabad go on harping about Pakistan's invincibility because of Dr. Qadeer, few have the courage to admit our political backwardness, vis-à-vis for instance India, in constitutional evolution under which even the courts, let alone those in other institutions of state, are too happy to agree that on some medieval perceptions of "state necessity" Constitutions can be torn asunder at any time by a local military commander."*[20]

Herein lies, in my view the genesis of the answer to the question of whether the current detente is for real and will last or not. Whether harmony and reconciliation is achieved and is far reaching in effect is in my view entirely dependent on the relevant characteristics of the two states that may now be very briefly analyzed in its essential component constituents.

Let us start with India. It is the largest working democracy in the world. Its state institutions, particularly its Executive, Legislature and its Judiciary work within their allotted constitutional spheres. I have never seen its Army being described as an "institution of state". It has many large minorities and has resultantly difficult problems. There are more Muslims in India than in Pakistan. Minorities have asserted, at times rightly in my view that they have suffered. The "core" issue of divergence between the two neighbours, according to the Pakistani Government, is that Kashmir, in Indian physical control since the creation of either country. It has since last few years India has a booming economy and out sourcing by many giant multinationals in its Bangalore region has made it a thriving prospect for financial houses of the world. In addition to the information technology this region has made astounding strides towards excellence in the manufacture of advanced biomedicines. This is amply reflected by growth rate of over 8% in its economy.

Pakistan, on the other hand, has most unsettled political processes in evidence, a non-existent observance of peoples' rights, weak state institutions including judiciary, and an over-bearing and politically minded army leadership that has repeatedly indulged in coups d' Etat.[21] In the economic domain, the decline in international interest rates and the after effects of 9/11 have combined to produce a bulging reservoir of foreign exchange. However, industry and investment are stagnant, and with inflation rising, poverty has actually increased from where it stood in 1999 when Musharraf took over.

So if the main irritant between the two countries *arguendo* were to disappear, or become a non-issue for the time being at least anyway, what immediate and long term affects the countries would encounter?

As far as India is concerned, politically it has to genuinely cherish such a goal. Not only an absence of tension allow its focus of attention to shift from being constantly on the look out for *ad hoc* political and military actions in its North Western frontiers, it can help it considerably in dealing perhaps constructively meaningfully with its large Muslim minority. In addition its economy will clearly benefit by a decrease in its non-development expenditures.

But there is a school of thought that maintains that the new Indian initiative was based on pragmatic grounds of domestic political compulsions. The BJP led Administration was cognizant of the fact that apprehensions existed in the rest of the Indian population, particularly in the Muslims of its staunch right wing religious sympathies. As such to negate the perception and indeed the impression that it had anything to do with the recent Gujarat riots in which 2000 Muslim reportedly perished or to deny the Congress of its traditional large Muslim electoral support, that Mr. Vajpayee and his think tank decided to turn a leaf in its relations with Pakistan. In sum, according to this view, the present Indian attitude is fundamentally guided by the electoral priorities that the BJP is currently faced with and not with any deeper considerations emanating from a sense of improving relations with Islamabad *per se*.

Personally, I discount this thinking altogether. Had such been the case, Mr. Vajpayee would never have come to Lahore in January 1999 and indeed gone to the Minar — a Pakistan and accept the nationhood of this country. Even otherwise the language used by him in talking of Pakistan has never been of the variety to hide any such feelings of animosity. I do not recall any rhetoric either where this scenario was reflected. But more importantly, in the last three years in the aftermath of 9/11 international developments, India never used in a meaningful manner, from its perspective, any issue that could have complicated Musharraf's volte-face on the point of Islamabad's long standing support of the Taliban. Similarly Mr. Vajpayee did not utilize the plethora of evidence that Pakistan historically had been a constant supporter of the "fundamentalists" in this region. In Pakistan most people still do not think that the description of "fundamentalist" should be used in a pejorative sense. Perhaps a majority of the Islamic populations also would be of the same view. However, there is no gainsaying the awareness that as a term of art as used by the Western press, this phrase does convey since the occurrences of 9/11 some element of aggression and rigidity.

An important factor in support of this perspective that Mr. Vajpayee has been quite upfront about this new attitude relates to the Pakistani attack on the Kargill in early 1999. The Indian Premier against Musharraf has never used this military and strategic misadventure reportedly undertaken by Islamabad in a way that could have been done. Diplomatically it could have proved most embarrassing for the military establishment in Pakistan in the aftermath of the international relations of the post 9/11 era since all powers in the country since October 1999 vest in Musharraf. I am thus of the view that Mr. Vajpayee has been substantially sincere in approaching his country's relations with Islamabad *de novo* with a view to the establishment of genuine cordiality between the two countries

Let us now take a look at Pakistan and the available theoretical and practical considerations to evaluate her *bona fides* in the current political progress. The most obvious point that has to be realized is a manifest realisation regarding Pakistan's formidable military prowess. Pakistan's raison d 'etre of possessing a substantial and large military establishment's is her professed fear of India.[22] If *ex hypothesi*, such a state of affairs were to emerge that such fears become irrelevant or not possible to realistically visualize, then how would one explain the present size or the maintenance of large expenditures on such an establishment that is a huge burden on the national exchequer?

My point is simple. How can the leadership of the size of the army that Pakistan possesses, demolish the very basis that justifies that size? With the meager resources of the country being largely taken in to support such a huge establishment, Islamabad has already, on numerous occasions, been advised by world monetary and financial institutions to decrease and cut down its non-development expenditures. Vital human and civil sectors of the country, dealing with such matters as health, education and communication are already receiving less than 3% of the total budgetary allocations of the country. Poverty *per se* is the largest source of unstable social conditions and the constantly deteriorating law and order situation that generally essentially prevails in the country.

In understanding this matter it is also crucial to keep in mind the tremendous political significance that the army leadership in the country has acquired by the sheer power of its resources in the body politic of the country. Is it realistically possible that any army leadership can relinquish all this bounty and largesse willingly?[23] Surely if the perceived *casus belli* with India were to hypothetically disappear or put in abeyance as a result of the current détente, the scenario I am envisaging would have to be faced by any military establishment in Islamabad.

As such it is not a mere coincidence that in the last dozen years on two important occasions when the purely civilian leadership tried to increase its level of friendship with India, the army leadership reacted with suspicion and distrust.[24] We cannot also be unmindful of the reality that at the time when the two previous major wars between the two countries took place the army leadership had the reins of political control in Islamabad. Since history is the surest guide to fore tell the expected future course of evolution, one has to carefully but with some degree of surety predict, that despite Musharraf's overtures of everlasting friendship to Mr. Vajpayee, when the crunch time arrives, the present Pakistani Government would not be as swift in moving ahead as some may think the present course of evolution may demand.

One has still to know for instance for sure what really happened in Kargill in 1999? Was it a misadventure indulged in by the civilian Pakistani Government under Prime Nawaz Sharif's orders?[25] Or, as has been hinted at by many including President Clinton, that it was the result of the thinking of only General Musharraf.[26] In sum, therefore, I am of the view that as long as Pakistan does not have a validly elected Government working under the Constitution, inter-governmental cordiality presently seen involving Pakistan is more an outcome of opportunistic outlook by Islamabad rather than a genuinely felt need of the history of this age.

What has been articulated above is fully in accord with recent history and deducible normative behavioral pattern of Pakistani motivations in approaching the current détente. However, I am also fortified in making this assessment also on the basis of available concrete evidence.

Is it, for example, not surprising that despite the present climate of high good will, all official TV channels of and from India are still forbidden to be seen here and cannot be broadcast by Cable operators in Pakistan by specific banning edicts of the Musharraf regime? Why? Is it not surprising that in the 9 PM daily news bulletin of the Official

Pakistan Television (PTV) India bashing is still very much an integral part of the Pakistani news? Does it not prove, as I see it, that the present Musharraf regime is keeping the anti-India rhetoric very much alive, though somewhat restricted for some patently non-deceptive motive? Is the Pakistani official electronic media to be used along with its dissemination apparatus, if a "need" arises? Conversely preventing the Pakistani public from seeing what officially the Indian channels are openly disseminating is tantamount to keeping them attuned merely to the PTV sermonized broadcasts?

I think another reality in this context is the fact that I believe that that the present military regime fervently wants to hide from the 140 million people of Pakistan the vibrant presence of democratic values in India. This is so for two reasons:

1. The fact is that we have currently no such representative system in evidence in Pakistan. Indian information about its system would prove highly embarrassing to an unrepresentative Administration still essentially controlled by the army in such a blatant manner that the country's "Prime Minister" refers to his Army Chief as his "Boss".
2. That it *prima facie* weakens Islamabad's case in the domestic and international fora for a plebiscite in Kashmir. If the people of Pakistan cannot have a duly and fairly elected Administration in the country, a case can hardly be made of having one in Kashmir through the same process despised by the military regime in the country itself.

Sadly, therefore the people of Pakistan are still being dished out blatantly the supposed benefits of Stalinist type ideas of governance through the state run and controlled media. It is a form of rulership that all military governments in Pakistan find most difficult not to extol and eulogize.

Such devices are, however, as faulty as they are bereft of any meaningful voice of reality. People in Pakistan, as in India may be poor and even largely uneducated. But they know the basic truths about their own governors. No amount of stopping the reaching of Indian TV stations can convince the people in Pakistan that non-elected Presidents and one man tailor made Constitutions are democratic.[27]

Thus a question arises: why did the Musharraf regime, manifestly after the 9/11 occurrence in the U.S., go so concertedly after a patch up routine with the Vajpayee Administration?

This fact is based on a realisation by Islamabad, I believe, on two important considerations. Before we articulate these two major motivations, however, it would be helpful to initially comprehend the ethos of the prevalent factual situation.

At the time of the 9/11 tragedies because of Musharraf's coup of October 1999, Pakistan already stood more or less internationally ostracized. The manifest absence of an elected Government in Pakistan at that time led to Pakistan's suspension from the Commonwealth. That suspension still continues. Similarly, Washington had imposed fairly crippling sanctions on Islamabad. This was a mandatory legal consequence as a result of the violation of the human rights clauses under which the U.S. cannot aid any country under it Foreign Assistance Act of 1961 if there is the absence of a civilian government in a country.[28] Similarly, the European Union had passed Resolutions criticizing the assumption of power of Musharraf.[29]

As such the Musharraf regime was in a literal sense desperate not to further antagonize India since it could not afford a confrontation of a political kind with both the secular forces[30] and the religious ones led by the Jamait-a-Islami (JI) and Jamai-Ulema-a-Pakistan (JUI) as well from across the eastern borders of the country. It was in a political sense a necessity that persuaded the military establishment to become "friendlier" with India to ward off any possibility of becoming more actively engaged in diverse fronts than could be handled at one time.

The two main reasons that certainly prompted Musharraf to cultivate India in this manner are therefore:

1. The realisation that by preventing India from agitating against the military government's domestic denial of civil liberties, it would gain at least time for undertaking more damage control measures for maintaining its domestic hegemony over political power in the country.
2. To ensure that in the much-changed international political environment, Pakistan got the necessary American support for its domestic agenda despite being admittedly a non-democratic Government.[31] Elections were held in Pakistan in October 2002 but with such extensive state control mechanisms and manipulation as well as under such changed constitutional provisions that no parliamentary system in the world functions as things are now occurring in Pakistan since these elections took place. No one really that matters, such as the Commonwealth, accepts that these elections have resurrected the civilian nature of the government in Islamabad.

As such the realities of the present detente as I see them are that while India would like this process to continue, it depends more on the political fortunes of the present military regime in Pakistan whether in fact that would continue to remain visible in the future

The process might well continue if the current political and regional *status quo* somehow maintains itself. But it surely is dependent on the chances of the continuity of the Musharraf regime. But one factor over which the Musharraf regime cannot probably reverse the process is the process that has now emerged as a result of the current enhanced peoples' contact.

One new element, however, deserves some comment. This has come to light, as I am about to complete the text of this article. As this element has intimate connection with the subject of this script, I may now briefly advert to it.

Newspaper reports suggest that on 19th April Musharraf visited Lahore and held long meetings with the Punjab Chief Minister, Governor and met many elected members of the ruling party from the largest Province of Pakistan. It appears that he is now setting his eyes on becoming the political head of the Muslim League, the collection of individuals belonging formerly to Nawaz Sharif but now handily available to his "successor" Zafarullah Jamali who is willing to extend his full support to the Musharraf regime. Despite being a Prime Minister in a parliamentary system, he has no qualms in accepting the role of the second fiddle when it comes to the running of the Federal Government. Musharraf has now apparently revealed overt ambitions of entering the political process as head of a political party of the country. Even after most reluctantly agreeing to step down as Chief of Army in 2004, Musharraf has now strongly indicated through several Ministers of the present Government that he is allowed to keep both his current position of Presidency and that of the head of the country's armed forces beyond the year 2004.[32]

This scenario does not auger well for Pakistan. Elections are won on different principles than Machiavellian maneuverings as a military dictator. The only way Musharraf, with all the help he may get in doing so by all State institutions, can win any type of election in contemporary Pakistan, is by adopting a visibly anti-U.S. and anti-Indian stance in any election that he may thus eventually contest. His political pitch in such an election, must of necessity also focus on Kashmir, which he has, somewhat mutedly of late still referred to as the "core issues" between India and Pakistan.

He can hardly expect India to accept this proposition as such. Resultantly it is not impossible to visualize a lessening of cordiality as a result of such an evolution from India as well towards the Musharraf regime.

This possible scenario is further strengthened by the slow but steady deterioration of Pakistan's relations with Kabul and indeed with the U.S. diplomats there. Although the strategic ingredients of this equation are different, yet for convenience Musharraf could easily lump them in India's lap. Already there are verbal battles going on between the U.S. envoy to Afghanistan Zalmay Khalizad and the Foreign Office Spokesman of the Pakistani Government. Both seem to blame each other for what Pakistan is allegedly doing or not doing adjacent to the boundary between Pakistan and Afghanistan.

With Musharraf seriously flawed record against the very concept of Rule of Law he can hardly expect to be in any position to win any non-military establishment support anywhere.[33] Even if all these maneuvers and intrigues alluded to above were to achieve successes, it will only firmly establish Musharraf as a military dictator who is willing to go to any extent to save his position.

I doubt whether President G.W. Bush, even if he wins the next election can stomach such a dictator *in simpliciter ad infinitum*; this "dictatorship formula" after all goes against his November 6th 2003 speech on the Middle East when he said he wished the establishment of genuine democratic Islamic regimes. Most observers think that remark was principally directed against Pakistan, rather than Arab states since in such countries "democracy' as such has another meaning.

In the context of the topic of this article, this scenario is hardly encouraging. Musharraf seems to be following in the exact footprints of the earlier military dictators of Pakistan, Ayub, Yayha and Zia. All three, in difficulties of their making, choose or tried to, go to embark upon hostilities with India and adopted strategies that failed them. In the process, Pakistan suffered irreversible damage. It lost its prevalent Constitutions in two cases and half the country in the third.

Hopefully, therefore, domestic politics in Pakistan and regional policies of the concerned powers do not allow this to occur under yet another military ruler in Islamabad. In this context he role that Washington might play is really crucial. As the sole superpower, it has larger interests in this region, as detailed earlier, to see that relations between India and Pakistan remain on harmonious footing. The American Government has already described India as "an emerging power". With Pakistan's "strategic need" for the U.S. bound to lessen soon enough,[34] and the issue of nuclear proliferation far from closed as some might wish it to be, there are fair chances, that despite the pessimistic possibilities pointed out by me, Washington may ensure that the blossoming of tranquil relations between the two countries is not jeopardized by usurpation tendencies of Islamabad's current military rulership.

In sum, good relations with India, from Pakistan's perspectives objectively, are dependent on the respect and prevalence of Rule of Law and Constitutionalism in Islamabad.[35] I am convinced that real questions of war and peace are better handled by representative governments as they have perspectives in view and interests at heart that can never be arrogated by self proclaimed protectors or by those who usurp public trust and authority. Lack of democratic system in Pakistan is thus not only a threat to the wider strategic prospects of peace between the two major South Asian countries, it poses acute dangers to the unity and cohesion of the country itself.[36]

REFERENCES

1. See Brands, *India, Pakistan & the Great Powers*, 1972, p. 158.
2. India was initially quite puzzled by non-manifest U.S. support keeping in mind the declared American position by which it considered China as a regional "threat". However, in a major speech in Delhi on August 8, 1962 Ambassador Galbraith explained his government's position and urged restraint lest it might worsen the cold war implications. Two former U.S. Ambassadors to India

Chester Bowles and John Sherman Cooper, despite their overt friendship with India had shared such views.

3. See Wayne A. Wilcox, *India, Pakistan and the Rise of China*, 1964.
4. *Ibid.*, p. 75.
5. See President Johnson's declaration that no further said would be given until India and Pakistan worked out an understanding for living more peacefully, *The New York Times*, September 30, 1965.
6. See Brands, *op cit.*, where it said: "We seldom recognize one unique aspect of America's experience in world affairs...its lack of involvement except when confronted with an acute threat to its security", p. 257.
7. This concern is based on the of repeated American pronouncements that (1) it considers it vitally important that Islamabad's nuclear assets do not fall into "wrong hands", (2) the internal security of Pakistan is very unpredictable, and (3) the lack of a settled political system on account of frequent military adventurism in the affairs of the State.
8. The "wana" operation started in Pakistan's Musharraf regime against "rebellious" foreign and local elements (of the fundamentalist variety) in South Waziristan on 15th March 2004, in military terms failed. The Economist opined that though Islamabad admitted to losing around 50 solders, actually lost over 150. This first major armed action within Pakistan by its military after 1971 has opened up another wide area of concern and raised many questions that have to be comprehended and understood by the Pakistan Administration if adverse fallout to the security interests of the state have to be avoided.
9. For instance in the 3rd week of April 2004 it was officially announced in Pakistan by the relevant quarters that American use of its airbases, particularly in Sindh at Shabaz had all but been given up by the US.
10. Testimony of March 30,1966, Foreign Assistance Act of 1966: hearings Before the Committee on Foreign Affairs, House of Representatives, p. 269.
11. See Brands, *op cit.*, "The same considerations suggest that the traditional American view that it is in U.S. interests that India and Pakistan retain their national identity and territorial identity was correct.", p. 267.
12. This has manifest relevance with regard to the nuclear status of the to major Sub-Continental states, to matters relating to nuclear proliferation and the potential position of India as an emerging regional "power".
13. The concept of "wrong hands" remains though its "identity" has changed. At that time it was the Communist dominated north, now conceivably the " Islamic fundamentalists" would be considered to be equally opposed to it by Washington.
14. See note 8 Supra.
15. Much stress has been laid in this respect by the Bush Administration to continue the war against "terrorism" as long as it takes. But it is doubtful if it will really be long-lasting keeping in mind the current crisis in Iraq and the rising spiral of anti-American feelings in the area.

16. See for instance the testimony of Richard Clarke, former Chief of Anti-Terrorism in the White House before the 9/11 Commission. He maintains that by going after other political targets like Iraq, "which had nothing to do with international terrorism", already U.S. has seemingly lost long-term interests in acting against international terrorism.
17. See, for instance, the statement of Foreign Office Spokesman of Pakistani Government in Nawa-I-Waqt, 25 April 2004.
18. See *The Nation*, 21st March 2004.
19. See *Op cit.* where I say: "No wonder in inter se comparisons with Pakistan, the highest Government functionaries of even the U.S. have to say that "India is an emerging Power." I do not think by this description they mean a nation with a few atomic and hydrogen bombs. They surely mean a country with a growing international clout with a settled democratic base."
20. See *Ibid.*
21. On 14 April in a BBC Hard Talk interview, Musharraf publicly admitted that in Pakistan the Office of the Chief of Army Staff was most important, as the Army was the most important institution of the State. Since this assertion is nowhere mentioned in the Constitution, it is manifest that open pronouncements of this nature can be made (clearly amounting to a subversion of the Constitution) because instead of principles, expediency has the upper hand in the Pakistani body politic. See further a monographic work of the author: *A Juridical Critique of Successful Treason, Stanford Journal of International Law*, 1984, 191.
22. However see Nawai-Waqt, 19 April 2004, which reproduces a Statement by Air Marshall (rtd.) Asghar Khan that both the 1965 and 1971 war with India was started by Pakistan and not India.
23. See note 4 Supra. It is astonishing that to a major foreign journalistic organization such as the BBC Musharraf openly admitted to this fact
24. In early 1990 when Benazir Bhutto was the Prime Minister and then in 1999 when Nawaz Sharif held this office, newspaper reports are supportive of the perspective that such moves towards "cordiality" vis-à-vis India were not approved by the army high command. Indeed, General Musharraf who held the highest army office in Pakistan in 1999 is reported to have refused to show the courtesy of appropriate protocol to the visiting Indian Prime Minister on his arrival at Lahore at the Wagah border.
25. See the Statement of former Primer Nawaz Sharif that a commission be appoint to see how Kargill crisis was created, Nawa-I-Waqt, 28 April, 2004
26. See The News, &The Dawn, 26 April 2000, detailing the speech made during the Islamabad 4 hour stop over by President Clinton regarding the coup of Musharraf against the Sharif Government. Also see note 23 ibid in which this scenario is impliedly contained.
27. On the advent of the New Year, 2004, General Musharraf, went through the

apparent "juridical" exercise of having the five Elected Assemblies of the Federation and the constituent Provinces repose "confidence in him to remain as "President" until 2007. He had on the previous date 31/12/03 signed into effect the 17th Amendment to the Constitution. This was to absorb his LFO (a military edict called Leal Framework Order) to gain a tailor made document through which he could feign, howsoever feebly, that he was the President of the Republic when dealing with the world community. The timing of this move was blatantly linked specially keeping in mind the SAARC conference in Islamabad between the 4th to the 6th January 2004. His initial "election" as President through the extra-constitutional Referendum that I had challenged on behalf of the major Opposition Political Parties in the Supreme Court had held this measure to be "extra-constitutional".

28. There has never been any election to the Office of the President of Pakistan since December 1997. As such there is no doubt that factually no election has been ever held in which Musharraf got elected to any Office, let alone that of the President. Whether it is the Referendum or the purported vote of confidence or a judgment of any court, no one ever contested any such an electoral tussle.
29. See e.g., 2003 EUEOM 99 page Report on the state of "democracy" in Pakistan.
30. Represented by Benazir Bhutto, of the Pakistan People's Party, and Nawaz Sharif, of the Pakistan Muslim League. Both have been Premiers twice each during the decade of the nineties in Pakistan. Both are in exile from Pakistan at the moment.
31. Important to note is the "voting" for the President's Office held recently for Musharraf's benefit. He was the only candidate to contest under the "amended" Constitution. Out of the total vote cast in the Federal Parliament; Mushharraf only obtained 56% of the vote suggesting that his landslide alleged showing, 97%, during the Referendum was entirely false. Secondly, he lost the majority vote in both the Frontier and Baluchistan Provinces. He therefore does not represent the Unity or the Symbol of the Federation, which is a constitutional requirement under Article 41of the Constitution. In the Federal Assembly he barely got the needed majority by gaining 191 voted which is one less than obtained by Prime Mister Jamali at the time of his confidence vote. Overall by proportionate calculations, the formula of which is contained in the Second Schedule of the Constitution, Musharraf only got 53.28 percent of the vote. So with all the arm-twisting, bribery and straightforward duress that the Pakistani Governments are infamous for historically for the self-perpetuation of an incumbent administration or office holder, Musharraf's showing is abysmal.
32. Under the 17th Amendment to the Constitution enacted by Musharraf himself, he must relinquish one of the two offices he holds by 31st December 2004.
33. Musharraf in January 2000 dismissed the Chief Justice and the six Senior Judges of the Supreme Court who refused to accept his new Oath of Allegiance

to him alone. It is still quite embarrassing that Pakistan, arguably the most important Islamic nation, has, a non-elected military chief of army staff as the country's President! On the other hand it cannot be denied that India has elected a Muslim intellectual to be the Republic's President.

34. But see the statement of Secretary of State Colin Powel on 16th March 2004 in Islamabad that because of its assistance to U.S. in its war against terrorism, Pakistan was "a non NATO ally." Exactly what this means is unclear and whether such a status can be conferred without congressional approval is questionable.
35. See generally present author's recent book, Pakistan: Constitutionalism Restored? 1997.
36. The National Security Act demanded by Musharraf was enacted into law in the Senate of Pakistan in less than three minutes in April 2004. A controversial head of state like Musharraf and a parliament that enacts such fascist type legislation which allows the four army chiefs to sit and advise and monitor civilian institutions in the country hardly augers well for the country's "democratic credentials". There is no gainsaying the fact that it is none of the business of the army of any country to so openly interfere in the politics of that state. It is more than likely that a serving general who has taken over the supreme authority of a state is more concerned with multifarious problems dealing with his "legitimacy" than with real and live substantive and delicate questions relating to diplomatic progress in a region.

2

Japan in South Asia
A Case Study of Japan's ODA Role in Nepal's Development

Pancha N. Maharjan

Foreign aid is a vital instrument for economic development. After the Second World War, U.S. foreign aid played a significant role in the economic development of the European countries and Japan. Between 1947 and 1951 U.S. had donated $ 14.2 billion under the Marshall Plan to sixteen Western European countries in order to help them recover their economy. Similarly, the U.S. had also played a major role to reconstruct the post-war economy of Japan. Under the war reparation scheme, Japan received first World Bank loan of U.S. $ 40.2 million to the power sector. In 1954 Japan joined the Colombo Plan. Later, it signed agreements with the countries — Burma, the Philippines, Indonesia, and South Vietnam. These countries were bound to buy the Japanese products under the agreement. For instance, in 1960 Burma imported 69%, the Philippines 31% and Indonesia 43% machinery products of Japan (Fuwa 1999: 3). Japan's war reparation agreements with these countries became most fruitful for Japan's economic development. In this way, foreign aid played a crucial role in the booming of Japanese economy. In a way, Japan started to increase its Official Development Assistance (ODA) to the developing as well as least developed countries. Japan's assistance is concentrated mostly in Asian countries from the very beginning. For instance, Japan's first ODA loan of Yen 18 billion was extended to India in 1958 (*Ibid*: 4). Similarly, this region was successful to drag 50% of Japanese assistance in 1961-64 and could maintain 70% during 1965-70 to 1980. But, after 1980 onward, its assistance slightly declined. Out of 44 major recipient countries of Japan's Bilateral ODA, mostly Asian countries are in top ten positions (Annexures 1 and 2). Observing the growing Japanese interest in South Asia, this paper tries to analyze the role of Japan in Nepal's development.

Japan and the SAARC

All the countries of South Asia fall under the status of developing nations. During the post world war period, economy of the countries was based on agriculture. Even in this millennium, only a few countries could proceed in an industrial process in a small scale and they are still dependent on agriculture. In the process of industrialisation, cordial relationship of the South Asian nations with Japan helped to mobilize foreign aid and also to transform technology. All of these countries had established their diplomatic relations with Japan only after 1950, for instance, India, Pakistan and Sri Lanka in 1952, Nepal in 1956, the Maldives in 1967, and Bangladesh in 1972. All these countries are successful to maintain good relations with Japan. The countries have not only maintained economic relations but have cultural relationship too. This is manifest from the exchange of people between the people in the respective countries of South Asia and Japan. For instance, 6422 Bangladeshi nationals are living in Japan and 412 Japanese are in Bangladesh. Similarly, 35 Bhutanese, 13 Maldivians, 3212 Nepalese, 5052 Sri Lankan, 6550 Pakistani, and 9067 Indian people are living in Japan. In its response, 47 Japanese people are living in Bhutan, 102 in the Maldives, 868 in Sri Lanka, 810 in Pakistan, and 2050 in India. Among the countries, Bhutan and the Maldives have less exchange of nationals living in the respective countries (See Table 1).

Regionally, though Japan has given a first priority of its ODA aid disbursement to Asia, South Asia comes only as the third priority — Southeast Asia is in the first, ASEAN in the second and Southwest (South Asia) Asia is in the third. For instance, out of Japan's ODA disbursement amount of $ 5,372 m. (62.4%) to Asia, Southeast Asia received $ 2,438 m. (28.3%), ASEAN received $ 2356 m. (27.4%) and South Asia received only $ 1,463 m. (17.0%) in 1998 (Annexures — 3 and 4). Similarly, Japan has made direct investment in Bangladesh with an amount of Yen 22.8 billion in 1999; Yen 23.2 billion in India in 1999; Yen 3,105 million in the Maldives in 1997; Rs. 840 million in Nepal during 1998. 7-2000.3, $ 13.9 million in Pakistan in 1999; and Yen 77.79 billion in Sri Lanka in 1999 (Table 1).

Table 1: Relation between the SAARC Countries and Japan

SAARC Countries	*Diplomatic Relations Established in*	*Nationals of SAARC Countries Living in Japan*	*Nationals of Japan Living in SAARC Countries*	*Direct Investment*
Bangladesh	1972	6422 (Dec. 1998)	415 (Oct. 2000)	Y 22.8 bil. ('99)
Bhutan	1986	35 (Dec. 1999)	47 (Oct. 1999)	—
India	1952	9067 (Dec. 1999)	2050 (Oct. 1999)	Y 23.2 bil. ('99)
Maldives	1967	13 (Dec. 1999)	102 (Oct. 2000)	Y 3,105 mil. ('97)
Nepal	1956	3212 (Dec. 1999)	408 (Oct. 2000)	Rs. 840 mil. (1998.7-2000.3)
Pakistan	1952	6550 (Dec. 1999)	810 (Oct. 2000)	$ 13.9 mil. ('99)
Sri Lanka	1952	5052 (Dec. 1999)	868 (Oct. 2000)	Y 77.79 bil. ('99)

Source: "Japan's Relations with SAARC Countries e.g., Japan-Nepal Relations", *http://www.mofa.go.jp/region/asia-paci/Bhutan,Bangladesh,India,Maldives, Nepal,Pakistan,Sri Lanka/*

Foreign aid from the U.S. and the European powers was basically concentrated mostly in the European countries. Similarly, Prime Minister Toshiki Kaifu's visit to European countries in January 1990 also facilitated an aid package of U.S. $ 1.95 billion to Poland (Molla 1997: 48). But, soon after his visit to Europe, his diplomatic tour in five countries of Asia — India, Pakistan, Bangladesh, Sri Lanka and India in May 1990, emphasis was given on Japan's ODA to Asia (*Ibid*: 49). As a result, South Asia was included in Japanese ODA priority list. And, within a very short period, India, Pakistan, Sri Lanka and Bangladesh from South Asia stood as the largest recipient of Japanese aid. However, Nepal, Bhutan and the Maldives fail to attract the Japanese funding. During 1996-1998, India, Pakistan, Sri Lanka and Bangladesh figured within the top ten positions among Japan's ODA recipient countries (Annexures — 1 and 2). In terms of aid and trade, growing dependency of SAARC countries with Japan is very high. For instance, top recipient of Japan's ODA in South Asia was India and aid to India from Japan increased to $ 504.95 million in 1998 from $ 21.91 million in 1985. In comparison to $ 93.31 million aid received by Pakistan in 1985, its aid increased up to $ 491.54 million in 1998. Among the countries, India, Pakistan and Sri Lanka received a high chunk of loan assistance from ODA. In comparison with these countries, Bangladesh received a low quantity of loan, and Nepal's loan with Japan is very nominal i.e., only $ 0.4 million, whereas, Bhutan and the Maldives got only grant aid (Table 2). Similarly, trade dependency of South Asia with Japan is also growing slowly. All these countries have trade deficit with Japan (Table 3).

Japan's investment in SAARC countries in sector basis is more or less the same. Japan has given a topmost priority mostly in the field of agricultural development, development of economic infrastructure, environment, human resource development, etc. (Annexure 5). After 1980s, it has also taken keen interest on the development of the democratic process and promotion of peace in the region. It has also disbursed some amount of ODA to improve and develop the democratic exercise in the region. In this regard, it has also tried to mediate to resolve the conflict between India and Pakistan. Similarly, it has also shown its great concern over the growing nuclear proliferation in the region.

Table 2: Flow of Japanese Aid in SAARC Countries
(Net disbursement basis: $ million)

Countries	*Grants in 1985*	*Grants After 1998*			
		Loans	*Grants*	*Technical Assistance*	*Total*
Bangladesh	$ 121.48	$ 50.13	$ 216.35	$ 22.83	$ 189.05
Bhutan	$ 1.59	—	Y 17.609 bil.	Y 5.09 bil.	Y 22.699 bil.
India	$ 21.91	$ 461.33	$ 23.10	$ 20.51	$ 504.95
Maldives	$ 2.08	—	Y 19.3 bil.	Y 3.7 bil.	(1997) Y 23.0 bil.
Nepal	$ 50.74	$ 0.4	$ 35.79	$ 21.49	$ 56.88
Pakistan	$ 93.31	$ 424.46	$ 53.47	$ 13.61	$ 491.54
Sri Lanka	$ 83.34	$ 121.47	$ 52.06	$ 24.32	$ 197.85

Sources: 1. Grants in 1985: Bam Dev Sigdel, "Japan's ODA To Nepal", in ed., K.V. Kesavan & Lalima Varma, *Japan-South Asia: Security and Economic Perspectives*, New Delhi, p. 21.

2. Grants in 1998: *Japan's ODA Annual Report 1999*, http:/www.mofa.go.jp/policy/oda/summary/1999/d_g2_02.html).
3. Grants in 1998 for Bhutan and the Maldives: *http://www.mofa.go.jp/region/asia-paci/Bhutan,Bangladesh/*

Table 3: Trade between Japan and the South Asian Countries

SAARC Countries	*Import from Japan*	*Export to Japan*
Bangladesh	$ 130 mil.	$ 130 mil. ('97)
Bhutan	Y 2,567 mil.	Y 19 mil. ('97)
India	Y 275.5 bil.	Y 255.4 bil. ('99)
Maldives	$ 9.233 mil.	$ 4.079 mil. ('99)
Nepal	Rs. 2.3 bil.	Rs. 230 mil. ('98)
Pakistan	$ 606 mil.	$ 252 mil. ('99)
Sri Lanka	$430 mil.	$ 160 mil. ('99)

Source: *http://www.mofa.go.jp/region/asia-paci/Bhutan,Bangladesh,India,Maldives, Nepal,Pakistan,Sri Lanka/*

Nepal-Japan Relation

Diplomatic relations between Nepal and Japan were established in 1956 and so far both the countries were successful to maintain their cordial relationship intact. Though, they have established their relationship only in 1956 on a diplomatic level, their relationship could be traced back to 1899, when Ekai Kawaguchi, a Buddhist monk visited Nepal and advised the then Prime Minister of Nepal, Chandra Shumsher, to develop Nepal with the Japanese assistance (Sigdel 2000: 33). Kawaguchi visited Nepal for three times in 1899, 1902, and 1912. Similarly, Nepal and Japan share some similarities in terms of geographical features, and in political, social, cultural and religious matters. Geographically, there is a similar feature between our *Tukche* village of Mustang district and *Tokugawa* village of Japan. Both of these villages are in Himalayan region of the countries. In this regard, both of these villages of Nepal and Japan have set a unique example of relationship in village (geographical) level. In order to maintain the relationship, there is a frequent exchange of visits by the people from these villages. Similarly, there is a social, cultural and religious similarity between the people of Japan and the hill ethnic people of Nepal. And, our Buddhist religion is a most attractive factor in Nepal to the Japanese people. That is why, since Kawaguchi to the present, people of Japan have taken a great interest in Nepal, which is cleared by the designing of master plan of Lumbini Development Centre (preservation of the birth place of lord Buddha) by a Japanese expert. Other examples are the monasteries build by the Japanese. On the other hand, both countries have constitutional monarchial system. Even before the establishment of diplomatic relationship between the two countries, Japan had trained 8 Nepalese students in 1902 (Sigdel *Op. cit.*). Similarly, training facilities to the Nepalese were provided in Japan under the Colombo Plan in 1954. In 1972 it provided 30 seats to the Nepalese under this plan out of the total of 409 seats. Even after the termination of the Colombo plan, it has continuously been providing training facilities to the Nepali students in Japan. For instance, about 1500 Nepalese are receiving training in about 80 courses every year in Japan, and on the other hand, about 43 Japanese volunteers are working in different parts of Nepal.

Nepal's Trade with Japan

In terms of trade, both these countries had trade relations before the Second World War. During that time Rana rulers used to import various goods from Japan. After the establishment of diplomatic relationship, Nepal's trade with Japan increased. From the very beginning, Nepal's trade with Japan was at a deficit level. For instance, Nepal's import from Japan was Rs. 115,696 and export was Rs. 5,814 in 1975. The gap of trade deficit increased in every year and reached the climax in 1999/2000 i.e., import is Rs. 2,891,860,649 and export is just Rs. 705,047,618 (See for detail, Table No. 4, Chart 1 and 2). On the item basis, Nepal had imported 89 categories of items and exported about 23 items in 1994/1995, whereas in 1999/2000, it has imported about 374 items and exported about 136 items (TPC 1995 and 2000).

Table 4: Nepal's Trade with Japan

Year	*Import from Japan*	*Export to Japan*	*Year*	*Import from Japan*	*Export to Japan*
1975/1976	115696	5814	1988/1989	1740303	25767
1976/1977	133261	26183	1989/1990	1628758	24072
1977/1978	245318	19215	1990/1991	3128465	29063
1978/1979	404795	66056	1991/1992	2872806	51554
1979/1980	404742	57811	1992/1993	2709286	84691
1980/1981	571794	31526	1993/1994	2737591	81175
1981/1982	574007	15628	1994/1995	3196411398	75444963
1982/1983	731577	11371	1995/1996	341898014	78982725
1983/1984	704803	9258	1996/1997	3955266692	100300756
1984/1985	886077	13539	1997/1998	2751584946	178531077
1985/1986	1473007	10284	1998/1999	2251572387	230801498
1986/1987	1437924	26956	1999/2000	2891860649	705047618
1987/1988	1607580	19457			

Sources: 1. For 1975/76-1993/94, Madhav Bhakta Shrestha, *Nepal-Japan Trade: Problems and Prospects*, Central Department of Economics, Tribhuvan University, Nepal, 1996 (unpublished M.A. Dissertation).

2. For 1994/95-1999/2000, *Nepal Oversease Trade Statistics*, Nepal Trade Promotion Centre, Nepal, 1994/95-1999/2000.

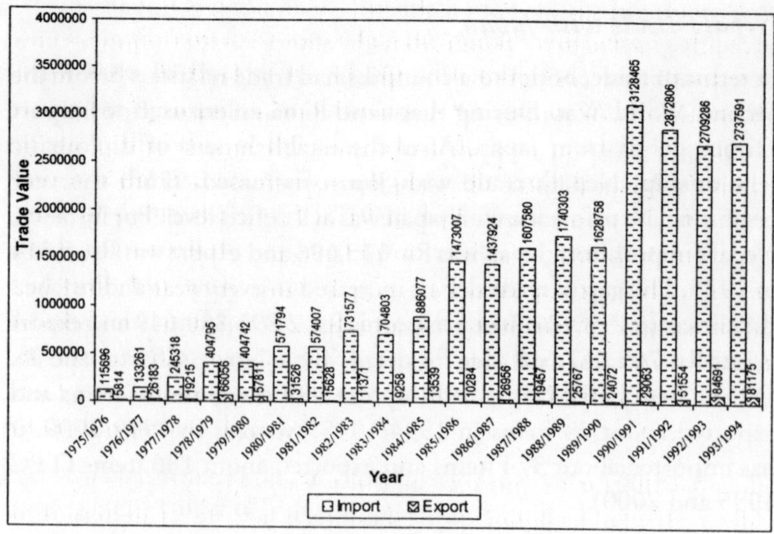

Chart 1: Nepal's Trade with Japan (1975-76 to 1993-94)

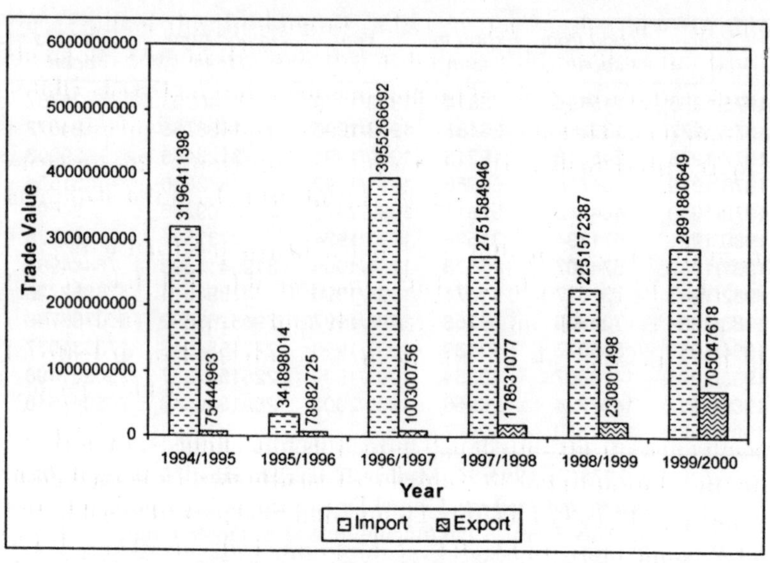

Chart 2: Nepal's Trade with Japan (1994-95 to 1999-2000)

Japan's Role in Infrastructure Development of Nepal

At first, Nepal started to receive foreign aid under the Point Four Programme of U.S. government after signing the agreement on 23 January 1951. Under this programme U.S. government provided the aid to the tune of NRs. 22,000,00 to Nepal. Since the very beginning, Nepal was dependent on foreign aid. For instance, after the dawn of democracy in 1951, planning was introduced in 1955 to launch the development programmes in a planned way. The First Five Year Plan (1956-61) was totally dependent on foreign aid. Similarly, 81.9 percent of total budget of the Second Two Year Plan (1961-62) was dependent on foreign aid. From the first plan to the present, more than 50% of allocated budget of the planning are being met by foreign aid. In this year, due to the failure of receiving foreign aid, as expected, the Nepal government was compelled to cut down the development budget in order to meet the increasing expenditure on security due to the Maoist insurgency problem.

As in other countries of Asia, Japan took a keen interest on Nepal's development and it started to provide aid since 1960s. Japan had helped Nepal to fill the gap of foreign aid in Nepal's development. In 1970 Nepal received NRs. 10 million aid from Japan (Sigdel *Op. cit.*, 35) and it increased up to $ 110.89 million in 1993, $ 118.75 million in 1994, and $ 127.6 million in 1995 (Table No. 5). Later, the flow of Japanese aid slowly decreased i.e., $ 88.8 million in 1996, $ 86.1 million in 1997 and $ 56.88 million in 1998 (Table 5). The main cause of the decline of Japanese aid is political instability in Nepal. For example, withdrawal from the multilateral funding agencies on "Arun III Hydro-electric Project" in Nepal is the genuine case. At that time, the major opposition party — Communist Party of Nepal-Unified-Marxist-Leninist, had asked the donors of the project to stop funding the project (Dhruba Kumar, 1997: 87). Among the members of the agencies, Japan was the biggest donor to the project. If the government could convince the Japanese government, Japan could help Nepal in influencing the multilateral funding agencies in this project. But, due to the political reason, the project was collapsed. Though, the importance of the project is obvious, Nepal is unable to move the proposal of foreign funding for initiating the project.

Table 5: Japanese Assistance in Nepal (Including Grant Assistance, Grant for Grassroots, Technical Assistance and Loan Aid)

Year	*$ million*
1993	110.89
1994	118.75
1995	127.60
1996	88.79
1997	86.15
1998	56.88
Total	1,406.96

Sources: 1. For 1993, Bamdev Sigdel, "Japan's ODA To Nepal", in eds. K.V. Kesavan & Lalima Varma, *Japan-South Asia: Security and Economic Perspectives*, New Delhi, India.

2. *ODA Annual Report, 1999*, http://www.mofa.go.jp/policy/oda/summary/1999/d_g2_02.html.

Japanese aid has played a vital role in building Nepal's development infrastructure. Main sectors of Japanese funding are Industries, power transmission and distribution system, roads, agriculture, horticulture, sericulture, floriculture, social sector, etc. Later, it has started to focus on human resource development, environmental conservation, cultural heritage, etc. In the field of Nepal's development, Kulekhani Hydro-electric Project, Tribhuvan University Teaching Hospital, Udayapur Cement Factory, Kathmandu Water Supply Facility Improvement Project, Construction of New Bridge of Bagmati including a number of important bridges of the Kathmandu Valley, Construction of Sindhuli Road, expansion of Kanti Children's Hospital, funding for primary schools, modernisation of Tribhuvan International Airport, Melamchi Water Project for the people of Kathmandu, expansion of the Rural Telecommunication Network in the

Northwest Region, are the most noteworthy projects funded by the Japanese grants. Major projects under the Japanese assistance are:

Completed Projects under Japanese Assistance

1. Kathmandu Valley Power Distribution System and Improvement Project
2. Teaching Hospital
3. Kanti Children's Hospital
4. Improvement in Load Dispatching Center
5. Construction of Food Shortage
6. National Tuberculosis Center
7. Expansion of Radio Broadcasting Network
8. Construction of Bridge in Kathmandu Valley
9. Kulekhani Hydroelectric Project
10. Second Kulekhani Project
11. Udaipur Cement Project
12. Kathmandu Bus Terminal
13. Improvement of Transport Capacity
14. Water-Induced Disaster Prevention Center
15. Modernisation of Tribhuvan international Airport
16. Kathmandu Water Supply Facility
17. Thapathali Bridge
18. Horticulture Development Project
19. Primary Health Care Project

Ongoing Projects

1 Rural Telecommunication Network in the North West Region

2 Construction of Primary School

3 Sindhuli Bardibas Road

4 Community Forestry Development Project

5 River Training and Road Protection Equipment

6 Reinforcement and Distribution System in Kathmandu Valley (Phase-II)

7 National Tuberculosis Control Program

8 Tribhuvan International Airport.

Source: http://www.nepalicongress.org.np/archives/np_jp_relations/economic_co.html.

Conclusion

Though, foreign aid is a major instrument of economic development, there is also a critical aspect — national interest of the aid donors. For instance, U.S. Marshall Plan was motivated to check the growing communism in the world. As in Marshall Plan, Japanese aid was concentrated on export promotion. At the beginning, Japanese aid was based on the principles of "reciprocity". It means its aid policy was concentrated to promote export and to secure import of important raw materials, which is proved by the statement of the Ministry of International Trade and Industry. It insisted on the "use of aid as a vehicle for Japan's own economic growth" and expected "discipline" from the recipients (Hook & Zhang 1998: 1052). This led to the booming of Japanese economy and Japan became an economic super power during 1970-1980. After being economic super power, it had to follow the recommendations of UN declared at the 25th anniversary meeting of the UN in 1970. The recommendations were — ODA target of 0.7% of GNP; relaxation of loan term; and promotion of untying aid. Now, Japanese ODA has considered three policies: (i) lesser consideration of geo-political factors, (ii) lesser intervention in policy issues, and (iii) strong emphasis on infrastructure support. (Fuwa *Op. cit.*, 6). And, lastly, Japan expects export promotion of the recipients rather than aid to them.

Even in the changed context of Japan's ODA policy in favour of Asia, South Asian countries, especially Nepal failed to exploit the maximum mobilisation of Japanese grants for its economic development. In this favourable situation, all the South Asian countries should think once more to mobilize more and more Japanese funding for their economic development. For this, all the SAARC countries should influence and attract Japan by creating a suitable environment for its funding in the region, which can be done by developing free trade system among the SAARC countries, minimizing political conflicts internally as well as externally within the region, and developing mutual understanding and cooperation among the countries.

REFERENCES

1. Dhruba Kumar, *Nepali State and Politics Inevitable Crisis and Harrowing Tradition* (unpublished report), CNAS, TU, Kathmandu, December 1997.
2. Fuwa, Yoshitaro, "Japan's ODA in Historical Perspectives", paper presented at International Seminar on *Japan-South Asia Cooperation during the Post-Cold War Period*, School of International Studies, Jawaharlal Nehru University and India International Centre, New Delhi, March 8-10, 1999.
3. Hook, Steven W. & Zhang, Guang, "Japan's Aid Policy Since the Cold War", *Asian Survey*, U.S.A., November 1998.
4. *Japan-Nepal Cooperation*, Embassy of Japan.
5. *Japan's ODA Annual Report 1999*, http://www.mofa.go.jp/policy/oda/summary/1999/d_g2_02_.html.
6. Maharjan, Bishnu Bahadur, *Nepal's Overseas Trade with Special Reference to Japan*, M.A. Dissertation, Economic Department, Tribhuvan University, Kathmandu, Nepal, 1989.

7. Molla, Gyasuddin, "Japan's Response to the Changing Need of South Asia", *South Asian Studies*, New Delhi, January-June 1997.
8. *Nepal-Japan Economic Cooperation*, http://www.nepalicongress.org.np/archives/np_ jp_relations/economic_o.html.
9. *Nepal Overseas Trade Statistics (1994/95-1999/2000)*, Trade Promotion Centre, Kathmandu, Nepal.
10. Shrestha, Madhav Bhakta, *Nepal-Japan Trade: Problems and Potentials*, M.A. Dissertation, Economic Department, Tribhuvan University, Kathmandu, Nepal, 1996
11. Sigdel, Bam Dev, "Some Aspects of Nepal-Japan Economic Relations" (in Nepali language), *The Journal of Nepal-Japan Studies*, Japan University Students Association, Nepal, Vol. 1, 2000.
12. ——, "Japan's ODA to Nepal", in ed. K.V. Kesavan, & Lalima Varma, *Japan-South Asia: Security and Economic Perspectives*, New Delhi.

Annexure 1

Major Recipient Countries of Japan's Bilateral ODA

(Net Disbursement Basis; $ million)

Rank	1996		1997		1998	
	Country	*Amount*	*Country*	*Amount*	*Country*	*Amount*
1.	Indonesia	965.53	China	576.86	China	1,158.16
2.	China	861.73	Indonesia	496.86	Indonesia	828.47
3.	Thailand	664.00	India	491.80	Thailand	558.42
4.	India	579.26	Thailand	468.26	India	504.95
5.	Philippines	414.45	Philippines	318.98	Pakistan	491.54
6.	Pakistan	282.20	Viet Nam	232.48	Viet Nam	388.61
7.	Mexico	212.84	Jordan	139.63	Philippines	297.55
8.	Egypt	201.32	Sri Lanka	134.56	Sri Lanka	197.85
9.	Bangladesh	174.03	Bangladesh	129.98	Bangladesh	189.05
10.	Sri Lanka	173.94	Egypt	125.40	Malaysia	179.10
	Total above 10	4,529.30	Total above 10	3,114.82	Total above 10	4,793.70
	Bilateral Aid Total	8,356.26	Bilateral Aid Total	6,612.59	Bilateral Aid Total	8,605.90

Note: As the figures in the table are rounded off, they do not necessarily add up to the totals.

Source: *Japan's ODA Annual Report 1999*, http://www.mofa.go.jp/policy/oda/summary/1999/d_g2_02.html.

Annexure 2

Major Recipients of Japan's Bilateral Assistance by Aid Type (1998)

(Net Disbursement Basis: $ million, %)

Rank	*Grant aid*			*Technical cooperation*				*ODA Loans*				*Total of bilateral aid*			
	Country/ Territory	*Amount*	*Share*	*Rank*	*Country/ Territory*	*Amount*	*Share*	*Rank*	*Country/ Territory*	*Amount*	*Share*	*Rank*	*Country/ Territory*	*Amount*	*Share*
1	Bangladesh	216.35	9.98	1	China	301.62	10.84	1	China	818.33	22.38	1	China	1,158.16	13.46
2	Indonesia	114.59	5.29	2	Indonesia	123.99	4.46	2	Indonesia	589.88	16.13	2	Indonesia	828.47	9.63
3	Tanzania	81.05	3.74	3	Thailand	121.74	4.38	3	India	461.33	12.62	3	Thailand	558.42	6.49
4	Philippines	78.34	3.61	4	Republic of Korea	96.39	3.47	4	Pakistan	424.46	11.61	4	India	504.95	5.87
5	Laos	61.61	2.84	5	Philippines	80.68	2.90	5	Thailand	418.12	11.43	5	Pakistan	491.54	5.71
6	Cambodia	58.35	2.69	6	Malaysia	59.53	2.14	6	Viet Nam	287.18	7.85	6	Viet Nam	388.61	4.52
7	Viet Nam	55.46	2.56	7	Brazil	53.02	1.91	7	Philippines	138.54	3.79	7	Philippines	297.55	3.46
8	Bosnia and Herzegovina	54.20	2.50	8	Viet Nam	45.98	1.65	8	Sri Lanka	121.47	3.32	8	Sri Lanka	197.85	2.30
9	Pakistan	53.47	2.47	9	Kenya	31.94	1.15	9	Malaysia	115.65	3.16	9	Bangladesh	189.05	2.20
10	Sri Lanka	52.06	2.40	10	Mexico	29.20	1.05	10	Ghana	94.33	2.58	10	Malaysia	179.10	2.08
Total Aid for 10 Countries		825.49	38.08	Total Aid for 10 Countries		944.08	33.94	Total Aid for 10 Countries		3,469.28	94.88	Total Aid for 10 Countries		4,793.70	55.70

(Contd.)

(*Contd.*)

Rank	*Grant aid*			*Technical cooperation*				*ODA Loans*				*Total of bilateral aid*			
	Country/ Territory	*Amount*	*Share*	*Rank*	*Country/ Territory*	*Amount*	*Share*	*Rank*	*Country/ Territory*	*Amount*	*Share*	*Rank*	*Country/ Territory*	*Amount*	*Share*
11	Yemen	50.44	2.33	11	Sri Lanka	24.32	0.87	11	Uzbekistan	89.59	2.45	11	Ghana	149.00	1.73
12	Myanmar	47.01	2.17	12	Paraguay	23.69	0.85	12	Kazakhstan	82.96	2.27	12	Brazil	104.55	1.21
13	Peru	45.83	2.11	13	Egypt	23.20	0.83	13	Brazil	51.53	1.41	13	Uzbekistan	103.00	1.20
14	Madagascar	43.29	2.00	14	Cambodia	23.05	0.83	14	Iran	41.29	1.13	14	Kazakhstan	95.21	1.11
15	Guinea	42.35	1.95	15	Bangladesh	22.83	0.82	15	Mongolia	34.48	0.94	15	Mongolia	93.99	1.09
16	Egypt	41.84	1.93	16	Tanzania	21.81	0.78	16	Botswana	29.21	0.80	16	Laos	85.57	0.99
17	Malawi	41.37	1.91	17	Nepal	21.49	0.77	17	Equador	23.14	0.63	17	Egypt	85.25	0.99
18	Palestinian Administered Areas	41.10	1.90	18	Mongolia	21.30	0.77	18	Peru	22.16	0.61	18	Tanzania	83.37	0.97
19	Ghana	39.25	1.81	19	Laos	20.90	0.75	19	Colombia	20.97	0.57	19	Cambodia	81.40	0.95
20	China	38.22	1.76	20	India	20.51	0.74	20	Egypt	20.22	0.55	20	Peru	80.14	0.93
Total Aid for 20 Countries		1,256.19	57.95	Total Aid for 20 Countries		1,167.18	41.96	Total Aid for 20 Countries		3,884.82	106.24	Total Aid for 20 Countries		5,755.17	66.87

(*Contd.*)

(*Contd.*)

Rank	*Grant aid*			*Technical cooperation*				*ODA Loans*				*Total of bilateral aid*			
	Country/ Territory	*Amount*	*Share*	*Rank*	*Country/ Territory*	*Amount*	*Share*	*Rank*	*Country/ Territory*	*Amount*	*Share*	*Rank*	*Country/ Territory*	*Amount*	*Share*
21	Mongolia	38.22	1.76	21	Argentina	19.11	0.69	21	El Salvador	19.46	0.53	21	Yemen	62.37	0.72
22	Mozambique	37.63	1.74	22	Bolivia	18.99	0.68	22	Papua New Guinea	18.44	0.50	22	Bosnia and Herzegovina	57.29	0.67
23	Nepal	35.79	1.65	23	Turkey	17.05	0.61	23	Syria	17.98	0.49	23	Nepal	56.88	0.66
24	Côte d'Ivoire	33.42	1.54	24	Chile	16.88	0.61	24	Kyrgyz	17.07	0.47	24	Kenya	52.59	0.61
25	Senegal	25.67	1.18	25	Syria	16.20	0.58	25	Morocco	16.71	0.46	25	Madagascar	51.96	0.60
26	Bolivia	25.18	1.16	26	Ghana	15.42	0.55	26	Tunisia	15.49	0.42	26	Syria	50.02	0.58
27	Mali	24.31	1.12	27	Pakistan	13.61	0.49	27	Chile	14.96	0.41	27	Equador	49.41	0.57
28	India	23.10	1.07	28	Zambia	13.12	0.47	28	Jordan	14.75	0.40	28	Iran	48.13	0.56
29	Zambia	22.97	1.06	29	Malawi	12.30	0.44	29	Benin	14.37	0.39	29	Malawi	47.41	0.55
30	Mauritania	22.01	1.02	30	Peru	12.15	0.44	30	Guatemala	14.26	0.39	30	Papua New Guinea	47.27	0.55
Total Aid for 30 Countries		1,544.49	71.25	Total Aid for 30 Countries		1,322.00	47.52	Total Aid for 30 Countries		4,048.32	110.71	Total Aid for 30 Countries		6,278.51	72.96
Bilateral Aid Total		2,167.60	100.00	Bilateral Aid Total		2,781.76	100.00	Bilateral Aid Total		3,656.54	100.00	Bilateral Aid Total		8,605.90	100.00

Note: Bilateral aid total for developing countries includes aid for Part II (Aid to Countries and Territories in Transition). As the figures in the table are rounded off, they do not necessarily add up to the totals.

Source: *Japan's ODA Annual Report 1999*, http://www.mofa.go.jp/policy/oda/summary/1999/d_g2_02.html.

Annexure 3

Types and Geographical Distribution of Japan's Bilateral ODA in 1998

(Net Disbursement Basis; $ million)

Region	*Type*					
	Grant Aid	*Technical Cooperation*	*Loans*	*Total ODA*	*Total ODA (1997)*	*1997/98 Growth Rate (%)*
Asia	935.37 (43.2)	1,072.52 (38.6)	3,364.14 (92.0)	5,372.03 (62.4)	3,075.60 (46.5)	74.7
Northeast Asia	76.44 (3.5)	427.36 (15.4)	707.31 (19.3)	1,211.10 (14.1)	529.92 (8.0)	128.5
Southeast Asia	437.85 (20.2)	489.31 (17.6)	1,510.49 (41.3)	2,437.66 (28.3)	1,416.06 (21.4)	72.1
(ASEAN)	(379.50) (17.5)	(466.27) (16.8)	(1,510.49) (41.3)	(2,356.25) (27.4)	(1,354.43) (20.5)	74.0
Southwest Asia	395.15 (18.2)	111.04 (4.0)	956.72 (26.2)	1,462.92 (17.0)	963.54 (14.6)	51.8
Central Asia	12.90 (0.6)	25.64 (0.9)	189.62 (5.2)	228.15 (2.7)	145.38 (2.2)	56.9
Caucasus	11.30 (0.5)	2.26 (0.1)	0.01 (0.0)	13.57 (0.2)	11.50 (0.2)	18.0
Other regions	1.72 (0.1)	16.92 (0.6)	0.00 (0.0)	18.64 (0.2)	9.21 (0.1)	102.4
Middle East	186.49 (8.6)	119.02 (4.3)	86.52 (2.4)	392.03 (4.6)	512.92 (7.8)	-23.6

(*Contd.*)

(Contd.)

Region	*Type*					
	Grant Aid	*Technical Cooperation*	*Loans*	*Total ODA*	*Total ODA (1997)*	*1997/98 Growth Rate (%)*
Africa	636.38 (29.4)	193.97 (7.0)	119.93 (3.3)	950.29 (11.0)	802.82 (12.1)	18.4
Latin America	215.38 (9.9)	(276.16) (9.9)	61.31 (1.7)	552.86 (6.4)	715.03 (10.8)	-22.7
Oceania	80.63 (3.7)	48.62 (1.7)	17.92 (0.5)	147.17 (1.7)	159.03 (2.4)	-7.5
Europe	79.34 (3.7)	62.73 (2.3)	1.46 (0.0)	143.53 (1.7)	133.76 (2.0)	7.3
(Eastern Europe)	(2.51) (0.1)	(40.86) (1.5)	(4.06) (0.1)	47.42 (0.6)	(53.49) (0.8)	11.3
Unspecified	34.01 (1.6)	1,008.74 (36.3)	5.26 (1.1)	1,048.00 (12.2)	1,213.43 (18.4)	–13.6
Total	2,167.60 (100.0)	2,781.76 (100.0)	3,656.54 (100.0)	8,605.90 (100.0)	6,612.59 (100.0)	30.1

Notes: 1. Regions are specified according to the Japanese Ministry of Foreign Affairs' criteria.

2. Unspecified technical cooperation includes survey teams sent to more than one region on a single mission, subsidies to groups that assist foreign students, administrative expenses, and costs of raising public awareness of development issues.

3. Including assistance to Part II (Aid to Countries and Territories in Transition).

4. Due to rounding of individual items, percentages do not necessarily total 100%.

5. Cambodia's 1999 accession to ASEAN has brought all 10 Southeast Asian countries under the ASEAN umbrella. The figures in this chart, however, refer to the ASEAN 9, excluding Cambodia. Viet Nam joined ASEAN in 1995, Myanmar and Laos in 1997.

Source: *Japan's ODA Annual Report 1999*, http:/www.mofa.go.jp/policy/oda/summary/1999/d_g2_01.html.

Annexure 4

Geographical Distribution of Japan's Bilateral ODA

(Net Disbursement Basis; $ million)

Region/Calendar Year	*1980*	*1990*	*1995*	*1996*	*1997*	*1998*
Asia	1,383	4,117	5,745	4,145	3,076	5,372
	(70.5)	(59.3)	(54.4)	(49.6)	(46.5)	(62.4)
Northeast Asia	82	835	1,606	0,869	530	1,211
	(4.2)	(12.0)	(15.2)	(10.4)	(8.0)	(14.1)
Southeast Asia	861	2,379	2,592	1,858	1,416	2,438
	(43.9)	(34.3)	(24.6)	(22.2)	(21.4)	(28.3)
(ASEAN)	703	2,299	2,229	1,694	1,354	2,356
	(35.8)	(33.1)	(21.1)	(20.3)	(20.5)	(27.4)
Southwest Asia	435	898	1,435	1,320	964	1,463
	(22.2)	(12.9)	(13.6)	(15.8)	(14.6)	(17.0)
Central Asia	—	—	67	80	145	228
			(0.6)	(1.0)	(2.2)	(2.7)
Caucasus	—	—	0	0	12	14
			(0.0)	(0.0)	(0.2)	(0.2)
Other regions	5	4	44	18	9	19
	(0.3)	(0.1)	(0.4)	(0.2)	(0.1)	(0.2)
Middle East	204	705	721	561	513	392
	(10.4)	(10.2)	(6.8)	(6.7)	(7.8)	(4.6)
Africa	223	792	1,333	1,067	803	950
	(11.4)	(11.4)	(12.6)	(12.8)	(12.1)	(11.0)

(*Contd.*)

(Contd.)

Region/Calendar Year	*1980*	*1990*	*1995*	*1996*	*1997*	*1998*
Latin America	118	561	1,142	986	715	553
	(6.0)	(8.1)	(10.8)	(11.8)	(10.8)	(6.4)
Oceania	12	114	160	198	159	147
	(0.6)	(1.6)	(1.5)	(2.4)	(2.4)	(1.7)
Europe	–2	158	153	200	134	144
	(–)	(2.3)	(1.4)	(2.4)	(2.0)	(1.7)
(Eastern Europe)	—	153	138	130	54	47
		(2.2)	(1.3)	(1.6)	(0.8)	(0.6)
Unspecified	23	494	1,303	1,200	1,213	1,048
	(1.2)	(7.1)	(12.3)	(14.4)	(18.3)	(12.2)
Total	1,961	6,940	10,557	8,356	6,613	8,606
	(100.0)	(100.0)	(100.0)	(100.0)	(100.0)	(100.0)

Notes: 1. Certain data were listed as "unspecified" because they could not be assigned to a single regional category: such aid includes survey teams sent to multiple regions, administrative expenses and costs of raising public awareness of development issues.

2. Five countries in Central Asia and three countries in Caucasus have become eligible for ODA since 1993 and 1994, respectively.

3. Data in parentheses are the percentages of the respective totals.

4. Due to rounding of individual items, percentages do not necessarily total 100%.

5. Cambodia's 1999 accession to ASEAN has brought all 10 Southeast Asian countries under the ASEAN umbrella. The figures in this chart, however, refer to the ASEAN 9, excluding Cambodia. Viet Nam joined ASEAN in 1995, Myanmar and Laos in 1997.

6. Including assistance to Part II (Aid to Countries and Territories in Transition).

Source: *Japan's ODA Annual Report 1999,* http:/www.mofa.go.jp/policy/oda/summary/1999/d_g2_01.html.

Annexure 5

Sectoral Priorities of Japan's Investment in SAARC Countries

SAARC Countries	*Areas of Development*
Bangladesh	1. Agricultural and rural development and improvement of agricultural productivity.
	2. Improvement of the social sector (human resources development and basic human needs).
	3. Improvement of the base for promoting investment and exports.
	4. Disaster prevention and management.
	5. Construction of bridges.
Bhutan	1. Agricultural development.
	2. Food Production.
	3. Telecommunication.
	4. Road maintenance and construction.
	5. Preservation of Museum.
India	1. Alleviation of poverty.
	2. Economic infrastructure.
	3. Environmental conservation.
	4. Construction of bridges and roads.
	5. Small scale industries and thermal power plants.
Maldives	1. Seawall construction.
	2. Water treatment plant.
	3. Electrification.
	4. Broadcasting: Voice of the Maldives and the T.V. Programme.
	5. Construction of primary school.
Nepal	1. Social sector.
	2. Human resources development.
	3. Agricultural development.
	4. Economic infrastructure.
	5. Environmental conservation.
Pakistan	1. Social sector.
	2. Economic infrastructure.
	3. Agriculture.
	4. Environmental conservation.
	5. Power plants: thermal and hydro power.
Sri Lanka	1. Building and improving economic infrastructure.
	2. Development of mining and manufacturing industries.
	3. Development of agriculture, forestry, and fisheries.
	4. Human resources development.
	5. Improving health and medical services

Source: *Japan's ODA Annual Report, 1999*, http://www.mofa.go.jp/policy/oda/summary/1999/d_g2_02.html.

Annexure 6

Japanese Funded Projects in Nepal

(¥100 million)

Fiscal Year	*Loan Aid*	*Grant Aid*	*Technical Cooperation*
1994	—	• Project for Extension and Reinforcement of Power Transmission and Distribution System in Kathmandu Valley (4.71) • Kathmandu Water Supply Facility Improvement Project (8.44) • Project for the Construction of New Bagmati Bridge at Thapathali (7.66) • Project for Modernisation of Tribhuvan International Airport in Kathmandu (8.76) • Project for Expansion of Kanti Children's Hospital (4.18) • Project for Providing Materials and Equipment for the Construction of Primary Schools (3.12) • Project for the Expansion and Reinforcement of Power Transmission and Distribution System in Kathmandu Valley (Phase II) (15.02) • Project for Equipment Supply for River Training and Road Protection (7.90) • Debt Relief (11.16) • Food Aid (6.00) • Aid for Increased Food Production (9.00) • Sports Equipment to the National Sports Council (0.50) • Grassroots Projects (3 projects) (0.20) (Total 86.65)	(Total 33.36)
1995	—	• Project for Construction of Sindhuli Road (Section I: Bardibas-Sindhuli-Bazar) (0.75) • Project for Providing Materials and Equipment for the Construction of Primary Schools (2.75)	

(*Contd.*)

(*Contd.*)

Fiscal Year	*Loan Aid*	*Grant Aid*	*Technical Cooperation*
		• Project for the Extension and Reinforcement of Power Transmission and Distribution System in Kathmandu Valley (Phase II) (0.77) • Project for the Construction of New Bagmati Bridge at Thapathali (4.75) • Project for Supply of River Training and Road Protection Equipment (3.18) • Project for Expansion of the Rural Telecommunication Network in the Northwest Region (0.46) • Project for Modernisation of Tribhuvan International Airport in Kathmandu (23.71) • Debt Relief (11.10) • Aid for Increased Food Production (9.00) • Equipment for Exhibition to the National Museum of Nepal (0.50) • Grassroots Projects (9 projects) (0.46)	
		(Total 86.65)	(Total 33.36)
1996	Kulekhani Disaster Prevention Project (III) (34.84) Kali Gandaki "A" Hydroelectric Project (169.16)	• Project for the Construction of Sindhuli Road (Section 1) (8.76) • Project for the Construction of Sindhuli Road (Section 4) (1.18) • Project for Providing Materials and Equipment for the Construction of Primary Schools (Phase II) (5.87) • Project for the Extension and Reinforcement of Power Transmission and Distribution System in Kathmandu Valley (Phase II) (19.59) • Project for Expansion of the Rural Telecommunication Network in the Northwest Region (5.95) • Project for Modernisation of Tribhuvan International Airport in Kathmandu (2.06) • Debt Relief (11.05) • Aid for Increased Food Production (8.50) • Grassroots Projects (17 projects) (0.48)	
	(Total 204.00)	(Total 63.44)	(Total 27.92)

(*Contd.*)

(*Contd.*)

Fiscal Year	*Loan Aid*	*Grant Aid*	*Technical Cooperation*
1997	—	• Project for the Construction of Sindhuli Road (Section 1) (12.36) • Project for Expansion of the Rural Telecommunication Network in the Northwest Region (12.69) • Project for the Construction of Sindhuli Road (Section 4) (6.13) • Project for Providing Materials and Equipment for the Construction of Primary Schools (Phase II) (5.71) • Debt Relief (5.48) • Debt Relief (5.44) • Supply of Television Programmes and Editing Equipment to Nepal Television Corporation (0.48) • Grassroots Projects (59 projects) (0.16) • Food Aid (5.87) • Aid for Increased Food Production (8.50) (Total 62.82)	(Total 23.43)
1998	—	• Project for Construction of Sindhuli Road (Section 4) (10.52) • Project for River Training (5.37) • Debt Relief (9.99) • Debt Relief (9.03) • Debt Relief (9.89) • Aid for Increased Food Production (7.00) • Grassroots Projects (5 projects) (0.22) (Total 52.02)	(Total 23.18)
	Total 583.95	1,291.09	406.76

1. Japan's ODA Disbursements to Nepal ($ million)

Year	Grants			Loan Aid		Total
	Grant Aid	Technical Cooperation	Total	Gross	Net	
1994	83.96	31.18	115.14	10.48	3.61	118.75
1995	95.38	29.42	124.80	10.27	2.80	127.60
1996	64.36	30.21	94.57	0.68	-5.78	88.79
1997	59.11	23.00	82.10	13.63	4.05	86.15
1998	35.79	21.49	57.29	11.95	-0.40	56.88
Total	873.76	325.27	1,199.04	270.12	207.91	1,406.96

2. Amount of DAC Countries' and International Organisations' ODA Disbursements to Nepal

i) DAC Countries, ODA Net ($ million)

Year	1		2		3		4		5		Japan	Total
1995	Japan	127.6	U.K.	25.6	Denmark	23.7	Germany	19.5	U.S.A.	19.0	127.6	266.1
1996	Japan	88.8	Germany	25.7	U.K.	23.3	Denmark	23.0	U.S.A.	15.0	88.8	236.2
1997	Japan	86.1	U.K.	28.6	Germany	24.6	U.S.A.	21.0	Denmark	18.0	86.1	233.5

ii) International Organisations, ODA Net ($ million)

Year	1		2		3		4		5		Others	Total
1995	IDA	74.3	ADB	48.9	WFP	8.3	UNTA	7.5	UNICEF	7.3	16.9	163.2
1996	ADB	57.9	IDA	53.8	WFP	12.7	UNICEF	8.5	UNDP	8.3	15.7	156.9
1997	ADB	86.5	IDA	45.2	UNDP	11.9	WFP	10.3	UNICEF	8.4	17.7	180.0

Source: *Japan's ODA Annual Report 1999,* http://www.mofa.go.jp/policy/oda/summary/1999/d_g2_o2.html.

3

India's Security Concerns in South Asia
A Case Study of Nepal

Prof. M.D. Dharamdasani

National Security is considered as a paramount, constant and compelling interest which a nation has to consider while formulating its policy vis-à-vis other countries particularly towards its neighbours. The achievement of favorable strategic frontiers and safeguarding neighbouring territories has been the traditional objectives to which states have been willing to commit huge resources because these areas if not properly defended could poss a major threat to nation's independence and territorial integrity.

In South Asia, the question of territorial integrity and preservation of national sovereignty has been projected as a major point of tension among the nations. Although South Asian countries share common colonial heritage except Nepal and are suffering from economic backwardness, there exist enormous diversities in their international and regional perceptions. Indeed there is no common security perception of the South Asian nations and their views differ from country to country keeping in view their domestic policies and geo-political compulsions. This is particularly true in case of periphery, states, which are small in size and poor in economic resources and military strength. For example, Pakistan's security framework is guided by its antagonism vis-à-vis India. Similarly, Nepal due to its landlocked position and excessive dependence on India is naturally obsessed with New Delhi's dominant role in its political and economic affairs. Bangladesh is also taking steps to reduce Indian influence by inviting western powers in its national development. Sri Lanka also till recently was relying on western support to ward off Indian influence particularly because of perceived Indian threat in the wake of ethnic turmoil. Thus conflicting interests of the South Asian Countries despite the formation of SAARC are largely responsible for the absence of a common security perception of South Asia as a whole.

An attempt is being made in this paper to examine India' s security perception of South Asia in general and its basic strategies to operationalise its security conception particularly in the context of the Himalayan Kingdom Nepal. The paper will also dwelt upon India's efforts towards Nepal within its security framework and to what extent Kathmandu in the past tried to break away New Delhi's security framework in order to assert its independence and identity in the international arena. The paper will also analyses the changing political scenario recently at the global and regional level and its impact on the security perceptions of India and Nepal.

India's Perception of the South Asian Security

Good neighbourliness is a basic tenet of India's foreign policy. This stems from India's awareness that its own security and welfare are closely linked with the security, stability and welfare of its neighbours. India' s relations with its South Asian neighbours barring Pakistan have not been marred by conflict and confrontation. Rather India has responded the call of its neighbours in distress by dispatching its own forces as happened in the case of Bangladesh, Maldives and Sri Lanka. However, due to their geo-political compulsions and domestic politics, and India's dominant position in the region on account of its size, economic and military capability has led these small neighbours to the policy of searching for option outside the region and thus inviting the extra-regional powers such as China, United States to intervene in the affairs of the region. There is also an impression that these small powers are also inspired by the non-regional actors attempt to contain India within the framework of South Asian regional cooperation.

Thus there are divergent models of security in South Asia which are not conducive to the evolution of regional security framework. One of the hindrance in the development of a security consensus is the fear psychosis developed in the small neighbours due to India's dominant position in the region; India's neighbours suffer from a sort of claustrophobia that the security model developed by their big neighbours might tie them to a new '*dependency model*' with India.

However, despite the divergent security perception of the small South Asian powers, New Delhi is trying to lay emphasis on three-fold strategy to achieve its security objectives in the region.

First: threat to the security of any nation should be considered as a threat to the security of other nation and stability of each should be concern of all. Late Mrs. Gandhi had rightly observed that India's effectiveness must rest on the secure home base of a peaceful South Asia.

Second: India is also against the South Asian nation's politico-strategic links with extra-regional powers, which it believes is detrimental to their national interests. For this purpose, India perceived that the South Asian states should not encourage super powers interference in their affairs, they should opt for a broad based political system and a policy of non-alignment in international affairs. Explaining India's concern over Pakistan's military pact with the United States, Nehru said:

> *of course they are a free country. I cannot prevent them. But if something affects Asia, India especially, and if something in our opinion, is a reversal of history after hundred of years, are we to remain silent... I say the return of armed forces from any European*

or American country is a reversal of the history of the countries of Asia.

Thus, the Indian perception had been that the interference of outside powers in the South Asian affairs would directly affect the security and integrity of the region. India must safeguard the strategic interests and for this purpose its dominant position in the region must be recognized by the states of South Asia as well as by extra-regional powers.

Finally: Commitment to peace in the region as well as world at large is a cardinal principle of India's foreign policy. Explaining the policy Nehru observed:

> *... Where freedom is menaced or justice threatened or where aggression takes place, we cannot be and shall not be natural. What we plead for and endeavor to practice in our own imperfect way is a binding faith in peace and an unfailing endeavor of thought and action to ensure it.*

Thus, India's policy towards its neighbours always has been to maintain peace in the region and for that it is instrument to achieve this peace was through non-violent methods and peaceful negotiate ions rather than to achieve peace through power.

India's Security Perception vis-à-vis Nepal

India's security perception vis-à-vis Nepal is primarily determined by later's strategic location in the Himalayas and its deep socio-cultural and historical relations with the Himalayan Kingdom. Since Nepal occupies an important strategic position between India and China, New Delhi has tried to keep the former within its northern security system and has tried to maintain 'primacy' in the Kingdom. Nehru had made the pointed reference to the fact when he observed:

> *"It is clear as I said that in regard to certain matters, the interests of India and Nepal are inevitably joined up, For instance, if I*

> *may mention it is not possible for any Indian Government to tolerate any invasion of Nepal from anywhere. It is not necessary for us to have a military alliance with Nepal... But apart from any pact or alliance, the fact remains that one cannot tolerate any invasion from any foreign country on any part of the Indian sub-continent or whatever you may like to call it. Any possible invasion of Nepal would inevitably involve the safety of India "*

Nehru further made it clear in the Parliament on December 6, 1950

...much as we appreciate the independence of Nepal, we are also interested in the security of our own country. From times immemorial, Himalayas have proved us with a magnificent frontier. Of course, they are no longer as impassable as they used to be, but they are still fairly effective. We cannot allow that barrier to be penetrated, for it is also the principal barrier to India.

It may be mentioned here that China has played an important role in India's security perception vis-à-vis Nepal. After the Chinese occupation in Tibet in 1950 and its historical claims over Sikkim, Nepal and Bhutan, the Chinese threat became more pronounced because it exposed northern border of Nepal to China. Nehru rightly believed that the Chinese threat to Nepal would not be restricted to that country but it would be also detrimental to India's border in the North. Besides, India's border with Nepal is open and without any natural barriers. India's richest agro-Industrial belt is also contiguous to the Nepalese border. Therefore it was natural that India's border with Nepal could be defended against a possible Chinese invasion in the north of Nepal. It may however, be argued that in modern times economic inter-dependence, nuclear warfare and means of rapid communication and advancement of technology, the entire concept of buffer has became redundant. But the behaviour of states shows that it is not the case as yet. Despite huge stockpile of nuclear armaments, conventional weapons have not lost their importance. Chinese interests in peripheral states, United States hegemony in Latin Americas, Afghanistan and Iraq even proposals such as "nuclear free zone" have at their base the buffer approach. Nepal, therefore, still remains an ideological and strategic buffer between India and China.

Thus, India still considers Nepal as an integral part of its defense mechanism. New Delhi's efforts in this direction were prompted by Nehru's conception of 'Area of Peace' which like the 'Munro Doctrine for America may be called as 'Nehru Doctrine' for the Himalayas.

The essence of this doctrine is that there is a 'minimum' interest, which India wishes to maintain in the sub-Himalayan region to preserve its security interests in this area. To achieve this objective, New Delhi tried to keep this area away from cold war politics so that any power inimical to Indian interests may not get an upper hand in Nepal. This 'primacy' has been expressed in various terms such as 'sphere of interest' or 'special relationship' and it has been maintained by various diplomatic means political, ideological and economic etc.

Evolution of India's Security Policy

Keeping in view its stakes in the Kingdom, India in order to lay down a security framework. concluded a Treaty of Peace and Friendship with Nepal in July 1950 wherein it was clearly mentioned that neither government shall tolerates any threat to the security of the other by a foreign powers. To deal with any such threat, the two governments shall consult each other and devise effective counter measures. Further it was also agreed by Nepal that she would secure arms and warlike materials from a country other than India with the prior permission and consultation with India.

The treaty of 1950 was indeed a bold step taken by Nehru to assert his country's special position in the Kingdom and thus to bring Nepal within India's strategic parameter.

India's security interests in Nepal were further consolidated by New Delhi's attempt to establish its military check posts along kingdom's northern border to safeguard the passes between Tibet and Nepal on one hand and Bhutan on Nepal on the other. Eventually in September 1951, seventeen check posts were established or manned jointly by Indian technicians and Nepalese army personnel in the villages of Gumshe, Mustang, Narnacha Bazar, 11am Bazar, Jhumla, Jhumshe, Clangchung, Dola, Muju, Simikot, Tinkar, Chepurwa, Thumshung, Raswa, Pushu and Setu Bash.

Along with the above efforts, the Indian Government tried to achieve its security objectives by persuading the Ranas to liberalize their political system. It should be noted here that it was Nehru's belief that the feudal system in Nepal due to its autocratic policies and narrow base would give rise to internal subversion and thereby would exposed to the external threat of China, Nehru therefore believed that stability in Nepal which was essential for India's strategic interests could be achieved only through a liberal democratic system. For that India played a decisive role in bringing about apolitical change in Nepal which initiated the process of democratisation in the Kingdom.

With the same objective, India in order to reorganize and train the Royal Nepalese Army established its Military Mission in Nepal. New Delhi also extended massive economic aid to Nepal so that the later can become so viable that it could achieve economic stability and thereby with stand the pressures of internal and external subversion.

In the aftermath of the revolution, New Delhi maintained its special position in the kingdom by persuading king Mahendra to establish parliamentary democracy in Nepal but the experiment could not last long. After the Royal takeover New Delhi again tried to ensure "stability through democracy" by covertly supporting the democratic forces against the Royal regime. But it failed to achieve its objectives which ultimately induced New Delhi to look at the Royal regime for stability in the kingdom. Thus keeping this approach in view, India came to important than democratisation of the policy. With this perspective India supported the Panchayat system of Nepal given by the King.

Despite Nepal's demand in 1969 to withdraw India's military personnel from Nepal's northern border and the revision of Treaty of Peace and Friendship, New Delhi's security interests were safeguarded by Nepal more or less till 1971. But after the emergence of Bangladesh and India' s decisive role in the crisis plus the assimilation of Sikkim induced Nepal to revise its security perception and relationship with India. Nepal now began to assert its independent position in world affair and tried to drift away from India's security parameter, which ultimately led to the crisis in Indo-Nepalese relations.

Troubled Indo-Nepalese Relations

The real cause of the impass between India and Nepal was deep rooted in the conflicting security perception adopted by Kathmandu vis-à-vis New Delhi. This conflicting security perception of Nepal was emanated due to some obvious reasons:

First: Impression set by the Indian ruling elite that Nepal belongs to that category of nations whose independence is only in the strict legal sense but not in the functional criteria so far as the security of India is concerned, induced Nepal to be cautious in its relations with India in pursuit of the preservation of Katmandu's national interests.

Second: A tendency to impose India's security perception on Nepal complicated the whole gamut of interaction between the two countries. It was Nepalese belief that India wanted their country to see China through the prism of New Delhi's strategic thinking and desire to block any type of relations developing between China and Nepal which the Indian policy makers think adverse to their interests.

Third: India's role in the domestic politics during the revolution of 1950 and during the I crisis in 1960-62 was also considered by Nepalese as symbol of high handed diplomacy adopted by New Delhi towards its small neighbours.

In view of the above assumptions Nepal believed that its security lies not in security treaties or pact, but in the improvement of general politico-economic conditions supported by a good foreign policy. Further Nepal also believed that it cannot play the big power card in South Asia, nor can it risk its independence by becoming a surrogate of any outside power. Indeed Nepal believed that India and China both are the real guarantors of its security. And this crucial aspect can be neither underplayed nor wished away. However since Kathmandu want to assert its independence and identity in international arena, it cannot be aligned with either neighbour, despite its extensive relations with India.

Thus in order to achieve the above security goals Nepal adopted three broad strategies:

a) a political balance between Nepal and its neighbours-India and China.

b) an adherence to the principles of the United Nations and non-alignment.

c) an effective use of its extra-regional as well as regional links (small powers of the region) to counterweight India's dominant influences in the region and thereby to reduce New Delhi's pre-eminent position in the Kingdom.

Nepal's stalemate with India in 1988-89 was the product of formers vigirous attempt to take some deliberate steps to follow its security perception to reduce later's dominant position in the Kingdom. Some of the issues. which have created uneasy situation between the two countries were: Nepal's proposal of zone of Peace, Securing Arms from China without India's prior knowledge and Kathmandu's deliberate attempts to nullify the provisions of the Treaty of Peace and Friendship.

While India believed that the above steps taken by Nepal were contrary to its basic security interests in the Kingdom, Nepal on its part considered these steps as manifestation of its identity which it believed could only be achieved by keeping away from India both in the security and economic affairs and to follow a tight rope policy between China as an alternative to India in the Himalayan region was also an irritating factor.

In the crisis India took strong stand by refusing to review the Treaty of Trade and Transit and by asking Nepal to discuss the entire gamut of Indo-Nepalese relations particularly New Delhi's concern over India's strategic interests in the Kingdom.

The Current Security Perspective

The political changes at the global level-end of cold war, dismemberment of the Soviet Union, adoption of liberal economic policies and introduction of new democratic system in Nepal have some positive impact on India's security perception vis-à-vis the South Asian countries in the general and Nepal in particular. Till now, New Delhi preferred to achieve its security goals by following a policy of non-alignment at the global level. As such New Delhi tried to refrain China as a major rival of India in the Himalayan region in particular and the United States to interfere in the South Asian affairs. In this effort, New Delhi got active support from Soviet Union, which is no longer, a super power making uni-polarity of the world a reality.

In view of the above changed scenario, New Delhi now has tried to reformulate and redefine its priorities and security perceptions vis-à-vis its South Asian neighbours so that it can evolve such a policy which could strive for a common regional security framework to checkmate the negative aspect of the unipolar world and at same time can safeguard her security interests in the region in general and Nepal in particular.

As a part of this strategy, India in order to consolidate its relations with the South Asian neighbours has articulated a doctrine known as 'Gujral Doctrine'. The major objectives of the doctrine is to adopt accommodating and generous attitude towards neighbours unilaterally to maximum extent possible without any demand of reciprocity.

Whereas India showed its magnanimity by accepting Nepalese demands for their economic development, New Delhi on its part expressed its concern over the proliferation of ISI activities in Nepal and suggested Kathmandu to take appropriate steps to check these activities. Regarding Nepal's demand of the revision of the Treaty of Peace and Friendship, India told Nepal to create consensus in the country and agreed to discuss the matter at Secretary level.

Thus, the confidence building measures adopted by India have undoubtedly enhanced India's popular image, which will indirectly safeguard India's security interests in Nepal. What is now needed is continuous dialogue between India and Nepal on security issues especially in view of emerging threat of Mao's insurgency to Nepal's political stability, so that any misunderstanding created in this regard should be sorted out in an atmosphere of good neighbourliness. While Nepal on her part should refrain from taking any steps which endanger India's security interests in the region, New Delhi should also extend its helping hand for safeguarding Nepal's national integrity and economic interests in the region.

4

Geographical Causation in Southeast Asian History

*Prof. Y. Yagama Reddy**

Southeast Asia is reckoned as an entity on the basis of certain common denominators which subscribe to an apparent regional homogeneity that tends to differentiate the region from the other regions of Asian continent. Yet, the complexity and the diversity of this area in many respects have inspired certain descriptive epithets like 'cultural shattered belt', 'political fault zone', 'Balkans of the East', 'bridge and barrier', and 'a region at the crossroads'. All these connotations ultimately point to the geopolitical significance of this region which underscores the need for an understanding of historical processes operating in this spatial realm. A two-decade long innings of my association with the Southeast Asian Studies has made me to develop a strong fascination for the long historical and cultural processes which entail political culture. The underlying cultural and political affinities sustained well for over a millennium during the pre-modern period and certain facets of economic history have persistently kindled my interest to gain an insight into the historical importance of geographical facts so that an estimate of geographical determinism on the historical momentum could be formed. This modest attempt

* Centre for Studies on Indochina & South Pacific, Sri Venkateswara University, Tirupati-517502, A.P.

at inquiring into the geographical causation in Southeast Asian history is thus based on my fairly comprehensive understanding of the historical processes (developments) in this region which have been analyzed from time to time by several eminent historians. It is evidently needless to make a citation of such a multitude of the historical accounts, especially as the inferences drawn from them, concern with this present study.

I. Etymological Significance of Southeast Asia

Notwithstanding its glorious past, the term 'Southeast Asia' is comparatively of a recent origin; and it was the Second World War that made this region prominent and visible and established the legitimacy of the name. But the Western colonial powers who were engrossed in their motives for accruing economic benefits from their colonial enterprises, hardly evinced any interest in getting the nomenclature standardized. It was an abject indifference of the colonial rule that led to the diffusion manifest in the loose or liberal use of the term, 'Southeast Asia' in multifarious forms. Western scholars looked at the region as a 'culturally shattered belt'; and the western statesmen were reluctant to think far beyond their impression of the term, as 'esoteric'. The callous attitude of colonial masters, evident from yet another fact that the colonial dominions, having obscured the pre-modern polities had totally ignored the logic of history and utterly disregarded the realities of geography in delineating the boundaries of their respective colonies has affected the evolved regional frame of Southeast Asia which has since then been at variance with the ground realities. The withdrawal of colonial rule had no doubt resulted in the independence to the Southeast Asian countries; but the post-war political map of Southeast Asia betrayed the otherwise illogical and illegal survival of the vestiges of Western colonial rule. Many scholars, who could not get reconciled to these glaring inconsistencies in the region-forming factors and processes, variously attempted to suggest the appropriate borders to this region on the basis of religion and history, ethnology and languages, geomorphology, biogeography and political science. Historical momentum being far ahead of these intrinsic realities, made the region contend with the existing borders which almost became the permanent features.

Southeast Asia, in its binomial expression, has also acquired much etymological significance. Far beyond the logic of compass that signifies the basic geographical connotation of the word 'southeast', there were variations in the very expression of the term. In English language alone, for instance, the term had once been spelt in a dozen ways, through the inclusion or exclusion of hyphen in the word 'southeast' and by an addition of the adjectival suffix 'ern' to southeast, besides varied preferences in capitalizing the initial letters of south and east. Of late, the term has become standardized by with the dropping of the hyphen (-) and the suffix (ern) to spell it as a single word and its initial letter (southeast), capitalized so as to be consistently used as southeast. About the same time, having endured trials and tribulations for over 30 years from the end of Second World War to Vietnam unification (1975), Southeast Asia came to be considered as a region comprising 10 nations — Myanmar, Thailand, Laos, Cambodia, Vietnam, Malaysia, Singapore, Indonesia, Brunei and the Philippines. The Association of Southeast Asia Nations (ASEAN) which was founded in 1967 for promoting regional cohesion and cooperation, had of late emerged as a full-fledged regional organisation (A-10) representing all the Southeast Asian countries, thanks to the reapproachment facilitated by the termination of Cold War. To this list may be added East Timor which achieved separate statehood following its cessation from Indonesia (2001). ASEAN has thus fulfilled the objective of achieving a regional identity to Southeast Asia. Yet, its historical geography, fully satiated with the positive and negative tendencies as a result of complexity and diversity in many aspects, presented a phenomenon of series of dialectical patterns that subscribe to the notion of paradoxes.

II. Physiography in Relation to Geological Structure

The physical make-up exemplifies the fact that the region is a realm of contrasts. Southeast Asia, as constituted into a peninsula and several thousands of islands, connotes territorial fragmentation into mainland (Indo-Pacific peninsula comprising Myanmar, Thailand, Lass, Cambodia and Vietnam) and insular Southeast Asia (Malayo-Indonesian archipelago consisting of Malaysia, Singapore, Indonesia, Brunei, the Philippines and East Timor). Equally half of this vast expanse of 9.2 million sq. km. is in the form of intervening seas which, throughout the period of history had served as a unifying factor rather than as a divisive force. Peninsular shape has made the trade easier as much as insularity facilitated maritime trade.

At the core of this physical character, lies the geological structure of the region. The north-south trending mountain series (of Mesozoie era : 225-65 million years ago) have bunched together and merged northwards into Yunnan highlands of China. Unlike these longitudinal ranges dominating the physiography of Mainland, the east-west trending horizontal structures of young folded tertiary series (65-2 m.y. ago) pervade the Malayan archipelago and merge with the western Pacific series running through the Philippines. This dichotomy corresponds to the division of Southeast Asia into a stable landmass (mainland) and an unstable insular region, the latter being exposed of cataclysm caused by earthquakes and volcanoes.

(a) Drainage — Glaciation — Landforms

That the drainage pattern broadly conforms to the geological structure is clearly seen as narrow and elongated valleys are formed by Irrawaddy, Salween, Chao Phraya and Mekong (all in the Mainland), as opposed to the multitude of short river courses in the insular region. Interestingly, notwithstanding this distinction, all these rivers remained part of the drainage system during the last glaciation period (about 17,000 years ago) when the exposed bed of South China Sea served as a platform (bridge) enabling the migration of plants, animals and the primitive man as far east as Australia. The post-glaciation phenomenon that lasted for 10,000 years (15,000 to 5000 years ago) resulted in the submergence of the hitherto exposed terrain and eventually in the formation of islands signifying the highly elevated grounds. In consequence, Southeast Asia had its land area shrunken to the present extent, besides being deprived of extensive depositional plains; and hence the scattered fertile plains or lowlands rather becoming an exception than a rule. If there had been changes brought in the coastline and thereby in the shape, the resultant physiography in the form of swamps, lakes, lagoons, flood-plains and marshes has facilitated the inland fishing undertaken to the extent of supplementing the diet composed of rice as the staple food item. Further, the long and sustained fluvial action of erosion and deposition in the context of tropical climatic rhythm and the recurring volcanic activity have produced complex landforms — steep and rugged mountain slopes, inter-mountane basins, subduced relief features like plateaus, flood-plains, deltas and coastal lowlands.

(b) Physiographic Divisions — Historical Process

The lowlands, though limited in their extent, have evolved as the centres of political and economic activity and as the clusters of population (about 75% of total population), repugnant to the expansive uplands (covering about 75% of total land area) as bearing of no economic and demographic significance. This lopsided relationship manifest in intraregional disparities in several aspects, has persisted all through the period of history. Regional imbalances owe much to inaccessibility, a persistent problem imposed by the deeply dissected mountain chains. Furthermore, the young folded mountains which had become an impenetrable barrier for the movement of goods and people to and from the Asia interior, had also imposed on Southeast Asia the ever-lasting impediments in the form of isolation and remoteness. Lowlanders too endured segregation on account of the transportation difficulties posed by the intruding mountain chains and the intervening river courses. The entire historical period witnessed a contrast between the lowlands and uplands in terms of agricultural practices.

(c) Geography — Emergence of New Kingdoms

The narrow constricted river valleys had for long played a vital role in the history of southward migrations. In the first instance, they had reduced the volume, if not the variety, of people who migrated into Southeast Asia. The people of Mongoloid stock from Tibeto-Yunan plateau started filtering slowly through these river valleys — a long process which resulted in the displacement of earlier settlers through subjugation by the new wave of migrants who later emerged as the dominant components in such potentially productive lands that could support high densities of population. It was the geographical proximity to Southern China that made Southeast Asia receive a variety of ethnic groups — Mons (from Southwest China), Karens (eastern Tibet) and Burmese (eastern Tibet and Yunan) through the Irrawaddy valley into different parts of Burma; Khmers (Southwest China) through Mekong valley into Cambodia; Thais (Southern China) along Salween into Shan region (Burma), along the Mae ping and Chao Phraya (into Thailand) and along Mekong into Laos. Mountainous geography as per the historical evidences, sustained the war-logistics of the new wave migrants infringing upon the earlier political dominions of lowlands. Repeated Thai conquests of Khmer territory were facilitated by geography. Thais took advantage of the ecology of mountainous terrain to the extent of inflicting a decisive defeat on the lowland — based Khmer empire, notwithstanding the latter's pervasive political power, economic prosperity and cultural pre-eminence. Similarly, geographical inertia manifesting in nature — imposed restrictions became all the more pervasive. The poorly endowed resources — extremely unhealthy highlands, limited rather compartmentalized fertile lowlands — restrained the highly civilized

Champa from achieving political unification and it eventually lost its prolonged battle against the invading Vietnamese from the north and Cambodians from the west.

(d) Mountains as Frontiers of Early Kingdoms

The political boundaries of ancient and medieval states were much in relation to the physical terrain; and the authority of the rulers was found diminishing from the capital towards the peripheries which had become the frontiers typified by criss-cross rugged mountains. Even today, mountains divide the people of Southeast Asia : Tenasserim mountain range divides Myanmar and Thailand; Annamite Chains remain an impenetrable barrier between Vietnam and Laos; Crocker mountains are between Indonesia and Malaysia in Borneo island while the Main range is between Thailand and Malaysia. But these mountainous frontiers had however served as 'shock absorbers' between the highly powerful lowland regimes which often extended their suzerainty of over-lordship on the ephemeral states in the peripheral uplands. Thus, physiography with centrifugal tendencies, though discouraged the settlement process, had contributed to the strategic significance in terms of the territorial security for the lowland regimes. The Mainland rivers enforced isolation in their upper reaches intercepted by rapids and waterfalls which thwarted the French attempts at discovering an inland navigable route to China all through the course of Mekong river. Nonetheless, its course through highly gradient slopes in the upper and middle reaches offered the scope for developing a multipurpose project to accrue the benefits thereof. The geographical setting and hydrographic character of the perennial rivers of the Mainland have formed the basis for achieving regional cooperation, as is evident from the efforts of riparian states concerned for over 4 decades ever since the establishment of Mekong Committee (1955) which, after having experienced trials and tribulations in the context of the cold war, has been transformed into Mekong Commission (1995).

(e) Maritime Geography and Strategic Significance

Besides being a source of means of livelihood like fishing, trade and piracy, the tropical seas are highly productive in matters of the marine wealth. Further, they act as a unifying factor rather than as a divisive force. The maritime character of Southeast Asia has acquired significance on account of the higher proportion of coastline (to the total land area) resulting from the territorial fragmentation. The peninsular shape and the insularity (cumulative factor of one thousand of islands) have made the oceanic shipping possible. Except the land-locked state of Laos, all the coastal fringes conferred the benefit of grater accessibility on the maritime-based pre-modern polities which developed several trading ports all along the lengthy coastline. Sea-borne commerce afforded as much economic strength to many a maritime power as agriculture could have sustained them. Southeast Asia's locational character at the maritime crossroads has predisposed the region to acquire the strategic significance. This locational factor alone exposed the region to external influences, though the insuperable barrier of lofty mountains had forbidden the establishment of an overland route between China and Southeast Asia. Similarly, Arakan Yoma impeded any possibility for an overland route between the geographically proximate regions of Assam (north eastern India) and Burma.

The physiography imposed isolation and inaccessibility, as discussed earlier, and denied the valley-based pre-modern polities of the normal contacts. The coastal routes being extremely circuitous, there began to emerge in the lowlands the ethno-linguistic states which were inward-looking with scant interest in the maritime pursuits. On the contrary, the insular political units, though confronted with the obstacles of intervening mountains, could establish communications with those on the opposite sides of a common stretch of sea. For all the limitations of smaller extent and instability, there was a semblance of unity attributed to the sealane communications and inter-insular trade.

(f) Political Power Based on Agricultural Prosperity

The development of early kingdoms was much in relation to the geographical location manifest in the centripetal influence on the process of people and converging in the potentially productive agricultural lands of valleys, deltas and plains. The advanced pattern of social and political organisation was essentially the product of agricultural prosperity of deltaic lowlands as, for instance, Tongking (Vietnamese), Meenam basin (Thais), and Irrawaddy and Sittang (Burmese). Similarly, the fertile soils of river basins in eastern and central parts of Java also formed the basis of political and cultural development. Together with the advantage of agricultural wealth, geographical modality of Cambodian (Toule Sap) basin enabled the Khmer empire to get itself equipped with natural defences through commanding easy routes to the upper Mekong, Korat plateau, Meenam basin and the coastal lands. Uneven spatio-temporal distribution of rainfall and a unique plain-land topography, were the peculiarities of geographical importance for the evolution of an irrigation system that facilitated the agricultural prosperity of immense economic wealth to the ruler and assured livelihood to the subjects. Of the two types of agrarian systems, "hydraulic-agriculture" necessitated the construction and maintenance of an elaborate irrigation and drainage system by the rulers, as opposed to the "hydro-agriculture" based on minor irrigation works essentially of local participation.

The inland agrarian hydraulic system was a magnificent one, developed by Angkorian rulers of the 9th century in the Cambodian basin characterized by the centripetal drainage and peculiar hydrographical conditions of Mekong river. The system, as per the study of aerial photography by Bernard Philippe Groslier which testified to the efficiency of water management, was designed 'to solve the problem posed by too much and too heavy monsoon water within too short a time'. It was capable of irrigating about 5.0 million hectares of paddy fields that could yield 3-4 harvests a year, besides regulating floods and meeting the drinking water requirements of the neighbouring township. Khmer's economic power based on its agricultural prosperity, was at the root of its unquestionable political prestige and cultural pre-eminence in the mainland Southeast Asia until the 13th century.

The Kyaukse irrigation system in the Central dry zone of Burma, was also formed of vital strategic importance to the successive regimes of Pagan and Ava. Similarly, water-logging conditions in the Red river delta of Tongking region necessitated the construction of dykes by the Vietnamese. This dyke system that ensured agricultural prosperity to Vietnam was designed to save the rice fields from flood — water raising 20-25 feet above the river banks. The cultivation of floating rice in the areas prone to inundation, points to the geography-driven economic history. Emergence of powerful kingdoms of Kedri, Singosari and Majapahit as well as of Mataram and Srivijaya was also ascribed to the irrigation development in eastern and central Java. Thus, the clusters of great population densities in these areas began to emerge as centres of political power and distinct cultural-areas, unlike the physically dissipated hill-states with emaciated population. The sea-empire of Madjapahit (13-15 centuries), like the land-oriented Mataram, had its political strength supported by an agricultural base. Soil fertility renewed by water-borne volcanic ash, facilitated the intensive agriculture and thereby economic wealth capable of supporting high densities of population. Like the maritime empire of Srivijaya (8-11 centuries), the two other dynasties of Sailendas (8 century) and Mataram (9-10 centuries) in Java rose to power on the basis of maritime trade, thanks to their locational advantage to the extent of controlling the coastal ports. Quite analogous to Malacca's strategic location was the central location of Java in the archipelago that enabled Java to gain access to products and to exercise control over an alternate trade route through Sunda Straits.

(g) Negative Phenomenon of Geography

On the contrary, geography had also its sway over the fall of many a kingdom in Southeast Asia. Sedimentation in the shallow sea and lower deltaic region of Mekong had cut off Tonle Sap from its contact with sea so as to get itself transformed into an inland lake. Furthermore, faster rates of deposition in the Mekong delta and storage tanks than the pace of maintenance capabilities set in motion the process of disintegration of Angkorian empire. The changing course of distributaries of Red river had virtually deprived Hanoi and Hai Phong of being accessible to sea. Similarly, the torrential rains used to bring down heavy loads of top soil from the steep slopes of young-folded mountains in the insular region and deposit the same along the coastal fringes. This constant process of sedimentation along the eastern coast of Sumatra and Malay peninsula, had eventually resulted in the decline of the powerful kingdom of Srivijaya which was based on the maritime commercial advantage owing to its location on the shortest sea route through the Straits of Malacca. So was the little but flourishing kingdom of Dharmavamsa (central Java) reduced to ashes following a volcanic eruption (1006 A.D.) and the subsequent mud-flows, which swept down from the volcanic ash, and washed off the settlements. In the recent times, volcanic eruptions caused heavy devastation in the archipelago region. The gruesome volcanic outburst at Krakatau in Sunda straits (1883) resulted in a human holocaust of 36,000 people, besides enormous loss of property. Yet another tragedy due to volcanic activity in Hibok-Hibok on Camiguin island (1948) rendered 35,000 people homeless.

III. Climatic Pattern

Though Southeast Asia is broadly identified with humid tropical climate, there are subtle climatic variations which divide this region into (i) equatorial Southeast Asia and (ii) monsoon Southeast Asia which is again categorized into two climatic zones manifest in the continental and insular rhythms. Southeast Asia gets itself differentiated from the rest of monsoon Asia because of the prevalence of two monsoon winds over Southeast Asia during the same period. This is a unique phenomenon resulting from the deflection of monsoon winds perpendicularly at the equator that passes through the large part of Southeast Asia. Thus, southeast monsoon (south of equator) becomes southwest monsoon (north of equator) during May-August; so does the northeast monsoon becomes northwest monsoon once it crosses into the region south of equator during September-November. An uneven distribution of the rainfall, being a natural feature, is due to the alignment of the mountains with windward slopes receiving heavy rainfall vis-a-vis raimshadow areas experiencing drought conditions. Equatorial location finds little diurnal and seasonal variations in temperature, humidity and rainfall which, being recorded on the higher scale, do not subscribe to seasonality. But the areas forming into tropical zone have distinct wet and dry seasons. If topicality gets replaced with sub-tropical or temperate climatic conditions owing to the increase in the altitude in the continental portion lying far beyond the Tropic of Cancer, it is the maritime influence that tends to sway over the insular portion of Indonesian archipelago region.

(a) Monsoon Climate — Spread of Indian Culture

Monsoon rhythm had been of tremendous historical significance of human geography — settlement pattern, population distribution, cultural evolution and economic growth besides trading relationship with the neighbouring lands. If narrow constricted river valleys of north-south trending parallel mountain chains had facilitated the historical southward migrations from Tibeto-Yunnan plateau region into the lowland of mainland Southeast Asia, these migrants who were preponderantly of Mongoloid stock of Southern Chinese origin got themselves attracted to the facets of Indian Culture. The process of Indian Cultural expansion into Southeast Asia was accomplished across the Bay of Bengal which posed no major climatic obstacles to the early mariners. The monsoon reversal winds over the Bay of Bengal and South China Sea facilitated the navigation all along the stretch of sea route between India and China. Much in accordance with the direction of winds during a particular period, navigators used to resume their return journey (in either ways) after a lapse of 3-4 months for change of winds. The process of Indianisation was an extensive rather pervasive spatio-temporal phenomenon that was sustained for about 1500 years from the beginning of Christian era and encompassed almost entire Southeast Asia. The spread of Indian culture, based on the precepts of Hinduism and Buddhism, was accomplished by Indian merchants, Hindu priests and Buddhist monks through a process utterly divorced from political conquest and economic exploitation. So was the spread of Islam into the insular region by the Indian Muslims. If the Philippines was the only country free from the Indian cultural influence, it was attributed to the surrounding deep sea trenches and the storm-ridden sea surfaces that deterred the early navigators from sailing across the turbulent waters to reach the indented coasts of the Philippines. This glorious chapter in the cultural history enkindled an overwhelming pride among a section of Indians as to float the concept of 'Greater India' much to the chagrin of Southeast Asians.

(b) Geographical Predisposition to Plural Societies

In fact, the geographical modality of Southeast Asia made the region become vulnerable to European domination in the form colonisation. Again the region's economic geography became so conducive to new innovative strategies and thereby to new economic opportunities that attracted the large scale immigrations of alien people — Chinese, Indians and Europeans — in 19th and early 20th centuries. Thus, Southeast Asia had become a bridge and barrier to a wide range of human contact, movement and ideas. This process of fusion and fracture of ethnic and cultural moves turned the region into a politico-cultural fault zone resulting in the formation of plural societies in every country. Marked by transition and instability, no unit in Southeast Asia is homogeneous either vertically or horizontally. Despite the fact that each of the nation-states represents a major ethnic group, racial purity is a myth rather a paradox.

(c) Climate — Disease — History

Its geographical location in the humid tropical belt has made Southeast Asia a region of endemic diseases and epidemics flared-up by natural calamities like floods and volcanic eruptions. Dense forests (both in uplands and lowlands) and marshes and swampy forests (in the coastal lowlands) have been the mosquito-infested areas endangering the very survival of people. High incidence of endemic diseases (like malaria and dysentery) accompanied by deadlier epidemics (like cholera and plague) took heavy toll of life reminding one of as much loss of population as in warfare and natural calamities. Such a high incidence of these diseases owed much to the climate (fostering fast bacterial growth), erosion and cloggings of water courses (leading to the breeding of malarial victors). Besides high mortality, these diseases in yet another form, diminished the people's stamina and productive capacity besides degenerating them physically. The malarial-ridden uplands discouraged the Annamities from seeking permanent settlement who instead preferred migrating all along the coast as far south as lower Mekong region. The defunct Khmer irrigation system induced high incidence of disease, eventually leading to the decline of man power required to fight against the invading Thais. Just as the fall of Chams and Cambodians entailed the disease, U?tong a Thai principality was devasted by the epidemic cholera in about 1350. Historiography also depicts the climatic hostility. Discomfort and disease on account of incongruent climate, took heavy toll of Portuguese troops within few days after their arrival at the Malacca port. The torrid climate being at variance with the European temperate climate became so inimical that forced the top-brass of colonial administration looking for summer resorts. Southeast Asia had therefore continued to suffer from under-population until and after the elimination of Malthusian checks of population (disease, welfare and natural diseasters) by the Western Colonial administration in late 19th century. Dry season offensive became a critical facet of the war-logistic pursued by the Cambodian rival factions (Coalition

Government of Democratic Kampuchea and the People's Republic of Kampuchea) during the civil war of 1980s.

IV. Biogeographical Factor in Historical Process

The peculiarities of Southeast Asian environment have undoubtedly been the products of geological structure, physiography, drainage and climate. If soils types point their genesis to the cumulative function of the above factors, forest types are found much in relation to climate. Thus, the broad forest types, viz., equatorial rain (evergreen) forests, tropical monsoon (deciduous) forests and temperate (montane) forests, conform mostly to the climate zones as being explicitly known from the above types. Yet, biotic environment also tends to divide Southeast Asia into Asian realm encompassing the continental portion together with the western half of Indonesia and the Australia realm covering the rest of archipelagic region. Though no such spatial division is discernible, soils too exhibit distinction in their spatial pattern. Zonal soils though preponderantly expansive, are of little value from the view point of agricultural productivity. On the other, a zonal soils, limited in their extent and highly scattered in their occurrence, are so highly fertile as to support populations of high density. Thus, dense forest cover and zonal soils coinciding with the uplands of mountainous terrain vis-a-vis the lowlands' physiognomy dominated by agricultural landscape have throughout the history been at the base of human settlement, population distribution and economic character of the region. Obviously, the rugged mountainous forests discouraged human settlement processes. This physical constraint led to the unending competition, confrontation and conflicts among the successive waves of migrants for acquiring a parcel of fertile lowland suitable for permanent (Sawah) cultivation. In this process which persisted almost throughout the first millennium, all those who were unable to resist the invasion of the northern migrants receded to the mountainous areas and remote islands and thenceforth continued to engage themselves in hunting, fishing, food gathering and seldom in shifting (Swidden) cultivation.

It is therefore a paradox to note that the expansive uplands could accommodate only about 25% population, as opposed to the concentration of 75% of population in the lowlands covering hardly 25% of land area. Besides this demographic imbalance, there has been diversity in the human environment in such matters as ethnicity, language and customs largely due to geographical isolation. The history of land use pattern had been simply a function of geographical determinism. Foremost of this has been monsoon rhythm that has exerted strong impact on the agricultural geography — cropping pattern and structure, crop typology, irrigation and drainage, all in essence depict the land use pattern. Multiple cropping also known as crop diversity with pronounced spatial variations over the entire uplands has been an insurance against natural calamities, besides portraying the principles of subsistence ecology. Preponderant monoculture of rice, in its historical context, had assumed significance as a source of economic power for many a state and as a means of subsistence for a large bulk of population in the lowlands. Furthermore, soil geography of the lowlands has facilitated the rice cultivation so much on commercial lines as to evolve onto the stage of exportation like rubber, oil palm, tobacco, coffee and indigo which were all introduced by the colonial masters depending upon their adaptability to soil and climatic conditions in different parts of Southeast Asia in 19th century. Broad similarity in agricultural pattern, owing to physiography, climate and recent history, have affected the prospects of intra-regional trade.

Geographical Determinism still Relevant in the Present Context

Geographical study, as is concerned with the spatial organisation expressed through processes and patterns, amply signifies the need for analyzing the historical processes (developments) as being influenced by certain geographical factors like location, areal extent, topography, climate and geophysical character. History provides us ample examples of defence strategies as having been predisposed towards geographical setting of the contending powers. In the modern context, many a state take cognizance of geographical imperatives in devising their foreign policy pursuits.

As for Southeast Asia, the complex geological structures and the intricate relief features (both signifying the physical make-up of the region) have for over millennia been inadvertently inert. Similarly, the configuration (in the form of a peninsula and the adjunct million islands) has remained unchanged for the last few thousand years. Just as the physiographic distinctions — uplands and lowlands — have remained static, the soil types and biotic life of this tropical realm have throughout the period of human history hardly responded to the anthropogenic influences. Needless to point out the prevalence of tropical monsoon rhythm (characterized by uneven distribution of rainfall and incidence of cyclonic storms) upon the Southeast Asian region through which equator passes for over 4000 kilometers.

It is therefore logical to conclude that the same geographical features as existed in the past continue to play their decisive roles even today. Arakan Yoma, for instance, is still a physical barrier between India and Southeast Asia. So are the mountain ranges within Southeast Asia impinging on the prospects of developing overland routes of any kind. In consequence, many parts still remain isolated rather inaccessible; and still sea serves as a means of communication and thereby a unifying factor than a divisive force. If the mountainous topography thwarts the attempts at expanding the farming land (being the lowest among the regions with comparable area), the hydrography of the rivers also frustrates the efforts to lengthen their navigable courses. Nor can it be contemplated to relieve Southeast Asia from the vagaries of monsoon and the onslaught of natural calamities (typhoons and volcanoes). Similarly agricultural practices (typology) do conform to the tropical rhythm than responding to the innovative agricultural strategies. Vietnam, like any other socialist state, claimed to have transformed subsistence farming into collective farming system, but met with the failure in bringing about changes in topology.

Southeast Asia's location at the crossroads had in the past facilitated the human contact and settlement and the cultural evolution. Under the Western colonial rule, the region acquired immense significance of maritime trade. Its pivotal position owing to the convergence of air and sea routes has conferred on it the paramount geopolitical significance to the extent of becoming itself a theatre of Second World War. During the Cold War, the two super powers indulged in a formidable task of gaining control over this region strategically located between the Indian and Pacific Oceans. Its immediate regional powers — India, China, Japan and Australia — too attached much importance to the geostrategic implications of Southeast Asia for their own security concerns.

Southeast Asia which formed a part of the inner/outer crescent of Mackinder's 'heartland' theory and of Spykman's 'rimland' theory, has thus entangled in centrifugal forces that resulted in dissensions and conflicts. Yet, a set of region forming factors sustained the region's identity as an entity. In the midst of trials and tribulations, the endeavour of forming a regional body resulted in the establishment of Association of Southeast Asian Nations (ASEAN) in 1967 with the initial participation of five nations. Though endured structural stagnation for a long period, the post Cold War situation has successfully accomplished the process of incorporating all the Southeast Asian nations into ASEAN and also geared up ASEAN for promoting regional security and cooperation.

ASEAN Regional Forum (ARF) — participated by 23 countries comprising all the ten ASEAN member states, 11 Dialogue partners plus Papua New Guinea and Mongolia — has ensured security of the region; likewise ASEAN's other initiatives too augur well for soliciting the support and cooperation from other ARF members. Of much significance are those propositions taking cognizance of geographical realities. Mention may be made of the Mekong Commission that has involved all the riparian states including China and the Indian initiatives of BIMST — EC and Mekong-Ganga Cooperation (MGC). ASEAN Free Trade Area (AFTA) is yet another well articulated device for promoting intra-regional trade through the reduction of tariffs.

Yet, ASEAN cannot altogether ignore the negative aspects of region's geography. Inaccessible mountains and remote islands are the fertile grounds for terrorist and insurgent activities. The geography of region also covertly subscribes to fostering non-military threats (like drug-trafficking, smuggling and sea piracy), even as ARF would provide a sort of insulation against external military threats. Broad similarity in economic strategies owing to tropical rhythm tends to inhibit the spirit of complementarity. Evolving common currency, on the lines of Eurodollar, would be a right step to achieve regional integration. Further, ASEAN's traditional restraint is called for to sort out their overlapping maritime claims. Thus, ASEAN is handicapped by the limited choices offered by nature than embarking on the chances ignoring the realities of geography.

Acknowledgement

I feel very much obliged to express my deep sense of gratitude to Prof. A. Lakshmana Chetty, former Director of our Centre and Vice-Principal of S.V. University College (Arts) for his encouragement and for having gone through the manuscript of this paper meticulously.

Suggested Readings

1. Cady, J. F., *Southeast Asia: Its Historical Development*, McGraw-Hill Book Co., New York, 1976.

2. Coedes, G., *The Making of Southeast Asia*, Routledge & Kegarn Paul, London, 1966.

3. Coedes, G., *The Indianized States of Southeast Asia*, (Trans-Susan Brown Cowing), University of Malay Press, Kuala Lumpur, 1968.

4. Crawfurd, J., *History of the Indian Archipelago*, (3 Vols.), B.R. Publishing Corp., Delhi, 1985.

5. Dobby, E.H.G., *Southeast Asia*, Univ. of London Press, London, 1958.

6. Dutta, A.K. (ed.), *Southeast Asia: Realm of Contrasts*, Westview Press, London, 1985.

7. Emerson, K., "Southeast Asia: What is in a Name?," *Journal of Southeast Asian Studies*, 15 (1), 1984, pp. 1-21.

8. Fisher, C. A., *Southeast Asia: A Social, Economic and Political Geography*, Methuen & Co., London, 1966.

9. Fisher, C. A., "South-east Asia," in : East, W.G., Spate, O.H.K. and Fisher, C.A., *The Changing Map of Asia: A Political Geography*, Methuen & Co., London, 1971, pp. 220-35.

10. Frayer, D. W., *Emerging Southeast Asia: A Study in Growth and Stagnation*, George Philip & Sons, London, 1970.

11. Hall, D.G.E., *A History of Southeast Asia*, MacMillan Publishing Co., New York, 1968.

12. Hill, R.D. (ed.), *Southeast Asia: A Systematic Geography*, Oxford Univ. Press, Kuala Lumpur, 1979.

13. Ng Shui Meng, *The Population of Indochina*, Field Report Series No. 7, Institute of Southeast Asian Studies, Singapore, 1974.

14. Sardesai, D.R., *Southeast Asia: Past and Present*, Harber Collins Publishers, New Delhi, 1987.

15. Spencer, J.E. and Thomas, W.L., *Asia, East by South: A Cultural Geography*, John Wiley & Sons, New York, 1971.

16. Tate, D.J.M., *The Making of Modern Southeast Asia*, (Vol. I), Oxford Univ. Press, Kuala Lumpur, 1977.

17. Tilman, R.O. (ed.), *Man, State and Society in Contemporary Southeast Asia*, Pall Mall Press, London, 1969.

5

Capital Flows in the ASEAN Countries

*Gautam Murthy**

Background

Regional co-operation and the formation of RTAs (Regional Trading Arrangements) are gaining increasing importance for both political and economic reasons. The economic or market factors for the formation of RTAs include opening out to new markets, attracting Foreign Direct Investment (FDI), and benefits from economies of scale. The political factors include greater diplomatic cohesion, counterbalancing other RTAs, commitment to internal reform, and greater synergetic networking of nations. There has been enormous proliferation of RTAs since 1995, with their scope and geographical reach expanding. Apart from removing tariffs on intra-bloc trade in goods, the newer arrangements tend to have deeper coverage.

Developing countries in Asia made a number of attempts at regional co-operation in the 1970s, beginning with the Asian Clearing Union of 1974 and U.N. ESCAP's "Bangkok Agreement" of 1975. However they failed to take-off because of limited coverage of membership, as well as in identifying products for tariff reduction. ASEAN (Association of South East Asian Nations) founded in 1967,

* Dr. Gautam Murthy is on the Faculty of the *Centre for Indian Ocean Studies*, Osmania University, Hyderabad.

is the most successful and dynamic cooperative forum, not only in Asia and for developing countries, but is also a trendsetter for all RTAs. The founding members of ASEAN were Indonesia, Malaysia, the Phillipines, Singapore and Thailand. Brunei joined in 1984. Vietnam became a member in 1995, followed by Laos and Myanmar in 1997. With Cambodia becoming a member in 1999, the ASEAN now includes all the ten countries of Southeast Asia.

When ASEAN was formed it sought not only to enhance co-operation, but also have a harmonised approach to issues of foreign policy and national security. The ASEAN member-states also take a coordinated and unified approach to security issues. Further, the ARF (ASEAN Regional Forum) discussing security issues, has enabled relatively smaller and less powerful ASEAN member states to engage China in the presence of powers like the United States on their territorial disputes in the South China Sea, where China has used its superior naval strength to assert its perceived territorial claims.

The first-ever India-ASEAN Summit held in Phnom Penh, Cambodia, in 2002, sets the stage for India to move purposefully in developing a broad economic and strategic partnership with the dynamic countries of South East Asia. In pursuance of India's "Look East" policy, the dialogue has moved from a limited sectoral partnership (1992) to full dialogue partnership (1995) and membership of ARF in 1996, culminating in the Summit.

India's economic potential and geo-strategic importance in Southeast Asia in the post-cold war world is today recognised as an important aspect of international economic diplomacy. India, needs to have a clearer "Focus" and even "Vision" with regard to its ties with the ASEAN. There is much scope for further expanding and deepening our cooperative agenda, synergising the economies of India and ASEAN and exploring new avenues for diplomatic complementarities.

SAARC continues to remain moribund because of ego clashes in the region. However, India has successful bilateral free trade agreements with Nepal and Sri Lanka. That a Free Trade Area in

South Asia remains a non-starter is not entirely the fault of Pakistan-India too has been reluctant to make the larger concessions that will make a more effective South Asia grouping. It is hoped that as India pursues and gives concrete shape to a free trade zone with ASEAN, other regional initiatives will also be reactivated, so that the Indian economy develops a multi layered set of net-works in the larger Asian and Indian Ocean regions.

The decision taken during the Fourth ASEAN Summit in 1992 to establish the ASEAN Free Trade Area (AFTA) by the year 2008 is an ambitious step for regional economic integration. The main mechanism for the implementation of AFTA is the Common Effective Preferential Tariff (CEPT). The CEPT is an agreed effective tariff, which is preferential to ASEAN member-states, and is to be applied to goods identified for inclusion under the CEPT scheme originating from member-states. AFTA has been complemented with other initiatives to facilitate movement of capital. These are the AICO (ASEAN Industrial Cooperation Organisation) and the AIA (ASEAN Investment Area).

The Asian Economic Crisis

The Asian financial and economic crisis affected many countries of the ASEAN. This first came to world attention in mid-1997, as the Thai baht rapidly lost value against the U.S. $. The interconnections among Asian economies led to its rapid spread to Indonesia, Malaysia, the Philippines, the Republic of Korea and Hong Kong. Many other countries In the region, such as Vietnam, Japan, Australia and Singapore, were also adversely affected.

Indonesia was worst affected by this economic crisis. According to the ADB, the GDP of Indonesia was estimated to have contracted by 13.2% in 1998. In 1999, however, the country's GDP increased by 0.9%, in 2000 by 4.8% and in 2001 by 3.3%. By 1999, the region's economies all began to recover. In 2000, ADB estimates placed

Singapore and Malaysia at growth rates of 9.9% and 8.5% respectively, while the economy of Thailand expanded by 4.2% and that of the Philippines by 3.9%. In 2001, however, owing to the global economic downturn (particularly in the electronics sector), Singapore's GDP contracted by 2%.

The predatory role played by currency speculators, and the extent of damage inflicted throughout the ASEAN region via the contagion effect, aggravated the financial crisis. There is certainly need to subject currency trading to some sort of surveillance, transparency, accountability and discipline, as the value of currencies traded far exceeds that of trade in goods and services across the globe. Heavy industries, including automotive and iron and steel were inefficient and under heavy protection. Unsound banking practices and poor corporate governance also contributed significantly to the financial turmoil. Massive outflow of capital in the form of "reverse investments" to finance long-term projects, with no prospects of early harvests exacerbated BOP problems.

The unpredictable nature of the crisis is certainly a cause for concern. In particular, the self-fulfilling nature of financial market expectations, chain reactions and herd behaviour tend to cause massive capital movements in a manner that is remotely connected to the fundamentals. All these have made high-flying ASEAN economies particularly vulnerable. While the crisis was clearly triggered by external forces, poor governance at home must share the blame to the extent that it has contributed to the vulnerability of these economies to external shocks. Sound prudential and banking norms, less crony-capitalism, and good corporate governance have put the ASEAN economies on the recovery track.

International Trade, Financial Flows and the LDCs

The slowdown of the U.S. economy has affected the growth performance of many LDCs, through a sharp reduction in their export earnings. Overall, GDP growth in the LDCs (excluding China) fell from close to 5% in 2000, to little more than 1% in 2001, mainly due to a sharp deceleration in most of Latin America and Asia. China was less affected, maintaining a growth rate above 7%. Elsewhere in Asia, only the Indian economy maintained the rate of the preceding year; in Latin America the Exception was Ecuador. Growth performance in Africa remained unchanged in 2001, but was again insufficient to achieve per capita income growth for the region as a whole.

In international capital markets, there has been an increase in risk premiums and less willingness by investors to lend to LDCs at a time when their external financing needs to meet rising current-account deficits have been growing. Even before the introduction, following 9/11, of more stringent and transparent reporting on financial transactions to fight illicit financial flows, capital flows to emerging markets in 2001 were forecast to fall to levels not since the early 1990s. This decline has been accompanied by considerably higher borrowing costs for several countries and the exclusion of others from international capital markets.

Thus, LDCs did not benefit from inflows of capital seeking alternative destinations or higher returns as the prospects for profits in financial markets in industrial countries deteriorated. Furthermore, the lower incomes due to the slowdown in exports and falling petroleum prices reduced fiscal receipts for many developing countries, and by cutting expenditures to keep their budgets in balance they further aggravated the downturn in economic activity. Finally, substantial declines in inflation rates and, indeed, the absolute levels of consumer prices, in a large number of developed and developing economies, such as Argentina, China, Japan, Korea and Singapore, in conditions of excess production capacity and excess supplies, have tended to limit corporate profitability and have reduced the likelihood of a return to high investment rates. Although declining inflation paved the way for a more aggressive anti-cyclical policy, most developing economies had little scope for autonomous action because of balance-of-payments constraints. However, some Asian countries loosened their fiscal stance and continued to pursue interest rate reductions designed to support domestic spending. Consequently, their cyclical growth performance was markedly better at the end of 2001 than the rest of the world.

Trade Flows and Balances

The slowdown of global growth during 2001 was accompanied by an even more marked deceleration of growth in international trade. This slowdown affected almost all-major regions. The economic impact of these declines was reinforced by downward pressure on export prices, leading to a pronounced deterioration, by an estimated 3%, in the terms of trade of LDCs in 2001. In Asia, the worst affected was the information technology (IT) sector, involving products such as semiconductors and consumer electronics. Despite the increasing optimism that the downturn in the developed economies outside Japan would be refersed in early 2002, growth in the volume of world trade is expected to recover to only about 2% in 2002 from 1% for 2001. Developing countries are particularly vulnerable to this sharp slowdown in the growth of world trade. With the value of exports falling more rapidly than that of imports, the current-account surplus attained in 2000 by developing countries as a whole almost disappeared in 2001.

In Asia, where recovery after the 1997 financial crisis was driven by exports, owing to the rapid expansion of investment in the IT sector, the fall in U.S. demand led to stagnation in export growth, rapid deterioration of current-account positions and declining growth rates in early 2001in all countries except India and China.

Financial Markets and Capital Flows

Capital flows to developing countries in 2001 remained at low levels, prolonging the downward trend that has persisted since the 1997

Asian financial crisis. In 2001, Latin America was the largest recipient of inflows; despite a substantial decline in flows to Argentina. Other regions, with the exception of the Middle Eastern countries and Turkey, also received positive inflows.

The interest rate reduction in the early 1990s followed a decade of historically high rates in the U.S. and it induced many investors to shift their investments to emerging foreign markets in order to maintain high returns. The attraction of these investments was supported by the rapid rates of economic expansion in Asia and the apparent success of adjustment policies in Argentina and Mexico in the early 1990s, and in Brazil in 1994. Liberalisation of financial markets in these countries also increased their attractiveness as investment alternatives.

As a result of increased global economic integration and the greater role of external trade in the economies of LDCs, the downturn in the United States has had a more rapid negative impact on their growth and export performance than in the past.

In many Asian countries recovering from the 1997 crisis, large external surpluses have been a source of increased deposits with international banks. Since 1998 repayments to banks by borrowers in all LDCs have exceeded new loans to them, and the total exposure of BIS (Bank for International Settlements)-reporting banks to such economies is now more than $200 billion lower than in 1997. Net repayments to BIS-reporting banks by borrowers in East and South Asia and in oil-exporting countries in West Asia have been accompanied by a large build-up of deposits by the two regions, which reflects substantial current-account surpluses; they have thus been a substantial net source of funds to the international banking system.

Financing for developing countries in the form of export credits also declined in 2001. Most of the decrease of $6.1billion was due to borrowers in Africa and Eastern Europe. This is shown in Table 1.

Table 1: Estimates of Net Capital Flows to Developing and Transition Economies, 1998-2002 (Billions of $) Estimates of IMF

Type of flow/region	*1998*	*1999*	*2000*	*2001*	*2002*
Total	69.6	59.6	8.9	20.1	59.8
Net direct investment	155.4	153.4	146.2	162.4	142.6
Net portfolio investment	–4.2	31.0	–4.3	–13.0	13.7
Other net flows	–81.6	–124.8	–133.0	–129.4	–96.6
Africa	10.0	11.9	7.0	9.5	10.0
Net direct investment	6.9	9.0	7.2	21.4	11.0
Net portfolio investment	3.7	8.7	–1.8	–6.3	4.2
Other net flows	–0.7	–5.8	1.6	–5.8	–5.2
Asia	–53.4	–7.6	–12.2	1.4	–3.1
Net direct investment	59.9	51.9	46.8	43.7	41.7
Net portfolio investment	–15.3	13.8	3.7	–4.7	3.8
Other net flows	–89.4	–74.4	–66.4	–46.0	–50.1
Middle East and Europe	11.8	–1.1	–22.4	–29.2	–0.7
Net direct investment	6.3	5.4	7.2	6.5	8.4
Net portfolio investment	–13.2	–4.2	–15.1	–9.6	–5.2
Other net flows	18.6	–2.3	–14.6	–26.1	–3.8
Western Hemisphere	71.7	43.6	37.9	38.8	39.5
Net direct investment	60.7	63.8	62.5	64.1	50.0
Net portfolio investment	16.5	9.8	4.6	4.0	7.6
Other net flows	–5.5	–30.0	–29.2	–29.3	–18.0
Transition Economies	21.0	13.8	2.2	7.6	15.0
Net direct investment	21.6	23.4	22.5	26.7	31.5
Net portfolio investment	4.0	2.8	4.3	3.6	3.5
Other net flows	–4.6	–12.4	–24.7	–22.7	–20.0

Source: IMF, *World Economic Outlook* (December 2001).

Recent Economic Performance of the ASEAN Countries

Key factors in the recovery path for all Southeast Asian countries were a resumption of domestic demand and consumption, rebuilding of the banking sectors to levels where financial intermediation can recommence, and the restructuring of private sector debt. With a need to restructure the corporate sectors, expunge bad debt, liberalise business regimes, strengthen institutions, and put in place better regulatory bodies, rapid growth took a secondary place. Healthy import demand from the United States has assisted their export growth performance, buoyed by the relative depreciation in the value of regional currencies against the U.S. dollar. In terms of potential domestic investment, local firms in Southeast Asia have been aided by the recent easing of interest rates in most countries across the region.

The Asian crisis has highlighted the need for most Southeast Asian policy-makers not to neglect their agricultural sectors, even when making concerted bids to develop their industrial and service sectors. Previously regarded as a sunset industry at best, the agricultural sector held up well during the regional economic downturn, and did much to cushion the social and economic impact of the financial crisis in some countries. Within the ASEAN-6 countries, the agricultural sector accounts for roughly 45% of total employment in Indonesia, the Philippines, and Thailand and just 20% in Malaysia. The figure is much higher for the transitional countries of Southeast Asia. With so many people still deriving their income from the agricultural sector in most Southeast Asian countries, policy makers now appear more cognisant of the need to support the development of this sector. On the road to modernity, allocating finite resources to IT clusters or rural areas should not become a zero-sum game.

The Macro-Economic Performance for the ASEAN-5 is given in Table 2.

The Asian Crisis has impacted the transitional countries of Southeast Asia harder than most had initially anticipated, and their economic reform programmes are in low gear as the leaderships debate how best to proceed. A coherent post-crisis recovery policy has yet to emerge from Indochina and Myanmar, leading us to believe that the transitional countries of Southeast Asia will lag the rest of the region in regaining full economic growth momentum. Recent sharp declines in foreign investment inflows and export earnings have placed added strains on these already weakened economies, and their fragile foreign exchange reserves in particular. A return to command economy policies is not a viable option, but the luster of market economies has also been tarnished, leaving doubts about the right policy-framework.

Vietnam's economy will need to counter the perils posed by a burdensome state sector, severe domestic debt problems and bank fragility, possible foreign exchange shortages, and rising urban unemployment levels from increasing migration of rural dwellers to cities.

Table 2: Macro-Economic Performance of the ASEAN-5

GDP Growth	*1997*	*1998*	*1999*	*2000*	*2001*
Indonesia	4.7	–13.2	–0.2	2.5	6.0
Malaysia	7.5	–7.5	4.0	4.5	5.0
Philippines	5.2	–0.5	3.0	4.5	4.8
Singapore	7.8	0.7	6.5	6.0	6.0
Thailand	–1.3	–9.4	4.5	5.0	6.0
Current Account (as % of GDP)					
Indonesia	–1.4	4.2	6.9	5.7	5.2
Malaysia	–5.3	12.9	13.6	6.2	3.5
Philippines	–5.3	2.0	2.5	1.3	0.3
Singapore	15.4	18.2	14.5	13.6	14.9
Thailand	–2.1	12.7	8.3	5.0	3.3
Gross External Debt (as % of GDP)		*1998*	*1999*	*2000*	*2001*
Indonesia		150.9	81.9	54.2	44.3
Malaysia		59.2	72.0	58.0	50.4
Philippines		74.3	70.3	73.5	75.5
Singapore		—	—	—	—
Thailand		76.8	58.3	51.9	46.9

Source: *Asian Development Bank*, 2002.

From Tables 3 and 4, it is clear that the ASEAN region is one of the most attractive investment locations in the developing world, and attracted a disproportionately large amount of FDI, particularly after 1985. This reorientation of the ASEAN economic cooperation is consistent with the national policies of the member countries i.e., economic development through market-based growth and greater participation of the private sector. The adoption of more outward oriented industrialisation strategies based on international trade and greater FDI is now being pursued in all the ASEAN members including previously inward-looking countries like the LCMV (Laos, Cambodia, Myanmar and Vietnam) countries. The impact of these large inflows of FDI into Indonesia, Malaysia and Thailand was impressive. Growth rates began to soar as these countries began to industrialise rapidly. The major investor countries in ASEAN were Japan, EU and U.S. The ASEAN nations like Malaysia and Indonesia faced disinvestments because of the financial crisis, but investments are now picking up.

Table 3: Financial Flows in the ASEAN Countries

($ millions)

Country	*Net Private Capital flows*	*FDI*	*Portfolio investment flows(Equity)*	*Bank and trade-related lending*
	1990 1998	1990 1998	1990 1998	1990 1998
Indonesia	3,235 3,759	1,093 356	312 250	1,804 3,512
Malaysia	769 8,295	2,333 5,000	293 592	617 3,017
Myanmar	153 153	161 70	0 0	-8 -83
Philippines	639 2,587	530 1,713	0 454	-286 269
Singapore	— —	5,575 7,218	— —	— —
Thailand	4,399 7,825	2,444 6,941	449 2,341	1,593 826
Vietnam	16 832	16 1,200	0 0	0 –368

Source: *World Development Indicators*, UN.

Table 4: FDI Flows in ASEAN Countries, 1987-2001

(U.S. $ million)

Countries	*1987-92*	*1993*	*1994*	*1995*	*1996*	*1997*	*1998*	*2001*
Brunei	1	14	6	13	11	5	4	244
Cambodia	—	54	69	151	294	204	140	113
Indonesia	999	2004	2109	4345	6194	4673	–356	–3277
Laos	4	36	59	88	128	86	45	24
Malaysia	2387	5006	4342	4178	5078	5106	3727	554
Myanmar	96	149	91	115	38	124	40	123
Philippines	518	1238	1591	1478	1517	1222	1713	1792
Singapore	3674	4686	8550	7206	7884	9710	7218	8609
Thailand	1656	1805	1364	2068	2336	3733	6969	3759
Vietnam	2060	1002	1500	2000	2500	2950	1000	1300

Source: *ASEAN FDI Data Base*, ASEAN Secretariat, Jakarta, 2002.

6

Emerging Trend of Economic Cooperation

The India — ASEAN Experience

*T. Nirmala Devi**

A fair multilateral trading system is all the way desirable, yet regional trading arrangements are increasingly accepted in the world due to the immediate economic benefits, particularly for the geographically contiguous countries. The decades starting from 1960s witnessed the emergence of various regional economic groupings and similar arrangements in the wake of the progress achieved in the Europe and North America. Regional cooperation is not an end in itself but as a means of fostering economic development and in this light, the regional cooperation efforts have been initiated in the Asia-Pacific region too in the 1990s, despite their soft and fragmented nature. The logic of the formation of a broader regional cooperation movements in Asia thus, stems from the emergence of powerful trading blocks such as European Union (EU) and North American Free Trade Agreement (NAFTA) which covered 60 per cent of the world trade, conducting on preferential basis.[1] A few sub-regional attempts in Asia, particularly the South Asian Preferential Trading

* T. Nirmala Devi, Professor, Centre for SAARC Studies, Andhra University, Visakhapatnam – 530 003.

Arrangement (SAPTA) are not thoroughly successful, due to the discrimination being faced in the industrial markets, apart from their own inherent weaknesses. All these efforts paved the way for the formation of regional trading arrangements, which are aiming at the acceleration of growth of the individual economies. In this context, the economic engagement of India with the ASEAN region is thoroughly desirable for attaining the fast growth. The 'sectoral dialogue' partnership of India with the ASEAN region in 1992; its upgradation to 'full dialogue' partnership in 1995; the membership in 'Asian Regional Forum' in 1996 and the increasing interaction in the first summit in 2002 were the important events of this growing engagement. This interrelationship not only reflects the good headway made by India in promoting greater cooperation with South-east Asia since the 'Look East Policy', enunciated in the early 1990s but also the emerging global trend of economic interaction with the neighbouring countries.

Introduction

In assessing the performance of the economy, besides other things, the degree of the development matters and in this light, there is a significant variation between India and the five major member countries of the Association of South East Asian Nations (ASEAN) viz., Indonesia, Malaysia, Philippines, Singapore and Thailand. Despite the geographical proximity, India and these members of the ASEAN differ markedly in the growth process as well as in the level of economic openness. If the size of the population of the two partners is compared, India is too big and the share of the ASEAN region as a whole increased from 37 per cent in 1990 to slightly above half of the population of India in 2000, not just because of the late entries into the regional grouping — Vietnam, Myanmar, Laos and Combodia — in the second half of the 1990s but also due to their relatively higher population growth rates as against India. On the other side, the Gross National Product (GNP) per capita of India which was about 10 per cent of the average of the major five ASEAN countries in 1990 fell to 7 per cent in the year 2000 due to the notable increase in the major five members, barring Indonesia and the four new members. The same per capita income if measured in PPP terms, the share of India amounts to 15 and 28 per cent of the ASEAN group of five and ten countries in 1995 and 2000 respectively. The Gross Domestic Product (GDP) of India varied from 83 to 85 per cent of the ASEAN region in 1990 and 2000 respectively, despite the inclusion of Vietnam and Laos in the latter year. Thus, it is interesting to note that India which experienced a relatively poor decadal growth rate of GDP in the past, registered a higher growth than that of the ASEAN's average in both the periods 1980-90 and 1990-2000, owing to the extremely poor performance of Philippines in the two decades together with that of Thailand and Indonesia in the latter decade.[2] The interaction between India and the other minor five member countries of the ASEAN region in the core area of trade and investment is not highly significant as compared to the remarkable economic relations with the major five member countries, hence India's linkages with the minor countries are not examined in this paper.

Theoretically, it may not be appropriate to compare India with the total or the average of the ASEAN grouping, as it constitutes a highly open and progressive economy Singapore followed by Malaysia, and a moderate economy Thailand and relatively weak economies Philippines and Indonesia. If the new entries are included in the late 1990s, a different picture was emerged and showing a relatively unimpressive economic scenario. Notwithstanding this, a general comparison is made between the two partners in this paper with a view to examine the impact of the recent developments in assessing the bilateral relations. Viewed against this background, the present paper attempts to address the core issue of trade between India and the ASEAN region as a whole on one hand, and India and the major five individual countries of the ASEAN grouping on the other, taking a note of the mutual benefits that are going to be accrued. The paper, then examines the aspect of how far the competitive nature of Indian economy is successful in penetrating the neighbouring South-east Asian markets by catching up their openness. This paper is arranged into two sections. Besides introduction, the first section deals with the overall economic performance of India in comparison with the ASEAN grouping as a whole as well as with the five major countries of the region and their dual engagement in the key trade issues. In the second section, the trade intensities — both export intensity index and import intensity index for the four year average periods, 1991-94 and 1995-98 are estimated to evaluate the bilateral trade orientation. The paper concludes with a few implications for policy and further research.

I. Overall Trade Performance

In Tables 1 through 7, the paper assesses the overall trade performance of India and the five individual ASEAN countries to the major extent possible with a view to examine the scope for future prospects. India's trade with the ASEAN grouping has not only been significant but also increasing as compared to the SAARC region throughout the 1990s (Table 1). India's imports from the ASEAN region were, by and large, gradually increasing in this decade, while the imports from the SAARC region were insignificant and not even constituting one per cent of its total trade, with the exception of the year 1998. However, the growth of India's exports was more steady in both the ASEAN and the SAARC regions, yet it was more striking in the former, barring the two subsequent years of 1997 financial crisis. It is apparent from the above table that India's trade orientation is more biased towards the ASEAN, despite its pre-eminence in the SAARC region.

Direction of exports, one of the important external indicators showed the surge in the share of exports of India as well as the major five countries of the ASEAN from 1985 to 2000 to the developing member-country group of Asian Development Bank which numbered around 40 (Table 2). The share of exports varied from a well above one-fifth in the case of India while it ranged between a well above

Table 1: Share of SAARC and ASEAN in India's Trade

(in per cent)

Year	*Imports*		*Exports*	
	SAARC	ASEAN	SAARC	ASEAN
1985	0.68	5.14	3.28	2.42
1990	0.39	6.76	2.73	4.25
1991	0.49	4.81	3.49	5.68
1992	0.83	6.64	3.89	6.61
1993	0.47	5.33	4.05	7.70
1994	0.51	6.91	4.22	7.35
1995	0.57	7.21	5.06	7.76
1996	0.61	7.50	5.08	8.69
1997	0.56	8.19	4.63	7.09
1998	1.10	10.18	5.05	4.91
1999	0.80	10.22	3.80	6.08
2000	NA	NA	NA	NA

Source: UN-ESCAP, Foreign Trade Statistics of Asia and the Pacific, various issues, Bangkok.

Table 2: Direction of Exports of India and ASEAN Countries

(% of Total)

Country	*Japan*		*U S*		*E U*		*Australia/ New Zealand*		*Others*		*DMCs*	
	1985	2000	1985	2000	1985	2000	1985	2000	1985	2000	1985	2000
India	11.1	5.4	18.9	22.8	16.7	24.0	1.4	1.1	43.0	24.5	8.9	22.2
ASEAN												
Indonesia	46.2	22.3	21.7	15.5	6.0	14.1	1.2	2.7	7.6	8.1	17.2	37.2
Malaysia	24.6	12.6	12.8	21.8	13.6	13.8	1.9	2.7	9.1	6.6	38.1	42.5
Philippines	19.0	14.7	35.9	30.2	13.8	16.6	2.1	0.8	9.7	6.9	19.5	30.8
Singapore	9.4	7.4	21.2	17.2	10.1	13.4	4.4	2.6	18.0	28.8	36.8	52.2
Thailand	13.4	15.7	19.7	22.6	17.8	16.7	1.9	2.8	20.1	9.2	27.1	33.2

Source: ADB, *Asian Development Outlook*, 2002, Oxford University Press, New York.

Note: DMCs — Developing Member Countries of ADB.

one-third and over half in the five member countries of the ASEAN. However, the improvement from 1985 to 2000 was not highly significant in Malaysia and Thailand, as most of the exports were directed to the U.S. The share of the U.S. in the exports of the rest of three ASEAN members was declining, in contrast to the moderate increase in India during the above period. There was no significant improvement in the share of the ASEAN's exports to the EU, except in Indonesia whereas India registered a sizeable growth during this one and a half decades. Japan had also lost its prominence as an export market of the above countries and the decline in its share was particularly pronounced in Indonesia followed by Malaysia.

Due to the external shocks, majority of the developing countries faced continuous deficits in the balance of their current accounts and the decline in the supply of concessional aid together with other external trade problems which aggregated their balance of payments situation in the 1980s. Most of the East and South-east Asian developing countries have been outwardly oriented and attached high priority to export promotion. In contrast, India along with the other South Asian countries registered a huge and increasing trade deficits with the outside world mainly due their inability to create export surplus. The bilateral trade balance of India with the five individual ASEAN members and the region as a whole in the 1990s revealed a mixed response of deficits and surpluses. India witnessed an unfavourable trade balance with the ASEAN region in this decade with the exception of the period 1991-95 and this deficit rose to formidable size in the later years 1998 and 1999 mainly attributing to the trade imbalance with Singapore and Malaysia, the two major importing sources from the region (Table 3). However, India enjoyed trade surplus with Thailand and Philippines, yet its surplus with Indonesia was restricted to half of the years of the above decade.

The share of five ASEAN members in India's total trade has been steady, notwithstanding the size. The share of India's imports from the major five countries of the ASEAN had been increasing in general, as compared to its share of exports, during the entire period starting from 1991-92, barring few years (Table 4). In the case of Singapore, India's imports ranged between 2.5 and 3.6 percentages while its

Table 3: India's Trade Balance with ASEAN Countries

(U.S. $ million)

Year	*Indonesia*	*Malaysia*	*Philippines*	*Singapore*	*Thailand*	*ASEAN**
1985	–27	–343	–5	–218	–46	–639
1990	28	–379	24	–116	181	–263
1991	80	–189	33	78	150	154
1992	87	–227	51	291	218	420
1993	115	–1	53	338	300	806
1994	–39	–202	88	63	235	56
1995	200	–505	122	45	302	152
1996	–5	–571	167	–137	250	–30
1997	–293	–687	215	–226	116	–926
1998	–644	–1288	81	–868	47	–2692
1999	–636	–1577	87	–865	122	–2854
2000	NA	NA	NA	NA	NA	NA

Source: As in Table 1.

Note: * 1985 = Total of the above five countries.
1990-93 = Total of the above five countries and Brunei.
1994-99 = All ten member countries.

Table 4: Share of ASEAN Countries in India's Trade

(in Per cent)

Imports from/Country Exports to	*1991-92*	*1992-93*	*1993-94*	*1994-95*	*1995-96*	*1996-97*	*1997-98*	*1998-99*	*1999-2000*	*2000-01*	*2001-02*
Indonesia	0.30	0.30	0.50	1.10	1.26	1.53	1.76	1.96	1.93	1.81	2.03
	0.80	0.70	1.10	1.10	2.08	1.77	1.25	0.56	0.88	0.89	1.23
Malaysia	2.00	1.90	1.10	1.70	2.46	2.66	2.84	3.80	4.07	2.30	2.22
	1.10	1.00	1.10	1.10	1.24	1.59	1.40	0.97	1.22	1.36	1.77
Philippines	—	—	—	—	0.06	0.04	0.07	0.09	0.11	0.13	0.18
	0.40	0.30	0.30	0.40	0.45	0.55	0.68	0.36	0.39	0.46	0.57
Singapore	3.60	2.90	2.70	3.10	3.04	2.72	2.89	3.27	3.08	2.87	2.53
	2.20	3.20	3.40	2.90	2.84	2.92	2.23	1.56	1.82	1.95	2.22
Thailand	0.20	0.30	0.20	0.60	0.46	0.50	0.56	0.64	0.66	0.63	0.83
	1.10	1.40	1.60	1.50	1.49	1.34	0.98	0.97	1.22	1.20	1.45

Source: CMIE, Foreign Trade and Balance of Payments, various issues, Mumbai.

a moderate fall in 2001-02 while its prominent export item gems exports varied from 1.5 to 3.4 percentages and registered a deceleration after 1997-98. Its share of exports to Malaysia was around 1 per cent in most of the years whereas the share of imports reached to 4 per cent in the later years of the decade.

The section-wise import and export trade of India with the ASEAN region clearly establishes the strong trade linkages in certain commodity groups. In India's trade with the ASEAN (Table 5), the imports of animal and vegetable oils, fats and waxes (Sec. 4) which varied from one-third to four-fifths constituted a prominent share, while crude materials (Sec. 2) and food and beverages (Sec. O) formed a considerable proportion of imports followed by machinery and transport equipment (Sec. 7). The latter section had occupied a sizeable share in India's exports also. India's exports in chemicals (Sec. 5), food and beverages, crude materials and unclassified commodity group (Sec. 9) were also noteworthy. Except in few cases, the expansion of imports from the ASEAN was not matched with the expansion of India's exports to the region. Furthermore, there was a deceleration in the latter and thus, causing a trade deficit with the region.

The share of top five products in India's trade with the ASEAN region from 1991-92 to 2001-02 (Table 6) shows that India's exports did not exhibit any increasing trend over the years, except in the share of its top export item gems and jewellery despite its erratic nature. The share of exports of electronic goods except for the year 2000-01; the share of oil meals and the share of machinery and instruments showed a declining trend in general. In the case of imports too, the trend was erratic with the exception of electronic goods, which registered a significant increase, particularly from the period 1999-2000. The share of other major import item vegetable oils, though oscillating, ranged between more than one-fifth and one-fourth of its corresponding total trade. The share of top two products in India's trade with the major five countries of the ASEAN for the three selected periods, 1991-92, 1995-96 and 2001-02 (Table 7) shows the preferential specification among the total products. The share of India's export of electronic goods to Singapore increased more than three times from 1991-92 to 1995-96, however, recorded

Table 5: India's Trade with ASEAN by Sections of SITC Rev. 2 (in Per cent)

Year		Sec. 0	Sec. 1	Sec. 2	Sec. 3	Sec.4	Sec.5	Sec.6	Sec. 7	Sec. 8	Sec. 9
1990	Imports	6.36	4.49	13.14	2.68	82.68	2.56	1.71	6.75	4.24	1.81
	Exports	5.13	1.56	5.04	0.13	1.37	6.57	4.77	12.49	1.27	20.23
1991	Imports	8.13	3.60	12.30	2.89	70.62	3.81	1.33	5.51	4.97	2.08
	Exports	10.32	2.06	5.49	0.12	0.46	7.08	5.18	9.88	1.35	5.38
1992	Imports	3.13	4.89	10.41	3.25	32.59	3.17	1.87	5.17	4.77	1.41
	Exports	13.55	1.25	7.58	2.74	2.28	9.80	5.77	11.92	1.22	3.17
1993	Imports	7.43	6.92	8.67	1.48	58.41	4.05	2.21	4.91	8.69	1.73
	Exports	14.18	1.72	11.21	8.25	3.81	8.02	6.23	13.62	1.68	2.64
1994	Imports	21.82	7.04	11.78	2.66	69.31	6.18	3.23	7.42	6.93	1.34
	Exports	13.22	3.64	6.99	7.43	7.52	9.67	6.47	14.12	2.11	2.33
1995	Imports	24.04	7.61	13.08	2.84	77.65	5.93	3.47	7.11	5.67	1.83
	Exports	17.64	3.73	8.04	5.06	4.60	9.36	7.10	15.76	1.73	4.01
1996	Imports	26.31	4.16	12.62	3.67	76.57	7.38	3.47	7.12	6.95	2.06
	Exports	15.56	4.65	14.63	0.65	4.90	9.54	7.12	14.66	2.00	3.18
1997	Imports	17.56	7.10	17.48	4.20	80.67	6.59	3.48	10.45	7.21	1.81
	Exports	11.50	7.18	10.72	0.87	8.61	8.24	5.88	13.89	1.94	4.29
1998	Imports	12.95	7.97	17.77	10.07	63.12	7.14	3.76	11.89	7.62	0.87
	Exports	7.67	6.67	4.65	3.00	4.66	8.88	3.84	8.52	1.96	5.05
1999	Imports	11.20	8.64	15.41	8.21	65.65	7.42	3.39	13.89	10.84	0.79
	Exports	8.60	6.60	9.09	18.71	6.60	10.88	5.20	10.85	2.07	2.47
2000		NA	NA	NA	NA	NA	NA	NA	NA	NA	NA

Source: As in Table 1.

Note: Sections 0 = Food and live animals chiefly for food
1 = Beverages and tobacco
2 = Crude materials, inedible, except fuels
3 = Mineral fuels, lubricants and related materials
4 = Animal and vegetable oils, fats and waxes
5 = Chemicals and related products, n.e.s.
6 = Manufactured goods classified chiefly by material
7 = Machinery and transport equipment
8 = Miscellaneous manufactured articles
9 = Commodities and transactions not classified elsewhere in the SITC

Table 6: Share of Top Five Products in India's Trade with ASEAN

(in per cent)

	1991-92	*1995-96*	*1996-97*	*1997-98*	*1998-99*	*1999-2000*	*2000-01*	*2001-02*
Composition of India's exports to ASEAN (%)								
1. Gems & Jewellery	5.20	12.18	10.11	7.60	11.47	13.55	11.41	10.94
2. Electronic Goods	9.65	7.52	6.14	6.05	5.92	6.20	9.34	9.37
3. Oil meals	13.40	13.92	17.64	15.43	11.62	7.74	8.33	8.18
4. Drugs, Pharmaceuticals & fine chemicals	5.63	3.18	4.25	4.76	8.11	7.42	5.83	4.71
5. Machinery & Instruments	13.14	4.44	5.78	7.96	7.30	5.22	4.60	4.48
Composition of India's imports from ASEAN (%)								
1. Electronic Goods	—	12.79	11.53	14.82	13.39	16.63	28.82	25.04
2. Vegetable Oils (edible)	5.73	20.27	22.04	18.00	28.06	25.32	22.86	20.22
3. Organic Chemicals	1.94	5.76	7.27	4.75	3.23	3.43	5.43	6.21
4. Wood & Wood products	9.54	3.06	3.45	4.62	3.20	3.22	3.79	5.59
5. Non-electrical machinery	5.85	3.75	3.78	4.09	2.97	2.46	4.83	4.79

Source: As in Table 4.

Table 7: Share of Top Two Products in India's Trade with ASEAN Countries

(in per cent)

Composition of India's Exports to:					*Composition of India's Imports from:*				
		1991-92	1995-96	2001-02			1991-92	1995-96	2001-02
Indonesia	1. Sugar	5.90	8.92*	15.35	Indonesia	1. Veg. Oils (edible)	7.70	14.48	37.53
	2. Oil meals	19.50	15.32	15.09		2. Coal, Coke & briquettes	0.00	18.93	11.05
Malaysia	1. Electronic goods	2.40	12.07	23.06	Malaysia	1. Veg. Oils (edible)	16.90	51.44	35.47
	2. Meat & Preparations	20.90	13.85	9.48		2. Electronic goods	0.00	6.66	25.36
Philippines	1. Wheat	—	0.61*	21.75	Philippines	1. Electronic goods	—	14.28	30.61
	2. Meat &Preparation	0.00	14.34	17.45		2. Inorganic chemicals	—	0.74	20.62
Singapore	1. Electronic goods	4.80	15.49	13.21	Singapore	1. Electronic goods	—	23.32	39.54
	2. Gems & Jewellery	10.90	10.61	12.57		2. Organic chemicals	1.60	8.11	9.79
Thailand	1. Gems & Jewellery	48.00	48.47	37.56	Thailand	1. Electronic goods	—	10.64	36.39
	2. Oil meals	8.90	13.51	11.16		2. Non-electrical machinery	15.80	5.96	12.18

Source: As in Table 4.

Note: * = 1996-97.

and jewellery showed marginal and sizeable decelerations in the first half and second half of the 1990s respectively. In the case of Malaysia, the share of India's export of electronic goods registered a tremendous increase in contrast to the export of meat and preparations. India registered growth in the exports of sugar to Indonesia; wheat and meat to Philippines; and oil meals to Thailand except for the period 2001-02, whereas it witnessed a decline in the exports of oil meals to Indonesia during the whole period and in gems and jewellery exports to Thailand from the period 1995-96 to 2001-02. The fall in the share of import of vegetable oils from Malaysia from the period 1995-96 was compensated from another ASEAN member, Indonesia. The share of import of electronic goods from the ASEAN, with the exception of Indonesia registered a very significant increase throughout the period under consideration. The share of organic chemicals from Singapore increased moderately, while the share of inorganic chemical imports from Philippines recorded a remarkable growth. The above two-way trade relations between India and ASEAN showed the active trading pattern and providing immense scope for closer economic integration. Some of the above tables reaffirmed the over representation of ASEAN members in the trade of India, particularly in imports. In essence, the pre-eminence of ASEAN in India's trade is clearly visible, especially in certain commodity groups.

II. Bilateral Trade Prospects

(a) Trade Intensity Indices

The trade intensities have been estimated for India — ASEAN countries for both exports and imports for the averages of 1991-94 and 1995-98 to evaluate the prospects of overall trade expansion, as shown in Table 8.

Table 8: Trade Intensity Indices of India with ASEAN Countries

	India's Export Intensity Index with ASEAN Countries		*India's Import Intensity Index with ASEAN Countries*	
Country	*1991-94 Average*	*1995-98 Average*	*1991-94 Average*	*1995-98 Average*
Indonesia	1.212	2.370	0.594	1.651
Malaysia	0.926	0.970	1.424	2.220
Philippines	0.756	0.827	0.231	0.144
Singapore	1.346	1.061	1.284	1.576
Thailand	1.176	1.130	0.359	0.508
ASEAN*	1.159	1.182	1.146	1.452

Source: Estimated from the basic data obtained from IMF, Direction of Trade Statistics Yearbook, 1998 & 1999, Washington D.C.

Note: * includes the above five major countries only.

The import intensity index is derived from the proportion of the country i's imports sourced from country j, divided by the ratio of country j's exports over total world exports net of country i's share.

The Import Intensity Index (mij) is defined as:

$$mij = \frac{Mij}{Mi} \Big/ \frac{Xi}{xw - xi}$$

where

Mij = Imports of country i from trading partner j

Mi = Total imports of country i

Xj = Total exports of country j

Xw = Total world exports

Xi = Total exports of country i

The export intensity index is derived from the proportion of country i's exports directed to country j, divided by the ratio of country j's imports over total world imports net of country i's share.

The Export Intensity Index (xij) is defined as:

$$xij = \frac{Xij}{Xi} \Big/ \frac{Mi}{Mw - Mi}$$

where

Xij = Exports of country i to trading partner j

Xi = Total exports of country i

Mj = Total imports of country j

Mw = Total world imports

Mi = Total imports of country i

As per the index, the value of more (or less) than unity of these indices indicate that a country is exporting/importing more (or less) to another country than might be expected from the country's share in world (export/import) trade.[3]

(b) Results

The bilateral trade orientation of India and the ASEAN region as a whole on one side and India with the five individual countries of the ASEAN on the other was, by and large, high during the periods 1991-94 and 1995-98 and particularly, the trade with Indonesia is striking in the latter period. The consistent importance of Singapore and Malaysia as key trading partners to India is also witnessed in Table-8. The table shows a considerable improvement in India's export intensities with the ASEAN as a whole and with the major five countries of the group from the first half of the 1990s to the second half. India's export intensity in general, was significant with these countries as the values were above unity in Indonesia, Thailand, Singapore and also in Malaysia in which the values were close to unity in both the periods, whereas the value of below unity in Philippines showed a less export trade orientation. In the case of Indonesia, the export intensity was quite remarkable in the latter period, owing to the increase of nearly twice of the value of the former period. Thus, the significance of the ASEAN as an important export market for India was revealed by the increase in the values, despite the marginal and moderate declines in Thailand and Singapore respectively in the latter period. The values of above unity in most of the cases indicate the positive signal for enhancing India's future exports to these countries.

The import intensity index of India on the other side, showed a slightly less trade orientation with the ASEAN countries, particularly with Philippines and Thailand, notwithstanding the marginal rise in the case of the latter country from the period 1991-94 to 1995-98. The results no doubt, revealed the importance of the ASEAN as an import source owing to the notable increase of a well below three times in Indonesia and a less than twice in the case of Malaysia followed by a moderate increase in Singapore and the ASEAN region from the former period to the latter. Though India had been giving priority to all the five major countries of the ASEAN, Indonesia surged much ahead of others in the latter period against the former. The significance of countries like Malaysia and Singapore as import sources to India was well recorded in the earlier years of the decade, but the latter country appeared to lose its prominence to some extent in the second period. Thus, the two-way trade transactions between India and the ASEAN witnessed a surge in the 1990s in relation to the rest of the world.

Conclusion

The protectionist policies of the industrial countries coming through the ambit of WTO under different guises have dimmed the export prospects of developing countries and called for an urgent need for the unification and enlargement of trade activities among the developing world. India's intensification of trade activities with the ASEAN region or the other way round in the coming future is essential to facilitate or safeguard the economic interests of the developing world. The existing trade relations between India and the ASEAN region clearly indicate the huge potential not only for further expansion of bilateral trade relations but also for other kinds of economic cooperation. The earlier study showed that the export and import trade intensities between India and the rest of SAARC countries were mostly politically dominated and reflected frequent fluctuations in the trade flows. This pattern has not lead to any clear conclusions, despite the better play of India's export trade intensity over import trade intensity.[4] In contrast to the above the trade intensities between India and the major five ASEAN countries estimated in this study have clearly pointed out the inevitability of free-trade arrangements or similar other economic interactions in the Asian region. Evidence shows that there is a vast scope for the enlargement of trade between India and the ASEAN in certain commodity groups. This may be in value added agricultural and manufactured products of India to ASEAN countries or in services sector goods. Studies also show that larger trade would lead to larger investment rather *vice-versa* in most of the cases.[5]

The formation of SAPTA and its ongoing transformation into South Asian Free Trade Area (SAFTA) cannot be the obstacles for this increasing economic engagement. The economic prospects of SAPTA/SAFTA have been dimmed in the wake of political misunderstandings in the SAARC region and in this background there is no other alternative for India at present except the 'Look East Policy'. Therefore, India's economic ties with the ASEAN grouping is crucial for strengthening its economy as well as its championing of the cause of the developing world in the industrial markets. On the other, ASEAN is also looking at India not just for its attractive potential market but also for the strategic partnership. It is visible from the above analysis that though India has a greater access to the ASEAN market, it has not been satisfying fully with the level of the two-way Indo-ASEAN trade owing to the slow pace of growth of trade. On the other, the ASEAN countries have yet to convince themselves fully the need for increasingly cooperating with India. Of late, the significant developments, particularly the ASEAN-India Summit which aims at increasing economic cooperation through regional trade arrangements and the signing of free trade pacts by India with some of the ASEAN members like Thailand indicate the change in the mind sets of the latter group of countries.

REFERENCES

1. Ramgopal Agarwala and Brahm Prakash, "Regional Cooperation in Asia : Long Term Progress, Recent Retrogression and the Way Forward", ERD Working Paper Series, No. 28, *Asian Development Bank*, Manila, October 2002.
2. World Bank, *World Development Report*, Various Issues, Oxford University Press, New York.
3. Charan D. Wadhwa *et al.*, *Regional Economic Cooperation in Asia : Bangladesh, India, Pakistan and Sri Lanka,* Allied Publishers Pvt. Ltd., New Delhi, 1987, p. 45.
4. T. Nirmala Devi, "Trade Intensities in SAARC: Need for A New Economic Outlook", paper presented at the International Seminar on *Economic Cooperation Among SAARC Countries — Challenges for the Second Decade,* organised by Centre for SAARC Studies, Andhra University, Visakhapatnam, March 24-26, 1997.
5. Sanjay Ambatkar, "An Evaluation of India-ASEAN Economic Cooperation Since 1985", *Regional Studies* (Islamabad), Autumn., 2002.

7

East Timor's Independence

*Jitendra Dhoj Khand**

East Timor (or Timor Lorosa's — the Tetum name for the area) is South-East Asia's newest nation. The territory of East Timor, a Portuguese colony since the sixteenth century (about 450 years) is located on the border of the Indonesian archipelago, between Southeast Asia, lies 300 miles north of Australia in the proximity of the South Pacific, occupying 24,000 square kilometers, and has a population of approximately 800,000 people.[1] The East Timorese voted overwhelmingly for independence on August 30, 1999 under the supervision and control of the UNAMET (United Nations Mission in East Timor). Formally East Timor became independent on May 20, 2002 after 24 years of Indonesian occupation and 32 months under the UNTAET (United Nations Transitional Administration in East Timor) stewardship. The Security Council (SC) passed a resolution 1410 on May 17, 2002 to establish UNMISET (United Nations Mission Support in East Timor) for an initial period of 12 months, starting on May 20. It is now a democratically governed independent nation with an elected President, Prime Minister, and Parliament. Against this background,

---

* Jitendra D. Khand is Professor in the Central Department of Political Science, Tribhuvan University, Kathmandu, Nepal, and President of the Nepal-East Timor Friendship Association. He was also in the Civil Service Academy, Dili under UNTAET Mission in East Timor.

an attempt has been made to analyze the role of United Nations to make independence of East Timor.

Agreement for Independence

United Nations had been contributing to make independence of East Timor since 1960. Firstly, the United Nations General Assembly (UNGA) added "Timor and dependencies" to the list of non-self-governing territories to develop self-government and take due account of the political aspirations" of their peoples. This step had realized by the Government of Portugal.

Portugal withdrew its administration from East Timor in 1975 after many violent clashes erupt between groups favoring independence and those favoring integration into Indonesia. In December 1975, Indonesian troops landed in East Timor and pro-Indonesian parties declared establishment of a "provisional government of East Timor." Later that month, both the Security Council and the General Assembly (GA) urged all the States to respect

East Timor's territorial integrity and inalienable right of its people to self-determination.

The GA requested the Secretary-General (SG) to initiate consultations with all the parties towards a comprehensive settlement in 1982. The Secretary General began the first of a series of tripartite talks involving Indonesia and Portugal, as well as consultations with Timorese representatives.

The Secretary General initiated a process in 1995 to promote a dialogue among East Timorese to improve the situation. Proposals emerging from the meetings were considered by the tripartite talks conducted by the Secretary General with Indonesia and Portugal. Annual meetings of the All-inclusive Intra-East-Timorese Dialogue (AIETD) also took place from 1995 to 1998. But in June 1998, Indonesia's President B.J. Habibie "proposed autonomy for East Timor on condition that the territory accepts integration into Indonesia". The proposal was rejected by East Timorese resistance leaders.

In August, following talks in New York between Secretary General Kofi A. Annan and the Foreign Ministers of Indonesia and Portugal, agreement reached to hold discussions on Indonesia's proposals for a special status based on a wide ranging autonomy for East Timor. The Ministers agreed to involve the East Timorese more closely in the search for a solution. They cited the Indonesian Government's intention gradually to reduce the level of its military presence in East Timor and to expedite the release of the East Timorese political prisoners.

In October, the UN submitted a proposal to the parties which could serve as a blueprint of self-administration in East Timor...either for a permanent or transitional autonomy. In subsequent talks, the proposal refined and enriched through consultations with East Timorese leaders.

President Habibie indicated in a public statement that "his government may be prepared to consider independence for East Timor on January 27, 1999". Talks began in New York on January 28 between the Personal Representative of the Secretary-General (PRSG), Jamsheed Marker, and the Directors-General of the Indonesian and Portuguese Foreign Ministries.

In the process, Secretary General Annan welcomed the understanding and the transfer of East Timorese leader Xanana Gusmao from prison to house detention on February 11. The Secretary General 's spokesman hoped that Gusmao's transfer would enable him to participate actively in the discussion about East Timor's future.

An agreement reached at ministerial-level tripartite talks in New York on use of a direct ballot to consult East Timor's people about whether they accept or reject the autonomy proposal. At a joint press conference with the Foreign Ministers of Indonesia and Portugal, the Secretary General expressed the continued concern of all the parties regarding the situation in East Timor, but he welcomed the positive steps to promote dialogue and reconciliation among East Timorese.

Secretary General Annan welcomed the signing of an agreement, initiated by Indonesia's National Human Rights Commission, which committed all the parties in East Timor—including the armed forces as well as pro-integration, pro-independence groups...to end violence in the territory. The agreement created a

Commission on Peace and Stability for East Timor, comprised of representatives of pro-independence and pro-integration groups, local authorities, local police commands, and the Indonesian Armed Forces (TNI).[2]

Ministerial-level talks in New York concluded with agreement on a settlement of the East Timor question involving a popular consultation on Timorese acceptance or rejection of the proposal for autonomy within Indonesia. Signing of the agreement was set for 5 May 1999, allowing the Indonesian Foreign Minister to secure final approval of Government authorities in Jakarta. At a joint press conference with the Foreign Ministers of Indonesia and Portugal, the Secretary General welcomed the Indonesian Government's reaffirmation that it would effectively carry out its responsibility for law and order and the protection of civilians. He also underlined the responsibility of all the parties that signed the agreement creating the Commission on Peace and Stability in East Timor.

Indonesian Foreign Minister Ali Alatas said that the Indonesian military and police "are determined to take their responsibility to keep law and order and peace and tranquility in East Timor". Thus, the Secretary General dispatched an assessment team to East Timor to evaluate the political and security situation on the ground. The team also discussed with the Indonesian authorities about the facilities available in Dili and elsewhere for the establishment of a United Nation mission. The information gathered to enable the Secretariat to draw up a detailed operational plan for the consultation.

The Secretary General stressed that the Secretariat was determined to ensure that the popular consultation "is free, fair and thorough". Noting that, under the agreement "security in East Timor is the responsibility of the Indonesian Government." He welcomed the assurances given by President Habibie that his Government would fulfill effectively its responsibility for law and order and the protection of all civilians. The Security Council adopted a resolution 1236 (1999) welcoming the May 5 Agreements. The resolution stressed the Indonesian Government's responsibility to ensure the safety and security of international staff and observers in East Timor, and to maintain peace and security in the territory.

UNAMET Mission

Indonesia, Portugal, and the United Nations signed the May 5, 1999 Agreement to the mandating of international intervention to check the violence through the ballot. Consequently, the Security Council formally established UNAMET at the end of August. Ian Martin was appointed for the post of the UN Secretary-General's special representative in the UNAMET.[3]

UNAMET Mission's basic goal was to success the referendum of the East Timorese a choice between autonomy within Indonesia or full independence. Mr. Ian Martin on his arrival on airport said that "the role of the UN in East Timor is to make sure that its people can choose their future after a fair campaign, in a secret ballot." He emphasized that "the UN is entirely neutral regarding the choice which the people of East Timor will be making" and that the UN neither supported the proposal for autonomy within Indonesia, nor its rejection. He added that "an end to all violence is essential for a fair campaign and ballot and appealed for an immediate end to violence and intimidation."

Secretary General Annan decided to delay the East Timor vote by two weeks due to violence and logistical problems. So registration was delayed to 13 July to allow time for the deployment of UN staff. Again, the Secretary General Annan postponed the start of voter registration for three days for the Indonesian government to resolve the remaining security problem. But after consultations with Indonesia and Portugal, Secretary General Annan decided to change the date for the ballot on East Timor's future to 30 August.

The Director of the Electoral Division in the UN Department of Political Affairs in New York, Carina Pirelli, told a press conference those 451,792 voters in and outside of East Timor registered for the vote. She also noted agreement on a code of conduct governing the activities of the 1,371 international and local observers officially accredited so far. Fifty Indonesian and fifty Portuguese official observers were allowed also to monitor the vote.

Meanwhile, East Timorese leaders from pro-independence and pro-autonomy groups also agreed to establish a 25-person commission to foster reconciliation and cooperation in the territory until the results of the UN-run autonomy ballot were implemented. Members were nominated by each side and appointed by the Secretary General . Supporters and opponents of the autonomy proposal for East Timor sign a Code of Conduct for the campaign period leading up to the ballot on 30 August. The United Front for East Timor Autonomy (UNIF) and the National Council of the Timorese Resistance (CNRT) signed the document in the presence of Bishop Belo, ambassador Tarmidzi, Chairman of the Indonesian Task Force responsible for liaising with UNAMET, as well as the heads of the Portuguese and Indonesian observer missions.

The Secretary General proposed a restructuring of UNAMET for the interim period between the end of the popular consultation and implementation of the voting results to build confidence and support stability in the territory. The Security Council extended UNAMET's mandate until 30 November. In a unanimous vote, the Council adopted resolution 126 (1999), endorsing the Secretary General 's to restructure the UN Mission in East Timor for the interim phase after the 30 August vote.

The UN intensified preparations for the ballot. An additional 50 UN Volunteers as polling supervisors were deployed, bringing the total number of UN Volunteers to 460—including medical staff—for polling day. 850 polling stations at 200 polling centers were planned, with UNAMET hiring more than 3,000 locals to assist in polling activities. Over 1,600 independent observers had also been accredited.

On 30 August, ninety five per cent of registered voters voted their ballots in the election (a total of more than 430,000). The voting was generally peaceful, although incidents at seven polling stations cause them to be closed for periods from 30 minutes to 3 hours. The polling was marred at the end of the day by the fatal stabbing of a local UN staff member after the polls closed. Secretary General Annan described the vote as an expression by the East Timorese of "their will as to their future." He appealed to all East Timorese groups to exercise the utmost restraint and patience in the post-balloting period.

In New York, the Secretary General announced the result of the vote: 94,388 or 21.5 per cent of East Timorese voted in favor of the special autonomy proposal and 344,580 or 78.5 per cent voted against. A total of 451,792 voters in East Timor were registered for the vote. In fact the UNAMET Mission was instrumental in implementing the ballot by a referendum on 30 August 1999, in the face of violent efforts to coerce the East Timorese to reject independence. The poll itself was with a historic 98.6% turnout and a 78.5% vote for independence.

Pro-autonomy East Timorous groups protested that the outcome was the result of UNAMET's pro-independence bias and presented a series of complaints of irregularities during the vote.

UNTAET Mission

The United Nations Security Council by resolution S/RES/1272 (1999) established the United Nations Transitional Administration in East Timor (UNTAET) on October 25, 1999 to administer East Timor's period of transition to independence. The Mission was comprised three main components: governance and public administration; humanitarian assistance and emergency rehabilitation; and a military component with an authorized strength of up to 8,950 troops and 200 military observers. Its mandate was the following objectives:

- To support capacity-building of self-government; and
- To assist in the establishment of conditions for sustainable development.
- To provide security and maintain law and order throughout the territory of East Timor;
- To establish an effective administration;
- To assist in the development of civil and social services;
- To ensure the coordination and delivery of humanitarian assistance, rehabilitation, and development assistance;

The Secretary-General appointed Under-Secretary-General for Humanitarian Affairs Sergio Vieira de Mello as his Special

Representative and Transitional Administrator. In the process, an election for the Members of the Constituent Assembly held on August 30, 2001 to make constitution of East Timor within a 90-day Constitution-drafting process. It was a tough task for the 88-member assembly in the face of some hard realities, like conceiving an economic road map for the new nation. Equally important was the assembly's take on identifying the mechanisms needed for a sustainable democracy. He also appointed the Second Transitional Government on September 20, 2001. The appointment of its 20 ministers, vice-ministers, and secretaries of state, all Timorese, broadly reflected the outcome of the elections as well as sect oral expertise, with an emphasis on youth and geographical representation. A Council of Ministers, led by a Chief Minister, Dr. Mari Alkatiri, presided over the Transitional Government and supervised the East Timor Public Administration (ETPA). This was a turning point in that the executive government in East Timor controlled by East Timorese, albeit under the overall authority of SRSG. The majority members of the Constituent Assembly also fixed sovereignty transformation of East Timor. Consequently, on October 31, 2001, the Security Council welcomed the political progress achieved to date towards establishing an independent East Timorese State, and endorsed the recommendation by the Constituent Assembly of the Territory that independence be declared on May 20, 2002. East Timor is now a democratically governed independent nation with an elected President, Prime Minister, and Parliament.

The United Nations has played a historical role to make independence of East Timor. It had contributed to East Timor in terms of political, economic, social, military, police, serious crime, land, border and judicial foundation through the UNAMET and UNTAET Mission. Until May 20, 2002 East Timor was under the authority of the UNTAET. But the significant role of former President Bill Clinton of the United States to make independence of East Timor can not be ignored although other big power countries were also supported it.

UNMISET Mission

Present mandate of the United Nations is resolution 1410 of May 17, 2002, the Security Council established the United Nations Mission Support in East Timor (UNMISET) for an initial period of 12 months, starting on May 20, 2002. Special representative of the Secretary-General is Mr. Kamalesh Sharma of India. Force Commander is Lieutenant-General Winai Phttiyakul of Thailand. Chief Military Observer is Brigadier General Sergio Rosario of Brazil. Chief of Civilian Police is Chief Superintendent Peter Miller of Canada.

The Mission was established by Security Council resolution 1410 (2002) of 17 May for an initial period of 12 months, starting on 20 May 2002, with the following mandate:

- To provide assistance to core administrative structures critical to the viability and political stability of East Timor;
- To provide interim law enforcement and public security and to assist in the development of a new law enforcement agency in East Timor, the East Timor Police Service (ETPS); and
- To contribute to the maintenance of the external and internal security of East Timor.

The Council also requested UNMISET to give full effect to the following three Programmes of the Mandate Implementation Plan as set out in section III A 3 of the report of the Secretary-General (S/2002/432) of 17 April 2002:

- Stability, Democracy and Justice;
- Public Security and Law Enforcement; and
- External Security and Border Control.

On December 4, 2002, emergency imposed in East Timor, Dili after police fired on student protesters, killing at least two people and sparking a rampage of looting and arson. Rioters burned down the house of Prime Minister Mari Alkatiri. Earlier, President Xanana Gusmao arrived at the scene of the riots, which were centered outside the National Police Headquarters, to try to restore order. The fighting continued, and he was escorted inside the building. Mobs also torched the Australian-owned "Hello Mister" supermarket which uses to sell mostly imported goods to UN workers and other foreigners in the country. At least one police car was also torched. They then looted nearby shops and hotels, taking televisions and motorbikes. United Nations peacekeepers were deployed, but were seemingly unable to contain the rioting.[6] This was the first violent incident since the independence of East Timor. Such destructive attitude tends to not only harmful to the East Timorese but also to the UNMISET Mission's participants countries.

Foreign Affairs

East Timor declared independence on November 28, 1975. Indonesia invaded East Timor on December 7. President Gerald Ford and Secretary of State Henry Kissinger met with Indonesian dictator General Suharto before the invasion. They gave Suharto a *de facto* green light for the aggression, beginning a long history of U.S. government complicity with Indonesian repression of the East Timorese. The U.S. continued its support for Indonesia's armed forces (then called ABRI, now TNI), supplying $1.1 billion in weapons in the 1975-99 period. [7]

Between 1972 and 1982, the United Nations passed two Security Council and eight General Assembly resolutions condemning Indonesia's invasion, calling for its immediate withdrawal, and supporting East Timor's self-determination. The U.S., however, was instrumental in blocking any additional UN action. In the aftermath of the U.S. defeat in Vietnam, Washington viewed Indonesia as a critical ally in the cold war. During the 1980s, concerns about repression in both East Timor and Indonesia were largely subordinated to U.S. geopolitical and economic imperatives in the region.

ABRI, which counted on U.S. aid and training, napalmed and displaced entire villages and disappeared, raped, tortured, and murdered civilians in an attempt to break the backbone of the resistance. More than 200,000 East Timorese, a third of the pre-invasion population, died as a result of this repression — either directly at the hands of the Indonesian police and military or indirectly as a result of starvation and disease.[8] Until 1991 the world community largely ignored these atrocities. On November 12, 1991, ABRI soldiers opened fire on a funeral procession, killing 270 East Timorese. This massacre, captured on videotape by British journalist Max Stahl, marked a turning point in East Timor's struggle for self-determination. International solidarity movements, like the East Timor Action Network/U.S., emerged to pressure foreign governments to withdraw support for Indonesia's occupation. East Timor's independence struggle gained wider recognition when, in 1996, Bishop Carlos Belo and exiled resistance leader Jose Ramos-Horta, both East Timorese, received the Nobel Peace Prize.[9]

It was only after visiting the United States, Canada, Japan (the main investor in Indonesia), Iran (important Muslim country) and Yugoslavia (founder of the Non Aligned Movement) and assuring himself of their support to the annexation, that General Suharto started to affirm, in public, that the Independence of East Timor would not be accepted.[10]

In 2001 East Timor had built a new Department of Foreign Affairs under the leadership of ETPA (East Timor's Public Administration) Cabinet Senior Minister for Foreign Affairs, Dr. Ramos Jose Horta. The establishment and organisation of the new department was to support the formulation and implementation of East Timor's future foreign policy. In order to determine the core functions of the Department of Foreign Affairs, decisions were needed at the

Government level to demarcate lines of jurisdiction between the Department of Foreign Affairs and other concerned departments.

More than one hundred countries of the world have been contributing to East Timor since 1999. The contributions are in the area of military, police, civil servants, money, goods, technology etc. Maximum authorized strength was Military 5,000 troops, including 120 military observers; CIVPOL (civilian police): 1,250; provision is also made for some 455 international civilian staff, 100 experts for the Civilian Support Group, 977 locally recruited staff and 241 United Nations Volunteers.

On May 31, 2002 the strength was 6,307 total uniformed personnel. Many countries have been contributing Military and civilian personnel in East Timor since the UN mission. They are Australia, Bangladesh, Bolivia, Brazil, Chile, Denmark, Egypt, Fiji, Ireland, Japan, Jordan, Kenya, Malaysia, Mozambique, Nepal, New Zealand, Norway, Pakistan, Philippines, Portugal, Republic of Korea, Russian Federation, Singapore, Slovakia, Sweden, Thailand, Turkey, United States, and Uruguay.

Similarly they have been contributing their Civilian and Police personnel in East Timor. They are Argentina, Australia, Bangladesh, Bosnia and Herzegovina, Brazil, Canada, China, Egypt, Gambia, Ghana, Jordan, Malaysia, Mozambique, Namibia, Nepal, Niger, Norway, Pakistan, Philippines, Portugal, Russian Federation, Samoa, Senegal, Singapore, Slovenia, Spain, Sri Lanka, Sweden, Thailand, Turkey, Ukraine, United States, United Kingdom, Vanuatu and Zimbabwe.

More than 213,000 of those who fled or were driven from East Timor in the aftermath of the September 1999 popular consultation have now returned to the newly independent country. First Foreign Minister Dr. Jose Ramos Horta who was the representative for foreign affairs in East Timor's transitional cabinet, made the remark in reference to Australia's position on the disputed Timor Gap Treaty. Reporting the comments, an article on January 26, 2002 *Financial*

Times also claimed "Mr. Ramos Horta is confident that Australia would be sympathetic to East Timor's requests".

The most serious such indication was Horta's call, during a January 22-24 2002 goodwill visit to Jakarta, for Washington to improve its military ties with the Indonesian armed forces. "Because of the sanctions in the past two years, [the Indonesian armed forces] are stretched and [facing] enormous difficulties in logistics and in the delivery of troops and police", Horta told journalists. According to a report by Lusa news service on January 24, 2002, Horta said he would urge the U.S. to partially lift sanctions on military cooperation with Indonesia. In the wake of Horta's visit, Indonesia's Foreign Minister Alwi Shihab told journalists on January 29, "I am optimistic that the military sanctions will be lifted because the Bush government is more pragmatic and realistic". Echoing comments made by Horta, Shihab claimed that the lifting of the sanctions was "necessary for the ongoing process of democracy".

Shihab planed to meet with the new U.S. secretary of state, Colin Powell to discuss the prospect of normalizing military ties between Jakarta and Washington. Both Horta and Shihab heaped praise on the Gulf War "hero" when his nomination for the post was announced in December.

Horta's proposal that the U.S. improve military ties with the Indonesian military, the British-based solidarity and human rights group summed up the feeling of many solidarity groups and activists world-wide. "If this is a correct report of what Jose Ramos-Horta said, it represents an extraordinary and highly damaging reversal of CNRT [National Council of Timorese Resistance] policy on military aid to Indonesia...We all need to re-double our efforts to ensure that the new U.S. administration does not decide to resume military aid to Jakarta". In reality, East Timor was occupied by the United States, Australia, United Kingdom, the Vatican, Japan and other powers, through Indonesia. Indonesia was not much more than an executor of a policy that interested the west.[11]

The Soldiers were Indonesian but the interests and the support were mainly the Western powers in the past. The Indonesian Government itself was not much more than the peon that, in the world geopolitical chess, the Western played against the International Communism in the defense of the interests, either global or specific of each state. In addition, the U.S. is playing a great role to eliminate the terrorists from the root of the world after the 11th September. This factor determined to formulate the foreign policy not only the government of East Timor but also other countries of the world.

Economic

East Timorese have begun their hard work of building a nation virtually from scratch. East Timor's oil reserves, tourism industry, and agricultural export sector (mainly coffee) provide a potential for a secure economic base for the new country, but over the next several years, East Timor will still depend on outside assistance. On May 25, 1999, General Assembly authorized $35 million to cover the initial requirements of the UNAMET. Later the Secretary-General submitted to the General Assembly a revised budget for UNAMET totaling some $52.5 million.

UNTAET was primarily responsible for coordinating, reconstruction and development activities in East Timor until an elected government takes over. UNTAET's operations had been criticized for including few East Timorese, neglecting rural areas, and giving inadequate attention to health care and other basic services. By late 2000, however, some positive changes had been made. The U.S. had played a more autonomous role in East Timor, declining participation in UN-led peacekeeping forces but contributing more than $25 million in assistance.

East Timor faces enormous challenges, including the provision of basic social services, the reconstruction of its economic infrastructure, and the strengthening of its civil society. The World

Bank is effectively coordinating numerous international donors and helping to design health care, education, and employment programs. East Timor's leaders have wisely pledged to avoid big foreign loans, for which East Timor will be eligible only after elections. Solidarity organisations are establishing themselves in East Timor, both to monitor international NGOs, financial institutions, and the UN, as well as to build genuine partnerships with East Timorese NGOs.

According UN News Service May 15, 2002, the Meeting at an event co-chaired by the UNTAET, governments and aid agencies pledged over $360 million to support economic development. The assurances of aid announced at the end of the two-day donor conference (Representatives of 27 countries, the European Commission and a wide range of multilateral groups attended the meeting, which was also co-chaired by the Second Transitional Government of East Timor and the World Bank) comes on top of the $81 million already available through the Trust Fund for East Timor and the UNTAET successor mission, the UN Mission of Support in East Timor (UNMISET). East Timor will now have access to over $440 million in international support for its three-year budget framework, which donors applauded for its emphasis on development.

On July 25, 2002 two institution, International Monetary Fund (IMF) and the World Bank announced that East Timor became the 184th members of IMF and Word Bank. East Timorese Prime Minister Mari Alkatiri signed the articles of agreement for the two Washington-based financial institutions in a ceremony at IMF headquarters, which is across the street from the World Bank? Besides, Prom Manila, Philippine announced that RDTL (The Democratic Republic of East Timor) became the 61st member of the Asian Development Bank (ADB).

To coincide with the event, East Timor Minister of Foreign Affairs and Cooperation, Jose Ramos-Horta, paid a courtesy call on ADB President Tadao Chino on 3 December 2002 and expressed appreciation for ADB's continuing involvement in the economic reconstruction of East Timor. President Chino assured Minister Ramos-Horta that ADB would continue to work closely with the government and donor partners to address poverty in East Timor, one of the poorest countries in Asia.

ADB plans to send a country consultation mission to East Timor shortly to formulate a medium-term assistance program. Although East Timor was not yet a member of the ADB during the pre-independence period, it was eligible to receive ADB technical assistance grants. Since 2000, ADB has approved 19 technical assistance projects for East Timor, amounting to $8 million from grant funds. Such projects were for project preparation, capacity building, and policy advice in key sectors and for economic management.

During the past two years, ADB also served as a co-administrator of the multi-donor Trust Fund for East Timor (TFET). ADB processed and supervised six TFET projects totaling $52.8 million, covering the restoration of physical infrastructure, particularly roads, ports, water supply and power facilities. ADB also prepared and administered a TFET-financed micro finance project.

The World Bank noted in the statement that the composition of the financial plan is strongly pro-poor, with 48 per cent of the core budget allocated by 2005 to health and education. The Timorese should continue to develop their own sources of revenue and to manage their resources in keeping with their track record. But East Timor should also continue to economic assistance.

East Timor and Australia share the Timor Gap oil and gas field that lies in the sea between them. They have signed a deal that will bring East Timor $ 7 billion over 20 years starting in 2005. Apart from the oil and gas, East Timor is one of the poorest countries in the world and survives on foreign aid. Coffee is the main export. Tourism, which started during later years of Portuguese rule, all but ended with Indonesia's invasion. At present, responsibility has come on the shoulders of people of East Timor, because the nation — state is still in its infancy which needs security, stability, peace, and economic development.

The Crimes against Humanity

The announcement of the result on September 4, 1999 was followed by a systematic campaign of organized killings, arson, destruction, and massive forced displacement of the population carried out by members of the Indonesian armed forces and police, and pro-integration militia. As many as 200,000 East Timorese went to West Timor, many against their will. On September 15, 1999, with the agreement of the Indonesian Government, the Security Council authorized the deployment of multinational force under Chapter VII of the UN Charter to restore law and order and to assist UNAMET to complete its mandate.

Militia attacked over several days at the end of June and into July—on the UNAMET regional office in Maliana, on a humanitarian convoy accompanied by a UNAMET humanitarian affairs officer and a local representative of the UN High Commissioner for Refugees (UNHCR)—and threats against UNAMET staff in Viqueque.

Violence also erupted outside the UNAMET compound in Dili as militia members attacked pro-independence supporters. Journalists witnessed the incidents seeking refuge at UNAMET Headquarters, along with several hundred internally displaced persons. Indonesian Police dispatched an armed patrol to secure the UNAMET perimeter. Two local UNAMET staff members were killed as post ballot violence spreads. UNAMET international and local personnel were relocated from the Mission's Headquarter in Dili to Darwin, Australia, along with more than 1400 people who sought shelter in the Dili Compound.

The wave of militia violence which swept over East Timor in 1999, culminating in massive deportations and destruction in

September was not the spontaneous response of those who favored integration, but the outcome of a decision by TNI Generals to counter the popular support in East Timor for independence, by means of intimidation and violence, and to prevent the loss of the province to the Republic of Indonesia. The campaign of massive destruction, deportation and killings in September was essentially an operation planned and carried out by the TNI, with militia participation, to punish the people of East Timor for their vote against integration.[12]

As a background to the events of 1999, it is important that the pattern of violations against the people of East Timor should be taken into account. From the very beginning of the military intervention, there were persistent reports of gross human rights violations. In the week following the invasion of Dili hundreds of citizens of the capital, almost all of them non-combatants, were summarily executed. These killings, some of which took the form of mass executions, included women and at least one foreigner, Roger East, a journalist from Australia. Mass executions at Linquica, Maubara, and Aileu and near Bobonaro were reported in the months following the invasion. According to reports received in Australia from Church sources, as many as 60,000 Timorese may have died in the year following the invasion, and as many as 200,000 in the subsequent four years, many of course from disease and starvation. Summary executions continued in the eighties and nineties, the worst known cases being the Creras massacres, where more than 1,000 East Timorese were killed by rampaging TNI troops, and the Santa Cruz massacre, which reportedly claimed the lives of more than 200 Timorese. There were also persistent reports of torture and sexual assault, which were given frequent attention in the annual reports of Ammenesty International[13] and, later, Human Rights Watch. However, until the Santa Cruz incident the response from the international community was negligible.

It is important that this pattern of behavior on the part of the Indonesian military be taken into account when judging the events of 1999. The relevance of the historical background was noted in the

KPP HAM report, which recommended that "a comprehensive investigation be carried out into all crimes against humanity committed in East Timor since 1975".[14]

TNI attitudes during this period clearly reflected a persistent disregard for basic human rights, especially when dealing with those suspected of being opposed to integration. The military's persistent brutal treatment of the East Timorese, including the mass killings, was evidently ignored or tolerated by the Government of Indonesia, a stance no doubt encouraged by the extremely low level of interest in the plight of the people of this remote and, at that time, little-known territory. There was, however, considerable international reaction to the Santa Cruz killings, but executions on a smaller scale, torture and other abuse in fact continued. In 1995 six East Timorese were executed in the Liquica area, although in this case a TNI officer was charged with the offense. From the outcome of these trials it was evident that the Suharto Government had not address what had become a culture of oppression and brutality in East Timor.[15]

Militia's violence against supporters of independence began early in 1999 and in April when Operasi Sapu jagad (Operation Clean Sweep) was launched.[17]) However, the main thrust of the violence occurred when the results of the referendum were announced in Dili, and the end of September, when the INTERFET force was able to restore security to central and eastern sectors of East Timor. This operation of massive destruction, ransacking and deportation was also devised by the TNI when it was realized that the referendum was likely to go against integration. Accordingly, the TNI began developing Operasi Wiradharma, the evacuation of East Timor, an operation which apparently also used the code-name, Guntur. The plan, which was devised at least two months before it was launched, was commanded by TNI Kopassus officers, with Major General Zakky Anwar Makarim and Adam Damiri playing key command roles. According to informed sources in Jakarta, it was planned to deport most of East Timor's population to West Timor, from where they would later be dispersed to other parts of the archipelago. The planners seemed to believe that the violence would persuade the MPR, the Indonesian Parliament, to reject the outcome of the ballot.

The training and use of Timorese in Para-military units goes back to the time of Indonesia's military intervention in East Timor in 1975. In that year the oldest of the militia units, Halilintar, was established following a covert military training programme conducted in West Timor by a special TNI military force, commanded by then Colonel Dading Kalbuardi.[18] In 1976, some months after the invasion of Dili, most of the Halilintar troops were redeployed to from the basis of Battalion 744, a regular territorial unit, which was later joined by Battalion 745. These units were largely made up of Timorese soldiers, but were staffed by Indonesian officers. Halilintar itself was disbanded in 1982, and was not reformed until 1998.(19) Basically international attention has been devoted to the killing of five newsmen from Australia at Balibo in October 1975, this incident was only the first of a serious of atrocities alleges to have been committed by Indonesian military units over tie ensuing 16 years. Until 1999 the only major incident to attract significant international attention was the massacre of more than 200 Timorese by Indonesian troops, following a peaceful demonstration at Santa Cruz cemetery in November 1991. In the face of international pressures some legal action was taken against a small number of troops. However, it is noteworthy that they were accused not of murder but of having disobeyed orders.

The best known militia of early units was Team Alpha (Tim Alfa) which, with Team Saka (Tim Saka), was formed in 1986 in the eastern sector of East Timor by a Kopassus officer, Captain Luhud Pandjaitan, reportedly acting on orders from his commander, then Colonel Prabowo. Team Alpha's members were trained and paid, and their operations against pro-independence elements organized, by Indonesian military officers. Another significant move was the setting up of the Gada Paksi (Gadu Pnenegak Integrasi — Guards to Uphold Integration) in 1994, also reportedly by Prabowo. The Gada Paksi was conceived as a way of mobilizing young pro-integration activists.

The formation of the militia was evidently yet another initiative of Kopassus, the TNI's Special Forces Command. This special military group became a select army within Indonesia's military force structure, at the time called ABRI (Armed Forces of the Republic of Indonesia). Its members were specially chosen, received special training and equipment, enjoyed privileges and were generally regarded as an elite corps, with to protect the integrity of he Indonesian state.

The organisational structure of the militia was virtually integrated into the TNI structure in East Timor. Militia units were formed in each of the 13 districts (Kabupaten), with the commanders being chosen or confirmed by the TNI command. These were as follows:

S. No.	*Militia*	*District*	*Commander*
1.	Tim Alfa	Lautem	Joni Marques
2.	Saka/Sera	Baucau	Serka Kopassus Joanico da Costa
3.	Pedjuang 59-75 Makikit	Viqueque	Martinho Fernandes
4.	Ablai	Manufahi	Nazario Corterel
5.	AHI	Aileu	Horacio
6.	Mahidi	Ainaro	Cancio de Carvalho
7.	Laksaur	Covalima	Olivio Mendonca Moruk
8.	Aitarak	Dili	Eurico Guterres
9.	Sakunar	Oecussi	Simao Lopes
10.	BMP (Besi Merah Putih)	Liquica	Manuel de Sousa
11.	Halilintar, Dadurus	Bobonaro/Maliana	Joao de Tavares, Natalino Monteiro
12.	Jati Merah Putih	Lospalos	Edmundo de Conceicao Silva
13.	Darah Merah Integrasi	Ermera	Lafaek Saburai

The above list is by no means an exhaustive one. In the Bobonaro/ Maliana districts, for example, there were at least six groups, with Halilintar forming the headquarters. While the plan to form these units was conceived and commenced in 1978, most were not operational unit April 1999. These units varied in size, the most prominent being Halilintar and Aitarak. Halilintar's commander, Joao

Tavares, a former Bupati of Bobonaro district, was appointed Panglima, or overall commander of militia chiefs in East Timor, an appointment said to have been made by TNI officers. Tavares had had a long association with Para-military bodies, having been a founder member of the Halilintar force, which accompanied Colonel Dading Kalbuardi's RPKED force on the TNI's first major military assault against East Timor in October 1975.

Aitarak came under the command of the flamboyant East Timorese, Eurico Gutteres. A much younger man, Eurico's earlier links had been with Fretilin. His parents had been killed by Indonesian troops, while he himself, when a teenager, had worked as a courier for Falintil before being captured by a Kopassus unit, which appears to have been responsible for the redirection of his loyalties.

As a matter of fact, if the truth about what was going on in East Timor was revealed, it would have been impossible to the governments, to silence the revolt of their public opinions and to maintain for so many years their support to a genocidal occupation so contrary to international law as it was the Indonesian occupation in East Timor. Besides, the so called free and democratic countries, where the freedom of the press is legally guaranteed, silence and lies were the motto of the governments and their representatives. Their involvement in the occupation was such that they accepted to cover up the murder of their own citizens, the six journalists, without a single formal protest.

Human Losses as consequence of Wars (estimates)

Countries	*Year*	*Number of people killed*	*Population at the beginning of the conflict*	*Percentage of people dead direct our indirectly*
East Timor (Indonesian Occupation) (20) (21)	1975-1995	> 308.000	696.000	> 44 %

It is a veritable holocaust, with more than 40% of the whole people eliminated during the first six years of occupation in East Timor. Twenty years after the invasion, and as a consequence of the Indonesian occupation, the martyred people of East Timor suffered the greatest genocide registered in the 20th century.

Several authors mention a number of two hundred thousand dead, taking into consideration the decline in the population registered in the first four years of the occupation, refer two hundred and fifty thousand dead in East Timor. Yet, they forget that the demographic statistics pointed out an increase of the population of 2.2% per year, at the beginning of the seventies.

Gabriel Defert, the specialist managed to study the several statistic data available either from the Portuguese and Indonesian authorities and from the Catholic Church statistics. He concluded in his book "Timor Est le Genocide Oublié"[20] that, even admitting that the rate of natural growth could have been reduced in a half during the first six years of occupation, between December 1975 and December 1981, an average of 308,000 Timorese would have lost their lives. This represents 44% of the population (696,000 inhabitants) in the territory before the invasion.

Curiously the Indonesian Professor George Aditjondro, from Salatiga University, in the island of Java, based on the Indonesian Army data, concluded, just as Gabriel Defert, that three hundred thousand Timorese would have had "disappeared" in the first years that followed the invasion.[21] Between 1983 and 1995 some several thousand Timorese have perished, therefore the total death toll will naturally surpass the figure of 308.000 dead.

Not even the Nazi Holocaust, perpetuated against the Jewish people between 1939 and 1945, managed to reach such a high percentage of people. The five million Jews murdered under the Nazism correspond, according to Professor Cecil Roth[22], from the University of Bar-Ilan, in Israel, to a third (33%) of the total number of Jewish people in the world, a percentage fairly behind the Maubere holocaust...

It strikes us to notice how a genocide of such dimension could pass unnoticed by the public world opinion. It was precisely the lack of knowledge of such reality and the information black out that contributed the most to the intolerable proportions of the East Timor drama.

Conclusion

East Timor is the world's newest independent nation-state after the Portugal, Indonesia, and United Nations rules and stewardship. The role of the United Nations to make independence of East Timor on May 20, 2002 was a kind of risk taking, painstaking, and challenging tasks. Consequently, Novel Peace Prize of 2001 had been awarded to Secretary General Kofi Annan and the Staff of the United Nations.

But the significant role of former President Bill Clinton of the United States of America to make independence of East Timor can not be ignored although other big power countries were also supported it. At present, East Timor has become a member of regional and international organisations.

The UNAMET Mission was established under the UN Secretary General's Special Representative Mr. Ian Martin to success the referendum of the East Timorese a choice between autonomous within Indonesia or full independence. In the referendum 78.5% of East Timorese voted in favor of the full independence and 21./5% voted for the special autonomy. Pro-autonomy East Timorese groups protested that the outcome was the result of the UNAMET's pro-independence bias. As a result, a systematic campaign of organized killings, arson, destruction, and massive forced displacement of the population carried out by the members of the Indonesian armed forces, police, and pro-integration militia.

The UNTAET Mission became successful under the UN Secretary General's Special Representative Mr. Sergio Vieira de Mello to achieve mandate by managing the elections of the Constituent

Assembly on August 30, 2001 and President on April 17, 2002. The Mission also became success to handover the sovereignty to the elected government of East Timor on May 20, 2002. Unfortunately, he died in Iraq in August 2003 due to terrorist explosion in the UN building.

The UNMISET Mission is going to success under the UN Special Representative Mr. Kamalesh Sharma of India to provide assistance to core administrative structures, political stability, democracy, justice, border control, maintenance of the external and internal security of East Timor. Perhaps, recent destructive incident in Dili has given a trouble to achieve the mandate of the Mission.

The World Bank noted in the statement that the composition of the financial plan is strongly pro-poor, with 48 per cent of the core budget allocated by 2005 to health and education. The Timorese should continue to develop their own sources of revenue and to manage their resources in keeping with their track record. But East Timor should also continue to economic assistance.

Naturally, a less developed country like East Timor tends to be less able than industrial countries to frame and execute the policy. It can not be a prime mover in global politics through its policy as the United States of America. Hence, the policy-makers of East Timor must learn about the past historical experiences and present development while making the future policy. Thus the leaders and people of East Timor must understand the value of ethics in relation to the foreign policy. Nevertheless, exchange of visits of high dignitaries between East Timor, Australia, Indonesia, USA and other countries of the world have benefited in terms of peace, stability, security, economic cooperation, and development.

The situation of serious crimes against humanity in East Timor is not positive. With the continued forced detention of those East Timorese in refugee camps in West Timor who wish to return to their homeland was one of the most serious crimes against humanity. The most serious crimes, such as the Creras and Santa Cruz massacres, are crimes of such magnitude that they must be considered of concern to the international community as a whole.

In fact, there are challenges, facing by the people in an independent East Timor. Much work remains to be done in rehabilitating and reconstructing both public buildings and private homes. The United Nations is the only institution which could have accompanied East Timor from occupied territory through devastation into transitional government, and independence to post independence. The credit goes to the three Missions (UNAMET, UNTAET and UNMISET)for the successful accomplishment of these trouble. It is hope that lessons learned over the past three years will help to both the government and international agencies to apply it more efficiently and effectively. Thus, the United Nations as well as leaders and people of East Timor had played a historically role to make East Timor's independence.

NOTES

1. East Timor — Consular Information Sheet, August 12, 2002.
2. lynn@etan.org
   (Lynn Frederickson is the departing Washington representative for the East Timor Action Network and the interim coordinator for the Indonesia Human Rights Network).
3. Foreign Policy in Focus, *East Timor*, Volume 5, Number 43, December 2000.
6. *The Himalayan Times*, December 5, 2002.
7. Foreign Policy in Focus, *East Timor*, Volume 5, Number 43, December 2000.
8. *Ibid.*
9. *Ibid.*
10. *Ibid.*
11. Benedict R. Anderson, The Importance of Liberating Indonesia from East Timor, Conference in Universidade Católica Portuguese, in Oporto em 27 May 1992.
12. A. Barbedo de Magalhães, East Timor, Indonesian Occupation and Genocide Oporto University 1992.
13. James Dunn, Crimes against Humanity in East Timor, January to October 1999, pp. 2-9.

14. KPP HAM report, Para 27, Press release. See also James Dunn, p. 10.
15. James Dunn, *ibid.*, p. 10.
16. *Ibid.*
17. *Ibid.* p. 11.
18. *Ibid.*, p. 12 sees also Tomas Conclaves: Transcription of testimony.
19. Battalion 744 came under the command of Major Yunus Josiah, who had led the attacking force into Balibo.
20. Gabriel Defert, Timor Est le Genocide Oublié, L'Hartman, 1992.
21. International Law and the Question of East Timor CIIR/IPJET, 1995.
22. Cecil Roth, Jewish History, in Chambers Encyclopedia, 1970. East Timor: A People Shattered By Lies and Silence.

8

Developmentalism and Environment in East Asia

A Comparison Between Developmentalism in Japan and ASEAN

Fumitaka FURUOKA & Mikio OISHI

Introduction

We are now at the vantage point from which the experience of the people in East Asia for the past decades may be reviewed critically, and from which a new version of East Asian development model is explored. This is particularly important during the time when the region undergoes economic downturn. The dominant paradigm in the region has been developmentalism, which is an ideology to industrialise a newly independent country with the massive use of state-power and nationalist rhetoric.

Japan is the first country that consciously adopted the ideology of developmentalism in order to survive a harsh international competition among imperialist states in the 19th century. This process was interrupted by World War II. After the war, Japan reinstated developmentalism ideology to help the country to recover from the chaotic economic condition.

Since the 1960s, other East Asian countries, both Asian NIEs and ASEAN countries, following Japan's example, adopted developmentalism and began implementing their industrialisation programmes. There are dozen of countries that have made considerable efforts to industrialise their economies, however, there are not many impressive success stories. East Asia's economic achievement was highly praised by the World Bank that, in 1993, described it as "East Asian Miracle" (World Bank, 1993).

During the current economic crisis, there have appeared signs that this paradigm is becoming increasingly irrelevant. There is a need to explore a new paradigm for the development which would take into account not only economic development, but also social, political and environmental issues. It is high time for East Asian countries to establish a sustainable dynamic balance between development and the environment through "social learning".

This paper will firstly examine developmentalism in Japan. As it was mentioned above, Japan chose this ideology as a national guideline since the middle of the 19th century and eventually became the first developed country in Asia. What lessons could ASEAN learn from Japan's experience?

The paper will also examine the underlying ideas and assumptions of developmentalism in ASEAN and look at various negative aspects of developmentalism. Finally, it will introduce bioregionalism as a new political trend that can effectively challenge the mainstream ideology of developmentalism. The chapter will discuss the basic principles of bioregionalism and their implications for the people in ASEAN.

Developmentalism

In this study, developmentalism is defined as the development-first policy at the expense of other national policies. If a government adopts the idea of developmentalism as a fundamental philosophy for the state-formation and nation-building, it will give top priority to economic development and pay less attention to other important agendas, such as environmental conservation, promotion of social integration and so on. Although it does not necessarily mean that the government chooses to ignore social or environmental issues, but rather that the government tends to consider "development" as the promotion of national welfare without taking into account its consequences. Thus, the government would implement various development projects under a slogan of "national interests".

Shibusawa *et al.* (1992, p. 53) point out two characteristics of "developmentalism" in East Asia: (1) pragmatism, and (2) an emphasis on economic goal. They argue that developmentalism in East Asia "is more a pragmatic policy choice, a concept designed to serve the purpose of state". The researchers maintain that developmentalism is not rooted in any ideological tradition of liberalism and an emphasis is put on the economic goal.

Developmentalism in Japan

The Japanese government consciously adopted "developmentalism" in order to compete with the Western colonial powers since Japan re-opened commercial and diplomatic relations with other countries in 1868. Also, the Japanese government used all available resources to achieve high economic growth in order to overcome a chaotic economic situation after World War II. As a consequence, Japan became the first instance of the "miracle" in East Asia and the first Asian member of the "rich countries clubs", such as the Organisation for Economic Cooperation and Development (OECD) and the Group of Seven (G-7). What made Japan's success possible?

The "Japanese Miracle"

Several reasons could be offered for Japan's success story. However, the crucial element of Japan's economic mechanism is the strong role of the government, or a "blue print" approach. In order to achieve high economic growth, the Japanese government implemented various industrial policies to guide the economy. By contrast, in the West, the governments, notably the U.S. government, tend to refrain from interfering into their economies. This is the reason why "industrial policy, despite its importance in many advanced capitalist countries (notably Japan and France) and some East Asian NICs (notably Korea, Taiwan and Singapore) during the post-war period, were largely ignored until the late 1970s in the English-speaking academic world. The concept of industrial policy does not seem to be recognised as a legitimate topic of academic discussion among economists" (Chang, 1994, p. 3).

Chalmers Johnson describes Japan's political and economic mechanism as the "developmental state" (Johnson, 1982). He claims, "The United States is a good example of a state in which the regulatory orientation predominates, whereas Japan is a good example of a state in which the developmental orientation predominates". In Johnson's opinion, the difference in the orientation between the U.S. and Japan rests on the timing of industrialisation. "In those states that were first to industrialise... towards the end of the nineteenth century the state took on *regulatory* functions in the interest of maintaining competition, consumer protection, and so forth... In states that were late to industrialize, the state itself led the industrialisation drive, that is, took on *developmental* functions" (Johnson, 1982, p. 19).

This means that the "developmental state" thesis could be regarded as a part of political economy theory of late industrialisation. Although there is no standard definition of developmental state, several common characteristics of this form of state can be pointed out. As Woo-Cumings (1999, p. 1) observes, "Developmental state is a shorthand for the seamless web of political, bureaucratic, and moneyed influences that structure economic life in capitalist Northeast Asia. This state form originated as the region's idiosyncratic response to a world dominated by the West... today state policies continue to be justified by the need to hone the nation's economic competitiveness and by a residual nationalism".

Japan is the first Asian country that transformed herself into a developmental state by ruthlessly promoting development at any cost. Johnson argues that the successful developmental states have been quasi-revolutionary regimes, in which whatever legitimacy their rulers possessed came from the "overarching social project their societies endorsed and they carried out... This one overriding objective — economic development — was present among the Japanese people after the war" (Johnson, 1999, p. 52).

To achieve its ultimate target, the Japanese government protected and promoted the interests of the big Japanese corporations and utilised the power of bureaucrats to guide the development projects. Pempel and Muramatsu maintain, "Japan's economic and political leaders have rather consistently embraced economic development as a national goal since the Meiji Restoration in 1868 and with redoubled vigour in the years immediately following World War II. Politicians, whether elected or not, have almost unswervingly identified their long-term viability as dependent on achieving high levels of national economic growth... Furthermore, the national civil service has generally been utilised as major instrument to achieve those goals" (Pempel and Muramatsu, 1995, p. 34).

Tripod System of Japan's Policymaking

Under a strong developmental orientation in her political setting, Japan has developed a "tripod system" of decision-making on the national policies. The three main actors of Japan's policymaking are: (1) powerful politicians from the Liberal Democratic Party (LDP), (2) national bureaucrats, and (3) big Japanese corporations. This system — a so-called "Iron Triangle" — has been dominating the Japanese politics for several decades. The system excludes other actors, such as civil society, small and medium industries (SMIs) and ordinary people, from participating in the policymaking process.

Tabb describes the "Iron Triangle" the real ruler of Japan. As he put it, "What is known as the "Iron Triangle" — the nexus of corporate interests, the LDP, and the bureaucracy, especially the Ministry of Finance and the Minister of International Trade and Industry — has ruled Japan for the last half century" (Tabb, 1999, p. 77).

Among the three actors, the national bureaucrats apparently occupy the dominant position. Although the Diet is stipulated to be the highest organ of state power and the sole law-making organ of the state, the national bureaucrats are said to have more influence in the Japanese policy-making system than politicians. For example, Terada (2000, p. 2) points out that although the Japanese Constitution accords the highest powers to politicians, Diet's deliberations have been ritualised. A prominent opposition politician, Naoto Kan (1998, p. 19) describes Diet as a colony of bureaucrats.

Bureaucrats rule the government and occupy a strong position in Japan's policymaking. Under the parliamentary cabinet system, the Cabinet has the right to control administration on behalf of the people and is the major policy-making apparatus. However, "In Japan the reality is that bureaucrats control even the Cabinet" (Terada, 2000, p. 3). Bureaucrats are involved in every stage of the policy-making process and "can manipulate the process to suit their interests" (Hosono *et al.*, 1999, p. 24).

Especially, the Ministry of International Trade and Industry (MITI) plays a pivotal role in Japan's policymaking process. Johnson described MITI as a strategist and planner of Japan's economic development in his book "*MITI and the Japanese Miracle: The Growth of Industrial Policy, 1925-1975*". Johnson argues that the real equivalent of MITI in the U.S. is not the Department of Commerce but the Department of Defence, which by its very nature and functions shares MITI's strategy. He points out that MITI-led Japan's industrial policy is similar to that surrounding the domestic expression "military-industrial complex" referring to a close working relationship between government and business to solve the problem of national defence (Johnson, 1982, p. 21).

Developmentalism and the Environment: Lessons from Japan

As the "Iron Triangle" has been busy shaping the Japanese national policy, other crucial agendas, among them environmental preservation, were set aside. As the consequence of the industrialisation process, a delicate balance between production and the environment was seriously undermined. The government implemented various mega infrastructure projects that aimed to facilitate the country's industrialisation and to provide business opportunities to private sector. Mason (1999, p. 190) claims, "Many of Japan's domestic environmental problems are attributed to the dominance of the 'construction state' (*doken kokka).* The so-called 'iron triangle' of business interests, politicians, and bureaucrats supports a vast public works empire".

Often, when deciding whether to implement a development project, the Japanese government overlooked or underestimated side effects the project would have on the local community. More precisely, while cooperating with private business the government was expecting local residents to sacrifice their rights for the sake of "development". As a result, environmental and social issues began cropping up.

The first Japan's major pollution case, the Ashio copper mine pollution, occurred in the beginning of the 20th century. The local population was unhappy about the pollution to such a degree that farmers from Ashio led by Shozo Tanaka held demonstrations against Furukawa Corporation, the owner of the copper refinery factory. According to Martinez-Alier (2000), Furukawa Corporation had been profiting from a "novelty and uncertainty of the chemical pollution in question, and from the closeness between the government and business in Japan. It was argued, Martinez-Alier points out, that public benefit that had accrued for the country from the Ashio mine far out-weighted any losses suffered by the local residents. The prevailing attitude was that the damage could in any case be adequately taken care of by compensation.

The Japanese government considered the demonstrators as "trouble makers" who threatened national security and took stern actions to control them. Ui (1992) claims that demonstrators who are the victims of the Ashio copper mine pollution were oppressed on the basis of so-called national security restrictions. Although the demonstrations were apparently held in vain at the time they did influence the Japanese government's environmental policy later. Ui argues that other mines, such as Besshi and Hitachi, which developed later than the Ashio mine, were more responsive to the demands of their respective pollution victims.

It often happened that even when pollution had become out of control and the consequences could not be concealed any longer, the government and responsible companies would ignore the pollution issue and would not admit their responsibility. Voose (1996) asserts that the government often ignored the demands of the pollution victims because it assumed that sooner or later the victims would stop their protests.

To sum up, the Japanese government has set "economic development" as the ultimate national target to be achieved by all means and has enlisted both bureaucrats and business sector for this purpose. Although Japan has successfully implemented various industrialisation programmes and became one of the richest countries in the world, she was not able to escape side effects that the "development at any cost" approach usually brings, i.e., environmental deterioration. This was a bitter experience for Japan. In this connection, the question is: can ASEAN countries as latecomers of "developmentalism" learn from Japan's mistakes and reduce the price of industrialisation?

Developmentalism in ASEAN

The prevalent form of governance in the contemporary age, that is, the institution of the state, was introduced from the West to Southeast

Asia during the colonial era. The political turbulence in European history since the age of Renaissance gave rise to the most fundamental principles of the state: its territorial sovereignty and non-interference in its domestic affairs. Guarded with scientific organising principles and equipped with the bureaucratic system and the military, it has been the most powerful institution that human beings have invented so far.

Once on Southeast Asian soil, this institution adapted to local conditions and transformed itself into the colonial state. It worked as a mechanism to exploit the natural and human resources of the region in order to feed the rising capitalism of the Western centres. Later, the colonial state's clearly demarcated boundaries helped the leaders of independence movements to form an "imagined community" in their collective consciousness — a nation embedded in its own territory (Anderson, 1991). With the achievement of independence, these leaders took over the state structure from the departing colonial masters, along with its bureaucracy, tax collection system, transportation system and military. The framework of a nation state was there, but it lacked a substance. The reality on the ground was a plural society in which divergent communities existed side by side, in many cases hardly related to one another, and there was a disparity between the rural and urban districts in terms of economy and the style of life. To give substance to the appearance, the elite initiated a twin process of state-formation and nation-building (Ayoob, 1991, p. 267). Their aspiration was to create within each country a unified nation protected by the state.

However, in the 1960s, Southeast Asian states were in turmoil, so the governments decided to adopt developmentalism as a means of achieving state-formation and nation-building. As a result, strong governments and economic development have been combined together. It may be said that this was an inevitable choice: except for communism, there was no alternative to developmentalism at that time, as the institution of the state was already there to stay, overhanging a diverse population and a vast territory.

As in the colonial days, the state under developmentalism has served as an instrument geared to the effective exploitation of local resources and maximum production, aimed at overseas markets. This time, however, the stress has been laid on industrial development with massive investments from foreign countries. Thus, natural and human resources within a country have been more systematically mobilised than before. The infrastructure, such as roads, highways, industrial estates, ports, airports and dams, have been built, and factories and offices, set up.

On the surface, the strategy of ASEAN states has been a great success. Their economy has been successfully integrated into the global economy,[1] and most of the countries in the region have registered high growth rates since the 1970s due to export-oriented economic policy (Dixon, 1991). As a result, condominiums and hotels are mushrooming in major cities. Luxurious cars fill the streets. Shopping complexes are crowded with shoppers. As a move to realise its founding fathers' dream of "ASEAN 10", the organisation has expanded to cover the whole Southeast Asia, and developmentalism has appeared triumphant over its erstwhile archrival, communism. A substantial segment of middle class has emerged out of the economic development. Its rise has contributed to a degree of democratisation of the government systems in the region.

However, besides some obvious benefits, developmentalism had negative impact on: (1) ordinary people, (2) the relations between a government and grassroots organisations, (3) the environment, (4) people's network.

Ordinary People

Due to development projects, it often happened that local residents had been dislocated from their traditional abode. Major causes of the people's marginalisation could be explained by the "blue print" approach that such a development strategy adopts. Development policy and projects are decided in the urban centres and implemented top-down according to blue prints. There is little room for consultation with the local people who would be affected, and little room as well for the bureaucrats to take local knowledge and wisdom into account. The development process tends to overlook cultural diversity and variety of human existence. Indeed, developmentalism regards diversity and variety as somewhat detrimental to industrialisation, because it requires large and homogenised markets, a standardised labour force and consumerist culture.

Prosperity has particularly affected the middle class people. Strongly influenced by the Western consumerist culture, their materialist lifestyle has been disseminated through the media, and has set a standard for a good life, which the general public, including those who are not so fortunate, are pressed to strive for.

It is true that the rising middle class has, to a certain degree, ameliorated some of the negative aspects of developmentalism by expecting government's accountability for balance between economic development and other social issues, such as environment conservation. However, these people are the main beneficiaries of developmentalism. Their concern is mostly confined to civil and political rights, which tend to protect their own interests rather than those of the socially and economically disadvantaged.

Government and Grassroots Organisations

With no effective mechanism for popular participation in the decision-making process, a government would lack the capacity to learn from the grassroots. Moreover, power will be overwhelmingly concentrated in the central government. As economic development has been linked to state-formation and nation building, developmentalism has other implications. For example, anyone who questions or opposes the national development policy or development projects might run the risk of being labelled as "excessively critical". Not equipped with the mechanism to fundamentally address development-related problems, the authorities would have no choice but to ignore these problems and miss an opportunity to incorporate feedback from the grassroots' organisation into the national policies.

The Environment

There have been signs for the deterioration of the environment due to excessive economic activities. This poses a risk of an increasing number of human-made disasters, such as flood, landslide, haze and water shortage, which would be more and more beyond human control if the balance between the environment and development is not achieved. Cleary, developmentalism does not possess the in-built mechanism to check environmental degradation, without humane corporate governance even more damage might be inflicted on the environment and human life. While agreement or a compromise can be achieved with affected people, the same cannot be done to nature, which sooner than later demands the balance sheet of misguided human acts.

People's Network in ASEAN

For a successful environmental conservation not only government's efforts but also the cooperation and networking between the people are needed. People in the region have much in common among themselves, they have lived under similar types of the governments. However, developmentalism has negatively affected people's perceptions. Nations and countries are judged according to their monetary wealth and prosperity. Historical and cultural similarities between people are often overlooked. There are rich and poor ASEAN countries in terms of GDP or per capita income. The different degrees of economic development among the regional countries have given rise to immigrant workers who seek jobs in neighbouring countries. Workers from poorer countries are not always treated well or with respect in richer countries where they are employed. The way in which immigrant workers and the local population encounter each other (such as house maids versus their employers, for example) at present is not very conducive for people's networking.

Comparison between Developmentalism in Japan and ASEAN

There are similarities and differences between developmentalism in Japan and ASEAN. A significant parallel is that the developmentalism ideology did work in both cases. Developmentalism made it possible for Japan to restore and reconstruct her war-torn economy by the 1950s, and gradually "catch-up" with developed countries. Moreover, Japan became one of the countries with the highest per capita Gross National Product (GNP). ASEAN countries that adopted developmentalism, such as Singapore, Malaysia, Thailand and Indonesia, used this ideology to overcome their economic problems caused by decolonisation. These countries were able to achieve exceptionally high economic growth and relatively good income distribution. This multi-tier industrialisation process came to be known as the "flying geese" pattern of industrialisation (Akamatsu, 1962).

The most noticeable trait of Japan and ASEAN's developmentalism is the leading role of the government in the economic development. As Shibusawa *et al.* (1992, p.54) put it, "The role of the state as the source, inspiration and expression of national development (in East Asia) is unquestioned.... The state has exercised an interventionist function as often as it deemed it necessary... If, in the West, that government governs best that governs least, the rule is turned on its head in the East to read, that government governs best that governs most".

The fact of East Asian governments' interference into their economies was noted by the World Bank. "In most these (East Asian) economies, in one form or another, the government intervened — systematically and through multiple channels — to foster development" (World Bank, 1993, p. 5).

It is important to note that East Asian development strategy — active government intervention into economy — could serve as an alternative development model for other developing countries. For example, according to Kurtz, Chile faced serious problems in industrialising its economy without the government intervention. Kurtz describes Chilean approach as "developmentalism" without "developmental state". He notes that without appropriate government intervention, "there is strong evidence to suggest that market forces are not reorienting the economy toward manufactured export or higher value added products". Kurtz concludes, "It requires a reinterpretation of the challenges facing developing nations that is more sensitive to the problem of market failure and the associated space for positive state intervention" (Kurtz, 2001, p. 18-19).

The most significant difference between Japan and ASEAN is the country's ethnic structure. Japan is a relatively homogenous society. Although there are ethnic minorities, the majority of the Japanese share a similar culture and way of life. Since the beginning of the country's industrialisation, the Japanese were forced to regard nation-state as a quasi-family and emperor as head or father of the quasi-family. Jun Ui (1992) observes that the emperor system, allied with the state religion of Shinto, provided the rationale for building a quasi-family nation-state.

After World War II, this basic structure was employed to restore Japan's economic power. This was achieved through a very close cooperation of public sector and private business that formed a sort of a quasi-company. According to Woronoff (1982, p. 14), Japan's international competitiveness is regarded as a reward for cooperation between public and private sectors, the special relation that is sometimes called "Japan Inc.". He maintains that the basic assumption of "Japan Inc." is the exceptional degree of cohesion that exists both among various companies and between them and the government.

By contrast to Japan, many ASEAN countries are multi-ethnic societies where people have different cultural, religious and ethnic backgrounds. In ASEAN, the nation-state normally is considered as a community rather than family or company. Nation-state in ASEAN can be described by the term "imagined community". According to Cohen and Kennedy (2000, p. 377), a nation is imagined because the member of even the smallest nation will never know most of their fellow members, but the nation is conceived of a deep, horizontal comradeship.

It might be easier for the political elite in Japan to mobilise people into the process of development due the country's ethnic homogeneity. But the situation is different in many ASEAN countries where it takes much more effort from the leaders to involve their people into the process of development. This is the reason why there is a relatively higher income discrepancy in ASEAN countries.

Regarding the environment, both in Japan and ASEAN development had a detrimental impact on the environment. Besides, rapid economic development in a country inevitably influences the traditional way of the life of its people. Excessive consumerism produces bigger amounts of solid waste while the industrialisation's by-product — industrial waste — causes pollution. In Japan, the magnitude of pollution has been much bigger than in ASEAN. The country faced a far more grave pollution and environmental deterioration during the industrialisation compared to ASEAN countries.

The difference in the degree of environmental deterioration can be attributed to the timing of industrialisation processes in Japan and ASEAN. Japan had started implementing industrialisation programme during the Meiji era while ASEAN countries introduced developmentalism in the 1960s. This could be advantageous for ASEAN countries for they could learn from Japan's mistakes and escape similar environmental problems with Japan. ASEAN countries have chance to utilize their "new comer" status to work out a better development strategy which would take into account negative effects of industrialisation to the environment.

Conclusion

It appears that the dominant political discourse in East Asia — developmentalism — has contributed to the "miraculous" economic growth in the region. However, developmentalism is not free of negative aspects. This discourse needs to be reappraised in order to achieve a balance between economic development and the environment. Japan was the first Asian country that had consciously adopted developmentalism in the middle of the 19th century and achieved high economic growth after World War II. However, this economic achievement was overshadowed by serious pollution cases in the 1950s and 1960s.

The political elite in ASEAN countries adopted developmentalism for the purpose of state-formation and nation-building. Unfortunately, this development-first policy gave rise to a similar with Japan problem of environmental deterioration, though its scope and gravity are different. In order to reduce the cost that development inflicts on the environment, ASEAN countries might utilize the position of "late comers" to developmentalism to their advantage and learn from other countries' experiences and mistakes.

NOTES

1. Ironically, this successful integration to the global economy has resulted in the over-dependence of the regional economies on global capital, enhancing their vulnerability to external forces.

REFERENCES

Akamatsu Kaname (1962), "A historical Pattern of Economic Growth in Developing economies" *The Developing Economies,* Preliminary Issue, no. 1, (March/August).

Anderson, B. (1991), *Imagined Communities* (Revised ed.): Reflection on the Origin and Spread of Nationalism, London: Verso.

Ayoob, M. (1991), "The Security Problematic of the Third World", *World Politics,* Vol. 43, (January), p. 267.

Chang, Ha-Joon (1993), *The Political Economy of Industrial Policy"*, New York: St. Martin's Press Inc.

Clements, Alen and Aung San Suu Kyi (1997), *The Voice of Hope*, London: Penguin Books.

Dixon, C. (1991), *Southeast Asia in the World Economy*, Cambridge: Cambridge University Press.

Holloway, R. (ed.) (1989), Doing Development: Governments, NGOs and the Rural Poor in Asia, London: Earthscan Publication.

Hosono, Sukehiro, Hideki Shiroyama and Hiroshi Suzuki (1997), *Chuo shocho-no seisaku keisei katei: nihon no kanryosei-no kaibo (Policy Formation Process in the Central Government: Anatomy of Japanese Bureaucracy)*, Tokyo: Chuo University Press.

Johnson, Chalmers (1982), MITI and the Japanese Miracle: The Growth of Industrial Policy 1925-1975, Stanford: Stanford University Press.

Johnson, Chalmers (1999), "The Development State" Odyssey of a Concept", in Meredith Woo-Cumings (ed.) (1999), *The Developmental State,* Inthaca: Cornell University Press.

Kan Naoto (1998), *Daijin (The Ministers),* Tokyo: Iwanami Shoten.

Korten, D.C. (1990), Getting to the 21st Century: Voluntary Action and the Global Agenda, West Hartford: Kumarian Press.

Martinez-Alier, Joan (2000), "Environmental Justice, Sustainability and Valuation", paper presented in Harvard Seminar on Environmental Values, March 21, 2000, from Harvard Seminar on Environmental Values' home page, http://www.ecoethics.nt/hsev/[accessed October 30, 2001].

Meas Nee (1995), *Towards Restoring Life: Cambodian Villages*, Phnom Penh: Krom Akphiwat Phum.

Pempel, T.J. and Michio Muramatsu (1995), "The Japanese Bureaucracy and Economic Development: Structuring a Proactive Civil Service", in Hyung-Ki Kim, Michio Muramatsu, T.J. Pempel and Kozo Yamamura (eds.) (1995), *The Japanese Civil Service and Economic Development: Catalysts of Change"*, New York: Oxford University Press.

Shibusawa, Masahide, Zakaria Haji Ahmand and Brian Bridge (1992), *Pacific Asia in 1990s,* London: Routledge.

Tabb, William K (1999), "The End of the Japanese Post-war System", *Monthly Review,* Vol. 51, No. 3, (July/August), pp. 71-80.

Terada, Takashi (2000), "New Aspects of the Politicians-Bureaucrats Relations in Japan: Diet Reforms and Implications for the Policymaking System", paper presented in International Conference on the Japanese Model, 29-30 March, 2000, Nikko Hotel, Kuala Lumpur, Malaysia.

Ui Jun, ed. (1992), *Industrial Pollution in Japan,* Tokyo: Untied Nations University Press, from http://www.unu.edu/unupress/, [accessed on November 8, 2001]

Vosse, Wilhelm (1996), "The Past, Present and Future of the Environmental Movement in Japan", paper presented in International Symposium on Environmental Education and Environmental Ethics, December 14, 1996, Konan University, Kobe, Japan.

Woo-Cumings, Meredith (1999), "Introduction: Chalmers Johnson and the Politics of Nationalism and Development" in Meredith Woo-Cumings (ed.) (1999), *The Developmental State,* Inthaca: Cornell University Press.

World Bank (1993), The East Asian Miracle: Economic Growth and Public Policy", New York: Oxford University Press.

Woronoff, Jon (1982), *Inside Japan, INC.*, Tokyo: Lotus Press.

9

Experiences of Economic Reform in China with Reference to Privatisation and FDI

*Dr. Bama Dev Sigdel**

Introduction

From the early 1950 to the late 1970s, China had a command economy that had focused on quantitative growth. Although Chinese industrial and agricultural growth figures looked impressive compared with these of other developing countries such is India, China's economic efficiency lagged behind not only of the western industrialized countries but also of the newly industrialized South Korea.[1] By the end of the cultural revolution, the majority of Chinese rural population lived in absolute poverty and did not have sufficient food to eat or warm clothing to wear. The rural per-capita disposable income in 1978 was only 285 Yuan for China and it was significantly lower than that of the poverty line of 454 Yuan fixed by World Bank.[2] Despite of launching of ambitious plans and programmes in the past during Mao's regime, China could not succeeded to grasp it. The launch of series of economic reform us programme particularly after 1978 marked a new stage in China's economic growth. The year of

* Dr. Sigdel is Deputy Director at Research Department, Nepal Rastra Bank, Visiting Professor, People's Campus and also the member at Central for Policy Studies, KTM.

1978 marked the beginning of a new era for China's modernizing programme, for it was when the country embarked on a road of reform and opening up to the outside World. By the late 1970's, reform minded Chinese leaders felt a great sense of urgency to improve economic efficiency and catch-up advanced nations. Deng Xiaoping was eulogized by his successors as the 'Chief architect' of China's reform programme and it's opening to the outside world. His commitment to the series of economic reform led him, throughout the 1980s, to open China to foreign investment and business result was un-even development of industrial and agricultural production. The main thrust of this paper is to discuss China's experience of economic reform with reference to privatisation and FDI.

Economic Reform and Economic Growth in China

Deng Xiaoping was eulogized by his successors as the 'Chief architect' of China's reform programme and is opening to the outside world. His commitment to economic reform led him, throughout the 1980s, to open the China to foreign investment and business to acquire the resources, technology, and expertise necessary to carryout his plans for modernizing the country. He instigated highly successful economic reforms in agriculture, dismantling the commune system in favour of household contracts and private farming.[3] He then moved to restructure the urban economy, introducing market incentives in industry, reforming price and wage systems and granting public and private enterprises more autonomy. In the transition to market economy, Chinese reformers have made efficiency the top priority. A guiding principle of Chinese economic reform is efficiency first while also taking equality into consideration.[4]

After careful consideration of Chinese characteristics, Deng proposed the strategy of allowing some people and some region to become rich first in belief that these people and region would set good example for the rest. The demonstration effect would encourages others to work hard and perform better. The regions that achieved great efficiency would also be able to help less-developed regions improve their economics, and ultimately general prosperity would increase. Thus, in Deng's Era, China transferred the income rights over agricultural production from collective to individual households. While this significantly enhanced the production incentives of peasants, the change deprived local governments of a major source of income. At the same time, China's fiscal reform granted local governments the right to retain part of the extra tax revenue, and the greater the income of local government. "Given such a stake in economic growth, local governments were motivated to mobilize and coordinate resources under their jurisdiction to engage in entrepreneurial endeavours. They established and ran rural enterprises and took the profits to pay for expenditures and re-investment. In such a way, local governments functioned like a large corporation with diversified business, thereby serving as the engine of China's economic reforms."[5]

China's new strategy for economic development initiated by Deng and his colleagues, as embodied in the policy of re-adjustment and reform showed the positive signals in the beginning of 1980s. Three years of practice gave China an endless beginning. From 1979 to 1981, total industrial and agricultural output value grew at an average annual rate of 6.7 percent; for total value of agricultural output rose by an average of 5.6 percent, the total value of industrial output rise by an average of 7.1 percent, which broke down to a 14 percent increase for light industries and 13 percent for heavy industries.[6] The openness and reform in China further improved the status or living standard of Chinese people in an aggregate term.

Since the early 1980s, a growing number of Chinese economists have followed the western practice of using the term "economic efficiency" to mean both technical efficiency, in terms of the best possible input-output relationship and efficiency in terms of the optimum allocation of China's market-oriented reforms started with gradual liberalisation of economic activities, step by step, and sector by sector. Some new market elements were welcomed, but the reforms of existing institutions, especially those that involved vested interests, met with strong resistance. Resistance also came from those in the government and the party who favoured a planned economy because they believed that such a system was more suitable for the People's Republic of China.[7] Economic liberalisation thus started in 1978 in China with the production and transaction of many agricultural products. Because most of Chinese poor people lived in rural areas and agriculture was the least centralized sector of the economy. Deng had decided to reform agriculture first, before moving on the reforms the urban and industrial sectors. Farmers were allowed to sell their products on the free market after marketing their quotas for procurement sales set by the state planners. Later such an agreement was also introduced into many industrial sectors on well. The implication of such policies in China was mere positive. Grain output had increased from 365 to 407 million tons over the period 1978 to 1984.[8] Similarly, real per capita income rose more than doubled.

Since the initiation of the reform and opening up programme in 1978, China has enjoyed an enhanced international standing with a rapidly growing economy and increasing comprehensive strength in the world. China's GDP rose from 362.41 billion RMB in 1978 to 7,477.24 billion RMB (US$ 900.87 billion) in 1977, a nearly twenty-fold increase.[9] Thus, in the two decades since Deng opening China to the world, Chinese GDP has risen 583 percent. Taking into account China's 31 percent rise in population in the same period, this means living standards have improved by 422 percent.[10] Openness in trade in increasingly being viewed as an important mechanism for steady economic growth in developing economies, especially, after the experiences of success stories in east and South-east Asian regions. In the east of China, the openness of the economy has dramatically increased since 1979, when Chinese government started pursuing the 'opening up' policy and economic reforms that follows. The sum of exports and imports as a percentage of GDP has risen from 8 percent in 1979 to 35 percent in 1993.[11] Most of the studies of China have also shown that export expansion and inducement of FDI in

China were the important factors continuing to the rapid economic growth in China. The change in economic policy from Mao to Deng involved a significant decentralisation of decision-making throughout the economy and a withdrawal of the state from interference in the daily life of the people. By the end of 1995, China was the world's seventh largest participant in world trade and FDI had gone to 233,564 enterprises in China, the foreigners accounting for 40 percent of US$ 739 billion invested in these enterprises.[12]

The Third plenum of the Fourteenth Central Committee in end 1993 had accepted of switch over to de facto market economy, it called for the development of modern enterprise system by the year 2000. The policy guidelines offered a sequential development that began with the pre-dominance of economic planning and sub-ordination of markets in the first phase of reform (1979-84), followed the combination of economic planning and market regulation in the second phase (1985-88), continued further with the state regulating the market and market guiding enterprises in he rectification programme (1988-91), and culminated in socialist market economy.[13] As the reforms in China in the late 1980s or the beginning of 1990s were frequently accompanied by considerable financial laxity, rampant corruption and speculation, significant inflation; viewing these bitter facts premier Zhu Rongij with the aid of prominent young Chinese policy advisors cracked-down hard on financial speculation and shifted Chinese macro-economic policy towards a conservation moderately tight money approach.[14] The most important reforms carried out under Zhu between 1993 to 1996 introduced new rules that at last principle applied equally to all economic actors.

During this period an entire series of reforms and regulation was rolled out that affected nearly every aspect of the economy. New laws were promulgated that covered labour, corporations, and the banking system. Some of these — such as foreign trade reform were immediately successful.[15] Viewing sluggish economic growth due to Asian financial crisis, Premier Zhu had announced an infrastructure spending programme expected to total some US$ 750 billion over three years (1997-2000).[16] Similarly, the Premier Zhu also announced plans to develop a mortgage backed commercial housing market, with banks able to dedicate up to 15 percent of their loans to home lending. Thus, between 1993 to 1998, Premier Zhu engineered a high successful shoft landing of the economy. The inflation rate fell from over 20 percent in 1993 to just 0.8 percent by the end of 1997, while the growth rate was reduced from an overheated 13.4 percent to a still impressive 8.8 percent in the same time period.[17] There were, however, some encouraging signs for Chinese economy in 2000. According to official statistics GDP for the half of the year was 8.6 percent and the annual GDP growth rate was expected to be 8 percent.[18]

China has become the world's largest producer of quite a few agricultural and manufactured products; it maintains the top position is steel, crude oil, chemical fertilizer, concrete, coal and television sets as well as grains, meat, cotton, peanuts and rapeseed. China started 1999 with a worshining economic situation. Export dropped by about 10 percent in the first half of 1999, relative to the first half of 1998, owing to week global demand, especially in Asia : private consumption demand stagnated owing to large lay-off by the SOEs, which led to a continued decline in price.[19] However, by Mid-1999 economic conditions had started to show improvement, including a significant turn-around of exports. External balances for China remained positive, although the current account surplus dropped by $ 10 billion in 1999 owing to strong import growth and relatively wear export performance.

Since the 1999, Chinese economic policies have increasingly been focused on efforts to further bolster domestic demand. New measures were adopted. Monetary policy become more accommodative. In mid-1999, the Central bank of China lowered reserve requirements and made its seventh and most aggressive reduction of interest rate in three years.[20] Particularly, economic reform since 1978 set China on a course towards market oriented economy and substantially increased her producing power, putting the economy on the track of high growth. But it must be noted that despite of this the figure for industrial nations already exceeds $ 10,000 (GNP per capita), and Japan's per capita GNP is as high as $ 40,000, or over 40 times that of China.[21] In short, despite of all these achievements, the level of Chinese economic growth still lags far behind from that of advanced industrialized countries of the world.

Economic Liberalisation and Privatisation Drive in China

Chinese policies towards private sector economies differ drastically between Mao's Era (1949-76) and Deng's Era (1977-1996). Before 1978, private economies in China were perceived as seedbeds for capitalism, and policies were designed to eliminate them.[22] The size of labour force in urban private business was reduced from 8,830,000 to 1,040,000 between 1952 and 1957, and to a mere 150,000 by 1978.[23] Meanwhile, State Owned and Collectively Owned Enterprises increased in number and thus become the only significant component of economy.

After the death of Mao in 1976, the rigidity in organisation, inefficiency in management, and poor productivity of the state-owned enterprises were seen as a hindrance to China's moderniation. The role of the private sector in China's economy was redefined as 'complementary to state and collectively owned enterprises' and their development would benefit production, market supply, and employment. An objective of reformer leader Deng Xiaoping in the initial stages of reform was to revive individual business as a part of efforts to promote growth while private enterprises reappeared during the early 1980s in China, the stigma of capitalism discouraged many individuals from stating business. From the beginning, owing to ideological barriers imposed by Mao's version of Marxist-Leninist socialist doctrines, SOEs reforms did not involved significantly privatisation of state assets.[24] However, major reforms increased enterprises in China accountability and autonomy, implementing a flexible wage system to link work efforts more directly with rewards. Post Mao-China confessed that State enterprises were inefficient and of capabilities to competed against growing domestic and international competition, thereby becoming a drag on growth and employment creation. These enterprises had received financial support through the fiscal and barking system,[25] which had affected periodically macro-economic stability in China in the late 1980s.

China's economic reform process officially began with the Third Plenum of the 11th Central Committee of the CPC in December 1978. At that time Chinese authorities recognized that administrative authority was unduly concentrated in the central government and enterprises lacked autonomy. As a result, the reform programme emphasized administrative decentralisation and the expansion of enterprise autonomy in China during 1979-84.[26] The 15th CPC Congress endorsed the process of enterprise transformation at the local level, which had actually been going on in China since the late 1980s. During the implementation of the Contract Responsibilities System (CRS), local governments at all levels expanded their central over SOEs by investing in the firms and sharing power with managers.[27] The objectives of the CRS was to increase productivity within the framework of continued state ownership by for their spreading the ownership of assets by the state from the management of SOEs. It covered 90 percent of SOEs, including 95 percent of large and medium industrial SOEs.[28]

A pattern of de facto property rights emerged, which was officially recognized by the central government in 15th CPC Congress strategy of 'letting go to small (fang-xiao)'. As many as 66,000 industrial SOEs in China fall under the control of provinces and lower administrative levels,[29] continues and township being the major 'owners' in rural areas, whereas cities play this role in more urbanized regions. Amendment of China's constitution in April 1988 gave further impetus for flourishing private enterprises slowly. As it spells, "The state permits the private sector economy to exist and develop within the limits prescribed by laws. The private sector economy is complementary to the socialist public economy. The state shall protect the lawful rights and interest of the private sector economy, while exercising guidance, supervision and control over the private sector economy."[30]

In 1983 most direct grants from the government budget to SOEs were replaced by interest bearing loans, and banking system became the primary channel through which the SOE's investments were financed. After reform, SOE's use of external sources for investment started to carry a cost in the banking system have also led to the emergence of more commercial banks and non-bank financial institutions, such as bonds, stocks, and inter-enterprises borrowings.[31] The final stage of enterprise reform at the local level implies the corporatisation of enterprises through the issuance of shares and total or partial privatisation. Enterprises take either one of the corporate firms contained in new company law (limited liability or joint-stock company), or the form of a shareholding cooperative, a hybrid[32] corporation from close to western cooperatives. In other cases enterprises were directly sold off to private investors or kept in state hands as wholly state-owned companies.

The Chinese government adopted further the privatisation friendly policy adopting a lease contract by which the manager leased the firm by paying the Chinese government a fixed proportion out of firms profit. The first significant case of lease contract happened in Wuhan Motor Company in 1986 when three people put 34,000 Yuan as collateral lease to the factory. By the end of the 1980s, lease contract were encouraged by the government as a means to reform small SOEs. A State Council regulation regarding the lease of small SOEs was issued in 1988. One direct consequence of the adoption of lease contract was the introduction of private entrepreneurs into the management of SOEs because managers could be recruited outside the enterprise.

The opening of the Shenzhen Stock Exchange in 1990 and the Shanghai Stock Exchange in 1991 enabled SOEs to issue shares to the public in a wide range. However, the Chinese government implemented restrictive measures to prevent the State from losing control of the listed SOEs. For example, it requires that a certain proportion of a firm's shares be held as corporate shares that can not be sold.

The growth of the private sector was further encouraged after Deng's Southern tour of China in 1992, in which he proclaimed the government's commitment to deepening reforms and operating up the outside world.[33] Thus, the real privatisation in China started after Deng's visit to southern China. As in the case of many other reforms initiatives, privatisation was first started from localities and then sanctioned by the central government. The most important impetus for local privatisation was the large amount of debt accumulated in the state sector. This was a more pressing problem in small cities because of the smaller size of their economy. For example, in Zhucheng city, Sandong province, among the 156 city owned enterprises, 103 were in red, and the total amount of loss was 147 million Yuan, equivalent to the city government's revenue in 1.5 year.[34] In 1993 the Chinese constitution was amended to indicate that the government's goal was to establish a 'socialist market economy' and that the private sector was a complement to it.

From 1998 onward, various types of property reforms have been applied to SOEs in China. According to a survey conducted by the State Statistical Bureau in 1998, among 13,716 enterprises that had been 'restructured', as many as 76 percent of them had undergone privatisation in the sense of buyout of state capital, whether all or partial.[35] As of the end of October 1998, 81.71 percent of small firms at city and country levels underwent various forms of property reforms. Micro privatisation proceeded quite rapidly particularly in Sichuan and Sandong provinces.

Following China's experience in transformation spanning in a period of 15 years, the CPC abandoned the centrally planned economy in favour of market economy. In this decision, the Chinese authorities set out their policy orientation to establish the so-called socialist market economy, which included the establishment of a more clearly defined property right structure of multiple ownership with public ownership as the core, a market system which unified and opened up the whole country, sound instruments of macro-economic management, income distribution, compatible with equity and efficiency, and social security networks at multiple levels including unemployment insurance, social insurance, social relief and welfare.[36] The partial restructuring of state industry created a gradual reform option for China's leadership.[37] The constitution was further amended in 1999 to state that private sector was an important component of China's socialist market economy. "Zhu's group has come to understand that Chinese economy today is not simply transitioning from plan to market. Nor is the policy challenge simply to dismantle the old machinery of state intervention so that free market forces can somehow spontaneously prevail. Rather, the Chinese system today after two decades of incremental reform already is a market economy, albeit on desperately lacking the governance measures that make modern market economies function smoothly."[38]

One of the hallmarks of reform in China has been what one study lies labelled its process of 'privatisation from below'.[39] In rural economy, the process is seen in the rise of privately owned enterprises alongside the dominant, collectively owned village and township enterprises. Some of the China's enterprise reform, although ad hoc, have been genuinely creative and have increased productivity. Moreover, despite an expansion of non state sector — urban collectives, township and village enterprises, individually owned firms, and foreign-funded ventures — propelled by reforms that have liberalized market entry, removed price controls eased investment restrictions, increased tax neutrality across different types of enterprises, and exposed the market to international competition, state owned enterprises remain the key drives of China's industrial sector.[40]

Financial liberalisation further fulled privatisation and open the avenue of more and FDI for China. There were three major driving forces behind the change in China's fiscal system.[41] The *first* is that the remarkable growth of non-state-owned enterprises — township and village enterprises (TVEs), dominance of state enterprises. Losses making states has been increasing and have great drain on the fiscal system. Thus, the Chinese government has been forced to run and alternative revenue sources. *Second*, the balance of political power has shifted towards local autonomy as a result of economic reform. It is natural for sub-national governments to demand a commensurate decision making power in fiscal areas as a consequence of their greater political autonomy. The *third* impetus to decentralize the fiscal system stem from purely economic reasons too.

There were different modes of enterprise reforms in China. The former SOE in converted into a limited liability Joint-Stock Corporation. In some cases, shares are distributed without charge to workers and managers (usually a maximum of 20 percent of shares is to be distributed this way). In other cases, workers receive only the right to purchase shares — sometimes all the shares of the new corporation, typically at a significant discount. In addition, sometime a financial interest in the firm is sold or assumed by other corporate or government, entities, and sometimes shares are sold to the public.[42] The remaining key hardcore problems for Chinese economy in the state sector, including SOEs, the state owned banks, and the government administration. Reforms in the state sector have mainly involved decentralisation of decision-making powers and managerial adjustments without change or ownership. These process have resulted in 'decentralized SOEs' and 'autonomous local governments', all playing increasing roles in determining resources allocation and income distribution within an unchanged ownership frame work for China.

Unlike reforms in the state sector, the past 1978 development of TVEs is largely spontaneous. The major form of ownership varies from region to region. In Jiangsu, most of the TVE as are owned by township or village government; in Guandong, there are large number of TVEs owned jointly by township/village governments, individuals and foreign investors; an in Wenzhou, most rural enterprises privately owned. The central and provincial governments have played a very limited role in encouraging the development of the TVEs, while he township and village governments provided active promotion efforts. Thus, the greatest achievement of China's economic reforms is probably the successful development of TVEs. The key strategy of Chinese reforms was to first effect a massive increase in income in the rural areas and then meets the demand for the consumer goods by encouraging the growth of TVEs.[43] In 1978, the total number of TVEs was just 1.6 million; by 1993, it rose up to 24.5 million. The real grown output value of TVEs rose by an average of 25.6 percent per year over the TVEs together 1978-1993.[44] With the rise of the TVEs together with other collective and privately owned industry, the share of state-owned enterprises in the real gross value of industrial output fell to 26.5 percent in 1997 (from 77.6 percent in 1978).

Sichuan provides an example of 'gaizhi'. In 1994, the provincial government began implement 'gaizhi', starting from country-owned enterprises. By the end of 1998, the province finished 'gaizhi' for 68.6 percent of the 42,681 firms that were targeted for 'gaizhi'. Among these transformed, 35.1 percent were transformed into employees-owned companies, 11.0 percent were transformed in to employees-owned cooperatives, 14.3 percent were sold out, 7.0 percent were contracted-out to the individuals, 8.5 percent were leased-out, 7.0 percent were bankrupt, and 5.0 percent were taken by other. firms.[45]

There are numerous indicators which point to the poor performance of state-owned industrial enterprises relative to the non-state sector. The SOEs accounted for 34 percent in 1981 but they covered 73.5 percent of all industrial investment.[46] In other words, the amount of capital used for each unit of output in the industrial enterprises and it is primarily due to the capital-intensive nature of these enterprises. A survey of 124,000 SOEs showed that asset losses and unaccountable expenses accounted for 11.6 percent of the assets of the firms sampled. In 1996 about 50 percent of the industrial SOEs incurred net losses; this proportion rose from the third in 1994.[47] The scale of the problems faced by China's SOEs has recently grown more evidence. Their total debt is estimated to be in the region of US$ 200 billion. Even in 1996, one third of SOEs were already technically bankrupt, and another one third suffered from serious liquidity problems.[48] Many state owned Chinese enterprises are technologically inefficient. Most remained obligated the provide cradle-to-grave social services to workers and their facilities.[49] They also carry a rising proportion of redundant employees and retirees on their payrolls.

Furthermore, after premier Zhu's three-year restructuring effort, China's poor-performing SOEs turned around in 2000 with 52.5 percent of SOEs and state-holding enterprises have been lifted out of financial trouble.[50] As a result of reforms implemented to date, the financial situation of the SOEs has improved. The total losses of the sector declined by 16 percent in the late 1999, and some large and medium-size enterprises in traditional industries (such as textiles, construction materials and railroad transportation) response profits. However, the large number of redundant employees, the problem of high indebtedness, and the heavy burden of provising social services still remained serious.[51] The SOEs laid off some 5.6 million workers in 1999, leading to the determination of consumer confidence and weak consumption demand.

Towards the beginning of 2000, the Chinese authorities adjusted their strategy for further reforming the SOEs.[52] *First*, reform will be implemented over a longer period and are to be completed by 2010. *Second*, SOEs will concentrate operations in a few sectors related to so-called lifeline of national economy. A large number of them will be organized in various types of ownership sharing arrangements. *Third*, debt-to-equity swaps will be implemented, and this will also improve the balance sheets of state-owned bonus. *Fourth*, SOEs will be gradually released from their functions as provides of social services. These measures, including training programmes for laid-off workers, are expected to alleviate the problems of SOEs in the long run.

Once Chi Fulin, the Executive Director of China Institute for Reform and Development in relation to Chinese privatisation drive suggested that "enterprises reforms in imperative especially in the telecommunications, civil aviation, rail way and power industries...ownerships should be separated from management. Once the weight of non-state investment increases, conditions for a level playing field can be created. The state should preserve its majority only in enterprises of strategic importance."[53] Broadman suggests that "reform should follow a two-track approach : strengthening the overall institutional framework, especially with respect to property rights, corporate governance incentives, and competition and other market-based forms of checks and balance; and further reducing the state's ownership in the enterprises to minority passive stocks managed by independent professionals."[54] In this regard, Matues also spells "China should impose effective fiscal and financial constraints on all local governments, and promote interregional competition and foster more equal regional development"[55] in order to accelerate meaningful economic liberalisation, privatisation and thereby sustained economic growth.

Economic Liberalisation and FDI in China

The Chinese economy considered as a command economy during Mao era, opened itself in 1979. China carried out massive economic reforms in an effort to restructure their economy main pillar of reform. The Chinese government has gradually liberalized its restrictions on FDI in order to reap the rewards of foreign investment; technology transfer modern managerial skills, and foreign exchange.[56] The outcome of the reform have been extraordinary. Thousands of multinationals have invested in China, bringing with them billions of dollars in FDI. Thus, China attracted a lion's share of FDI flows among the developing countries as it was considered one of the lucrative location for FDI in the world.[57]

During the 1980s, capital inflow to China were mainly in the form of foreign loans of foreign capital inflows. After joining WTO, China promises to provide national treatment to foreign enterprises, open its service market to foreign ownership, and improve its investment climate and policy to facilitate foreign investment. Coupled with the potential demand from China's domestic market, China has thus become much more attractive to investors from all over the world.[58] According to reports, one-quarters of the FDI which flowed into the developing countries over 1991-2000 went to China while about three-quarters of China's cumulative inbound FDI has came from Asian economies.[59]

For several year, local government in China too has been engaged in infrastructure investment to attract foreign investors. In addition, some regions have granted preferential treatment of various kinds to the investors, involving tax retreats exemptions, subsidies and other fiscal and financial incentives. The accession to WTO has made China more attraction destination in FDI. Furthermore, FDI has become one of the important factors contributing the rapid growth of China's export. Most of the economists also agree that the continued active introduction of foreign capital is of great importance for China's economic prosperity, reforms and thereby the meaningful globalisation of Chinese economy. Foreign capital inflows, especially FDI is becoming an increasingly important aspect of the development and globalisation process. FDI and portfolio investment helps the developing countries by supplementing the domestic capital resources. FDI also provides modern technology, improves workers skill and could help boost up exports.

China had succeeded to attract US$ 13.5 billion worth FDI in 1989-1994. FDI for China rose tremendiously over the years and stood at US$ 46.8 billion in 2001. During this period, India in contrast failed to draw more FDI for her economy. She succeeded to attract just US$ 3.4 billion worth FDI in 2001. A higher level of FDI in China is also reflected in higher ratios like FDI/total domestic fixed investment, FDI stock/GDP, value added by MNEs/GDP, and FDI employment/total employment.[60] By June 2002, the cumulative contracted and realized values of inward FDI for China reached US$ 784 and US$ 420 billion respectively. China in now the largest host of FDI in the developing world.[61]

During the period between 1979 and 2001, FDI in China was mainly from Hong Kong (47.3%), followed by U.S. (8.7%), Europe (8.1%), Japan (8.1%), Taiwan (7.4%), Singapore (4.7%) and Korea (3.2%). Various studies have pointed out that overseas direct investment into China has been almost dominated by ethnic Chinese from Hong Kong, Taiwan, Macao followed by USA, Japan, Europe, South Korea and Thailand. In terms of geographical distribution, the FDI pattern in China shows a great disparity among the regions. The eastern region (accounting for 64 percent of GDP) took up nearly 88 percent of FDI to China while the central region (29% of GDP) took up 9 percent and the western region (23% of GDP) attracted only 2 percent. This pattern stems from the FDI policies prescribed by the Chinese authorities and reflect the incremental nature of the reform process in China.[62]

The major reasons for foreign investors desire to move direct investment in China are: (*i*) China has been the world's biggest potential moment; (*ii*) China has abundant cheap labour force and abundant resources; (*iii*) China is eager to have true FDI because she could be benefited from western advanced technology and managerial talents, which could be massively utilize for internationalizing the economy.

Sum Up

Thus, on can say that China's future development will greatly depend upon how successful these corporate reforms measures can be implemented. It is also important to realize that the health of business enterprises has a major influence on the state of bonus and of the social welfare system. Besides, the transition towards a developed and efficient market economy should be a comprehensive, and synchronized transition of institutions, economy, culture, society and polity. Piecemeal and disjoint reform programmes may merely create an illegitimate market economy. Some Chinese analysts maintain that the growing un-employment resulting from the reform of SOEs will constitute the biggest threat to stability. Some SOE's will go bankrupt, putting all of their workers out of a job while others will have to drastically downsize to survive. With China's economy being continuously privatized, the Chinese government reform programmes may will be likely to sustain, so the synergy of a private ownership based economy and a sound state governance structure could be formed. As China is steadily improving the transparency of its trading regime to meet the standards set by WTO and giving more secured access of Chinese goods in the overseas market, more foreign investors would intend to establish export manufacturing operations in China particularly in eastern central regions including Hong Kong. China's accession to WTO would transfer technology to China and establish procurement centre and R and D center there. Furthermore, opening up distribution in China will attract retailors, and the opening of banks, insurance and telecommunications will attract additional FDI as well as FPI. China's success in attracting FDI inflows has been primarily due to her large special economic zones with various incentives and facilities. China's large domestic market, low wage cost, and improved infrastructure, complemented with open FDI policies, especially the establishment of OEZs, seems to have major determinant factors in attracting FDI. It is expected that China's gradual market opening through various economic liberalisation measures and robust economic growth will positively as well as negativity affect the major and emerging economies of the world.

Table 1: Major Indexes of National Economy during 1991-2000.

Indices	*1991*	*1992*	*1993*	*1994*	*1995*	*1996*	*1997*	*1998*	*1999*	*2000*
GDP (one hundred million dollar)	12617.8	26638.1	34634.4	46622.3	58260.5	67885.0	74463.0	78345.0	81911.0	8940.0
GDP per person (dollar)	1866.5	2273.4	2922.3	3890.0	4810.1	5569.0	6048.0	6374.0	6513.0	690.0
Fixed asset investment of the whole country (one hundred million dollar)	5508.8	7855.0	11829.1	17042.9	20019.2	22914.0	24941.0	28406.0	29855.0	3261.0
Total amount of export and import (one hundred million U.S. dollar)	1356.3	1655.3	1957.0	2366.2	2808.5	2899.0	3251.0	3240.0	3607.0	4743.0
In which £° export	718.4	849.4	917.4	1210.1	1487.7	1510.7	1827.0	1838.0	1949.0	2492.1
Import	637.9	805.9	1039.6	1156.1	1320.8	1388.4	1424.0	1402.0	1657.0	2250.9
Foreign exchange reserve (one hundred million U.S. dollar)	217.1	194.4	212.0	516.2	736.0	1050.0	1399.0	1450.0	1547.0	165.0

Source: www.chinaFDI.org.cn

Table 2: Shares of State and Non-public Sectors (%)

	State Sector Gross Industrial Output	*Fixed Capital Investment*	*Urban Employment*	*Non-public Sector Gross Industrial Output*	*Urban Employment*
1978	77.6	–	78.3	–	0.2
1980	76.0	81.9	76.2	0.5	0.8
1985	64.9	66.1	70.2	3.1	3.9
1990	54.6	66.1	62.3	9.8	5.7
1995	34.0	54.4	59.0	29.4	24.5
1996	28.5	52.5	56.7	32.1	28.0
1998	28.2	54.1	43.8	40.0	46.7

Note: Non-public sector means all sectors other than state and collective ones.
Source: China Statistical Yearbook, various editions.

Table 3: SOE Efficiency and Profitability

Indices	*Wage share (%)*		*Profit-Tax Ratio (%)*		*Average Wage (yuan)*		*Labour Productivity (10000 yuan)*	
	1985	*1995*	*1985*	*1995*	*1985*	*1995*	*1985*	*1995*
Total	25.14	33.10	35.06	15.64	1042	5,086	1.277	7.492
State-owned Enterprises	22.02	37.08	32.94	13.45	1164	5,546	1.598	6.739
Elective-owned Enterprises	34.84	33.15	46.96	22.26	863	3,811	0.799	6.170
Private Industry		16.83		50.71		4,086		9.797
Joint Industry	21.08	32.79	64.44	18.45	1051	5,491	1.681	9.196
Share-holding Industry		26.22		25.63		6,891		12,482
Foreign Founded Industry	23.16	17.80	31.9	20.29	2138	7,590	4.693	19.548

Source: Calculated from Chinese Industrial Census, 1985, 1995.

Table 4: FDI Inflow into China and India

(In billion US$)

Year	*China*	*India*
1989-1994	13.5	0.3
1995	35.8	2.1
1996	40.1	2.5
1997	44.2	3.6
1998	47.7	2.6
1999	40.3	2.1
2000	40.7	2.3
2001	46.8	3.4

Source: World Investment Report, 2002.

Table 5: Shares of Major Source Countries of Relaised FDI in China (1986-2000)

(In per cent)

Year	*Hong Kong/Macao*	*Taiwan*	*Japan*	*US*	*EU*
1986	59.22	—	11.74	14.54	7.96
1987	69.08	—	9.50	11.36	2.28
1988	65.60	—	16.11	7.39	4.92
1989	61.24	4.56	10.50	8.38	5.53
1990	64.87	6.38	14.44	13.08	4.23
1991	56.96	10.68	12.20	7.40	5.63
1992	70.03	9.54	6.45	4.64	2.21
1993	64.91	11.41	4.81	7.50	2.44
1994	59.75	10.04	6.15	7.38	4.55
1995	54.64	8.43	8.28	8.22	5.68
1996	50.95	8.33	8.82	8.25	6.56
1997	46.46	7.27	9.56	7.16	9.22
1998	41.64	6.41	7.48	8.58	8.75
1999	41.35	6.45	7.37	10.46	11.11
2000	38.92	5.64	7.16	10.77	11.00

Source: http://www.chinafdi.org.CN.english.

NOTES

1. Liu, Gooli, *The Politics of Marketization: In equality vs. Efficiency*, in 'Asian Affairs', Heldret Publication, Vol. 24, No. 3.

2. Quoted in Sigdel, Bama Dev, *Nepal's Relation with Japan and China,* Centre for Policy Studies, Kathmandu, 2003, pp. 88-89.
3. Bader, J.A., *China after Deng Xiaoping: Prospects for Continuity or Change*, in 'Asian Affairs', Vol. 24, No. 2, USA, 1997, p. 41.
4. See, Wang, Weichen, and Lianzhon Li, *A Courses in the Socialist Market Economy*, Peking University Press, Peking, 1995, p. 389.
5. Oi, Jean C., *Fiscal Reform and Economic Foundations of Local State Corporatism in China,* in 'World Politics', Vol. 45, October, 1992.
6. Hong, Ma, *New Strategy for Chinese Economy*, New World Press, Beijing, 1983, p. 151.
7. Gang, Fan, et.al., *People's Republic of China: Economic Performance and Prospects,* in 'Asian Development Review', Vol. 15, No. 2, Manila, 1997, pp. 54-55.
8. Suije, Yao, *Economic Development and Poverty Reduction in China Over 20 Years of Reform,* in 'Economic Development and Cultural Change', University of Chicago, Vol. 48, No. 3, April, 2000, p. 44.
9. *March Towards 2000*, Information Office of the State Council of PRC, Beijing, 1999.
10. Jun, Lim Suk, *Can China Build a Future on the Foundation of Its Past*, in East Asian Review, Institute for East Asian Studies, Vol. 12, No. 4, Winter 2000, pp. 37-53.
11. Sun, Haishun and Dutta Dillip, *China's Economic Growth during 1984-93: A Case of Regional Dualism* in 'Third World Quarterly', Vol. 18, No. 5, UK, 1997, p. 847.
12. Dernber, Robert F, *The People's Republic of China at 50: The Economy,* in 'China Quarterly: An International Journal for the Study of China', University of London, No. 159, September 1999, p. 611.
13. Quoted in Singh, Surjit, *Economic Reforms and State Enterprises in China,* in 'China Report', Saga Publications, New Delhi, Vol. 34, No. 2, April-June 1998, p. 199.
14. Naughton, Barry, *China's Economy: Buffeted form Within and Without,* in 'Current History', USA, Vol. 97, No. 620, September 1998, p. 274.
15. *Ibid.*
16. *Asian Outlook, 1998*, ANZ, Philippines, 1998, p. 7.
17. Fewsmith, Joseph, *China in 1998: Tacking to Stay the Course,* in 'Asian Survey', Vol. XXXIX, No. 1, January/February 1998, p. 103.
18. Cheng, Li, *China in 2000: A Year of Strategic Rethinking,* in 'Asian Survey', Vol. XII, No. 1, January/February 2001, p. 81.
19. See, UN, *World Economic and Social Survey 2000*, United Nations, New York, 2001, pp. 101-102.
20. *Ibid.*
21. See, *APC Journal of Asia Pacific Studies*, Japan, No. 6, March 2000, pp. 7-8.
22. Han, Sun Sheng and Pannell C.W.; *The Geography of Privatization in China,*

1978-1996, in 'Economic Geography', Clark University (USA), Vol. 75, No. 3, July 1999, p. 274.

23. *Ibid.*
24. Yao, Shujie, *op cit.*, p. 450.
25. See, World Bank, *China: Macro-economic Stability in a Decentralized Economy,* World Bank, Washington D.C., 1995.
26. Zengxian, Wu, *How Successful has State: Owned Enterprises Reform Been in China,* in "Europe-Asia Studies", University of Glasgow, Vol. 49, No. 7, 1997, pp. 1237-1262.
27. See, Granick, D, *Chinese State Enterprises: A Regional Property Rights Analysis,* University of Chicago Press, 1990.
28. Zengxian, Wu, *op cit.*, p. 1239.
29. Quoted in Matutes, J.S., *Privatization and Local Governments in Mainland China: A Critical Assessment,* in 'Inter-Economics', Review of International Trade and Development, HWWA, Hamburg, May/June 2000, p. 138.
30. Han, Sun Sheng and Pannell C.W., The geography of privatization, *op cit.*, p. 278.
31. See, *Policy Environment for State and Township Village Enterprises,* http:// members. aol.com/Junmanew/ch4.htm,1988, p. 1-11.
32. Matues, J.S., *op cit.*, p. 138
33. *Transition*, The World Bank/The William Division Institute, November-December 2000/01, p. 13
34. Zhao, Xiao, *Competition, Public Choice and Privatization in China,* CCER Working Paper Series C 1999025, Beijing University, 1999.
35. Nakagane, Kastsuji, *SOE Reform and Privatization in China: A Note on Several Theoretical and Empirical Issues,* University of Tokyo, Tokyo, November 2000, p. 17.
36. Wu, Zegxian, *op cit.*, p. 1240.
37. Jefferson, G.H., *China's State: Owned Enterprises did Their Job-Now They Can Go,* in 'Transition' WB/Development Research Group, World Bank, Vol. 10, No. 5, October 1999, p. 31.
38. Stinfield, Edward S; *Beyond the Transition: China's Economy at Century's End,* in 'Current History', Vol. 98, No. 629, September 1999, p. 272.
39. Harrold, Peter, *China's Reform Experience to Date,* World Bank Discussion Paper, Washington D.C., 1992, p. 35.
40. Broadman, Harry G; *The Chinese State as Corporate Shareholder,* in 'Finance and Development', A Quarterly Publication of IMF, IMF, Vol. 36, No. 3.
41. Lin, Zhiqiang and Liu, Zhiqiang, *Fiscal Decentralization and Economic Growth in China,* in 'Economic Development and Cultural Change', The University of Chicago Press, Vol. 49, No. 1, October 2000, p. 4.
42. Naughton, *op cit.*, p. 276.

43. Pant, Manoj, *Sequencing of Reforms: Lessions from China*, in 'The Economic Times', New Delhi, February 1, 2002.
44. Yao, Shujie, *op cit.*, p. 454.
45. Yao, Yang, *Government Commitment and Outcome of Privatization in China*, China Centre for Economic Research, Beijing, 2001, p. 3.
46. Singh, Surjit, *Economic Reforms and Sector Enterprises in China*, in 'China Report', Sage Publication, Vol. 34, No. 2, New Delhi, June 1998, p. 200.
47. *Ibid.*, p. 201.
48. World Bank, *The Chinese Economy: Fighting Inflation, Depending Reform (Country Paper)*, Washington D.C., 1996.
49. Broadman, Harry G., *op cit.*, p. 52.
50. Cheng, L., *China in 2000: A Year of Strategic Rethinking*, in 'Asian Survey', Vol. XLI, No. 1, January-February 2001, p.81.
51. UN, *World Economy and Social Survey*, United Nations, New York, 2001, pp. 101-102.
52. *Ibid.*, p. 102.
53. Fulin, Chi, *China's Infrastructure Needs Great Leap Forward*, in 'Transition (The News Letter About Transforming Economies)', World Bank, Vol. 11, No. 6, November-December 2000/01, p. 12.
54. Broadman, H.G., *op cit.*, p. 55.
55. Matutes, Jacint Soler, *op cit.*, p. 144.
56. Berkum, Sandra, *Foreign Direct Investment in China*, May 7, 2001, pp. 1-2.
57. Sahoo, Dukhabandhu and Mathiyaz M.K., *et al.*, *Is Foreign Direct Investment an Engine of Growth; Evidence from the China Economy*, in 'Savings and Development', No. 2, Vol. XXVI, 2002, p. 419.
58. Yen, Tzung-Ta (*et al.*), *SEACEN Supplementary Research Project on The PRC in the WTO: Impact on Trade and Investment in Selected SEACEN Countries*, Economic Research Department, Central Bank of China, Taipei, March 2003, pp. 66-67.
59. Singh Arvinder, *China and Global Economic Slowdown*, in 'China Report', A Journal of East Asian Studies, Institute of Chinese Studies, New Delhi, Vol. 30, No. 3, July-September, 2003, p. 383.
60. Agrawal, Pradeep and Sahoo, Pravauar, *China's Accession to WTO: Implications for China and India*, in Economic and Political Weekly, June 21, 2003, p. 2547.
61. Wei, Yinggi, *Foreign Direct Investment in China*, Lancaster University Management School, UK, 2002, p. 1.
62. Tseng, Wanda and Zebregs, Harm, *FDI in China: Some Lesson for Other Countries*, IMF Policy Discussion Paper, IMF, USA, February 2002, p. 5.

10

Japan's Relations with Africa

Dr. (Mrs.) Aparajita Biswas

In the recent years, one notices a major shift in Japan's Africa relations. In January 2001, Yoshiro Mori made history by becoming first ever Prime Minister to visit three countries Kenya, Nigeria and South Africa in the African continent. During his visit he made an important policy statement on Africa. He emphasized on Japan's total support for development, conflict resolution and refugee aid in Africa. He reiterated that "there will be no stability and prosperity in the world of the twenty first century unless the problems of Africa are resolved", and that "the problem of Africa is one of the most important issue of our global foreign policy".[1] However, there are apprehensions and speculations regarding its time and purpose of his visit. This was because so far Japan showed very minimal interest on African Affairs. In the 1960's and 1970's Japan's initial endeavour towards the African countries was mainly revolved round Japan's rudimentary Official Development Assistant (ODA) Programme. This programme began in the 1960's when Japan concluded "economic cooperation" agreement with number of Asian states who had been victims of Japan's aggression before or after World War II.

The second stage started from late 1960's to 1973-74, when Japan's aid was making inroads into the other regions of the world. It was in the third phase i.e. between the years 1974-85 Japanese aid diplomacy had acquired a wider significance in terms of Japan's overall foreign policy objectives. The period coincides with the oil shocks of 1973-74 and 1979. The year 1974 was important in the sense that since 1974 Japan realised the vulnerability of its resources as oil was projected as a political weapon by the Organisation of Arab Petroleum Exporting Countries (OAPEC) against the United States and its allies, including Japan. Japanese government, during this period began to establish cordial relations with the countries which were richly endorsed with mineral resources. In the African region, in early November 1974,

Japanese Foreign Minister Kimura Toshio, visited the countries like Ghana, Nigeria, former Zaire and Tanzania. This was the first Japanese cabinet minister tour to Africa. The foreign minister's trip to Africa was a response to the new developments in the international political economy, in addition to the threats from the countries which were in possession of certain important raw materials and energy resources upon which Japan mostly dependent on at that time. Following foreign minister trip to sub-Saharan Africa, Japan had doubled its official development assistance to Africa.

However, Japan's ODA programme in sub-Saharan Africa was placed under heavy criticism mainly on two grounds. First critics insist that Japan was only interested in disbursing aids to those states in the African region which were richly endowed with mineral resources such as former Zaire, Zambia, Niger and Zimbabwe. Also Japan was interested in cultivating friendly relations with the countries like Kenya and Tanzania for their geo-political significance in the African region and their influences in the United Nations. Second burning issue was Japan's rising trade surpluses with apartheid South Africa.[2]

Infact Japan had considerable economic linkages with South Africa since early 19th century. It should be appropriate to mention here that the Japan-South Africa relations flourished since the year 1930's when South Africa faced with great economic difficulties. Japan was granted the status of 'Honorary White' where Japanese had access to all white commercials and residential areas and cultural activities.[3]

Thus as Morikawa in his article explains "by identifying themselves with prevailing racial prejudices Japan provided psychological support to the minority regimes."[4] Since 1960's the co-operation between the two countries further extended and deepened. It was the time when apartheid South Africa was becoming a pariah state in the world community. Between 1962-1980's, trade grew phenomenally from U.S. $ 178 million to U.S. $ 3.5 billion.[5]

For Japan, South Africa was an attractive trading partner. South Africa was not only a major supplier of primary resources but also a substantial export market. Japan imports included large quantities of coal, iron ore, manganese ore, platinum, gold, maize, sugar, wool from South Africa. In 1977 the percentage rate of dependency on South African imports was as follows: Silo-chrome, 99.1, ferro-chrome, 76.1, iridium, 56.2, rhodium 49.8, ferro-manganese, 48.7, platium 33.9.[6]

Again Japanese export to South Africa include not only capital goods, such as motor vehicles, electrical and mechanised equipment, and iron and steel but also consumable items such as textiles, chinaware and toys. Although South Africa's share of Japan's total overseas trade remains constant at around 1.5 percent, certain industries rely greatly on this market. In 1969, South Africa was the second largest foreign buyer of Japanese goods and the fourth largest purchaser of passenger cars, and by 1981 had become a more important trading partner than France.[7] Thus by the early 80's South African market was so important to Japan that when contradiction emerged in Japan-South Africa relations in the later years economic interest generally took precedence over ideological commitment or issues of morality.[8]

The significant year of Japanese South African trade was 1987, when due to South Africa's isolation and international sanction, South Africa's trade with United States and United Kingdom shrunk. At this time, Japan seized the opportunity and Japan — South Africa trade soared from $ 3.6 billion in 1986 to U.S. $ 4.3billion in 1987.

Japanese exports increased by 37 per cent and its imports raised by 8 per cent vis-a-vis South Africa.[9] By 1989 Japan had become South Africa's second largest export market with a 13.6 per cent share of all South African exports and its goods constituted 12.6 per cent of South African imports.

Japan-South Africa's relations irked the leaders of sub-Saharan African States. Incidentally in May 1973, the African States through their Ambassador in Tokyo, had delivered a warning to Japan to the effect that the latter would be isolated from the Afro-Asian group if it did not support the African States in their struggle against minority government in South Africa. Indeed, they further threatened to refuse Japan access to the raw materials in Africa, if it continued expanding economic relations with South Africa.[10]

In 1974, responding to the pressure and also to the threat of Third World economic pressure as demonstrated by Organisation of Petroleum Exporting Countries (OPEC) oil embargo in 1973-74, Japan also took decision to suspend sports, cultural and sporting exchange with South Africa and refuses to issue visas to South African citizen. This gesture, however was an eyewash because business and tourism did not fall within the scope of these ban. Moreover, Tokyo downgraded its diplomatic relations with Pretoria from the ambassador to counsellor level. However strong diplomatic relations were continued. Japanese two consular offices in South Africa were considered to be more important and active than other embassies located in the African region, either in Nigeria or Kenya. As Morikawa notes that according to Japanese Ministry of Foreign Affairs in 1982 there were only 11 official in its Nigerian embassy and 12 in Kenyan embassy, two of Japan largest while 66 officials and family members were station in South Africa.[11]

Not only trade but, Japanese government and Japanese companies have been decisive actors in the development in several key sectors of the South African economy. Although officially Tokyo banned direct foreign investment in South Africa in 1965, but as Nestor explains that several Japanese firms with indirect encouragement from Ministry of International Trade and Industry actually have invested hundreds of millions of dollars in scores of manufacturing, mining and service industries in South Africa.[12]

On one side, Japan maintained its relations with South Africa by keeping economic realities separate from its political rhetoric. Simultaneously, on the other, in order to offset international criticism of its ties with South Africa, Japan's external Trade Organisation encouraged Japanese companies to invest in other African region in the mid 1974. Following years since1980 to date with Ohera Masayoshi governments followed by the Suzuki Zenko administration, Japan extended its aid programme in Africa as a diplomatic instrument.

However, the period between 1974-1988 also witnessed increasing rhetoric of Japan's relations with South Africa. During this period, Japan's policy often appeared inconsistent and contradictory.[13] In 1985, Japan followed the United States and the European Community in supporting the UN condemnation of Preteria's declaration of the state of emergency. Same year, Japanese Ambassador at the UN Mrs. Kurokochi, called for abolition of apartheid, the release of Nelson Mandela and all political prisoners and urged Pretoria to negotiate with the ANC. She strongly condemned South Africa for its apartheid policy and called the institutionalised racial discrimination "the most serious and systematic denial of freedom and equality anywhere in the world."[14]

Moreover, Japan took measure to curtail the export of computers to South Africa's apartheid-enforcing agencies, following South Africa's declaration of the state of emergency and the internal violence in 1985. The apartheid-enforcing agencies designated by the Government of Japan are Ministry of Defence, the Defence Force, the Ministry of Law and Order, the Police, the Armaments Development and Production Cooperation, the National Institute for Defence Research, and the Ministry of Justice.[15] It also put restriction in 1986, on iron-ore imports and steel and asked its businessmen for "voluntary restrain" their imports of Krugerrands and gold coins from South Africa. However, there were deliberate loose ends. As Sasaki notes that the major strategic items were excluded from the ban and those that were insignificant were marked. This symbolic gesture hardly affected bilateral trade and the trade data showed that Japan as the largest trading partner of South Africa in 1986.[16]

In 1988, United Nations General Assembly strongly criticised Japan for its economic relations with South Africa. Although Japanese government tried to justify the relations on the ground that trade was basically private sector initiatives and not the government, nevertheless because of growing international criticism it forced to call on its leading business houses to restrain their economic ties with South Africa.

In the sub-Saharan African region as mentioned before, since 1973, greater emphasis has been placed on finding critical mineral resources especially uranium, iron ore, cholorium and oil. One of the most active firms involved in maximum exploration and mining is the Power Reactor and Nuclear Fuel Development Corporation which has operations in Mali, Niger, Guinea, Gabon and Zambia. Niger regarded as the most promising source of Uranium, is already a producer. Overseas Uranium Resource Development company, a Japanese Consortium, the Niger government, Congema of France and Spain's Enus are mining uranium at Akouta and Tokyo Uranium is searching uranium deposits in Mauritania. In Sudan's Ingesana Hills, the Japanese government is co-operating Sudan's chromium exploration efforts. Japanese firms are also helping exploration of iron ore in the countries like Liberia, Senegal and Mauritania. In Gabon, Mitsubishi Petroleum Development Company and Itogh are helping Elf-Gabon France to increase oil production level.[17]

In manufacture sector, Japan invested mainly in motor vehicles, textiles, consumer electronics, fishing nets and motor bikes. Japan views Africa as potentially significant market, especially for automobiles. Its vehicle export to Africa have increased in such a large extent that over 60 per cent of all cars sold in Africa are Japanese.

Besides theses, economic assistance to the region increased significantly during the second half of the 1980's : from $ 252 mn in 1985, to $516 mn in 1987 i.e., more than 100 per cent.[18] By 1989 it had reached $ 1.04 bn, until it started descending. In1993, Africa took 24.4 per cent of Japan's grant aid. As part of its development, Tokyo provided a $ 500 mn non-project grant aid to eleven countries in sub-Saharan Africa in 1987. And in 1989, the government established a system to support the Structural Adjustment Programme undertaken by the donor nations in Asia and Africa. The Plan was supported with a $ 600 mn grant, which was further extended for three years beginning in the fiscal year 1990. The new system succeeded the non-projected programme initiated in 1987.[19]

In the sub-Saharan Africa, Japanese economic assistance was mainly in the form of Grant aid and technical assistance as demonstrated in Table 1 and the following figures. The table shows that Kenya and Tanzania were the main recipients of loans from Japan. In Tanzania, Japan's grant aid was primarily earmarked for basic human needs projects and emergency food aid. The projects included agricultural and industrial development, road and bridge construction and rehabilitation, public health projects, tele-communication projects among others.

Table 1: Leading African States Receiving Japanese ODA — Cumulative to 1986. 100 m. (Exchange rate was Between 187.88 and 160.29 = $ 1)

1.	Kenya	549.17	Tanzania	283.40	Kenya	205.74
2.	Zambia	495.50	Kenya	236.59	Tanzania	125.58
3.	Nigeria	401.00	Zambia	193.74	Ghana	65.63
4.	Tanzania	353.57	Senegal	171.39	Zambia	56.70
5.	Zaire	344.96	Niger	159.90	Malawi	50.47
6.	Madagascar	239.66	Ghana	149.61	Zaire	46.85
7.	Malawi	146.69	Zaire	114.95	Nigeria	40.12
8.	Ghana	118.00	Somalia	110.6	Ethiopia	36.46
9.	Guinea	111.50	Madagascar	108.20	Senegal	30.36

It should be noted here that inspite of Japan's growing trade with South Africa and African leaders annoyance over the issue, Japan was tactfully establishing relations with other sub-Saharan African countries. It was reflected during Japanese Foreign Minister visit to Tanzania. During his visit then Tanzanian foreign minister, John Maleselia assured him that 'being full aware of Japan reliance on external trading, Tanzania had no intention of requesting Japanese to call an immediate halt to normal trading with South Africa.' He then...urged "Japan to boost its economic aid to African state bordering South Africa and Rhodesia."[20]

Tanzania's foreign minister's comments was directly contradicted the stand of other African states mentioned earlier. As Kweku Ampiah mentions "that with this particular Tanzania behaviour as a point of reference, it can be assumed that issue of Japan's relations with South Africa did pose a problem of interests among the African states because Malecelia's assurance can be seen as having defined a relationship between Tokyo and Dar-es-Salaam."[21] Tanzania became one of the leading receiptant of Japanese aid in sub-Saharan Africa in 1980's. Apart from this Japan International Co-operation Agency had sponsored 600 Tanzanians to attend training courses in Japan, in addition to about 200 Japanese experts and 450 volunteers who had extended their technical skills to Tanzania. President Nyerere himself commended the Japanese for their assistance to Tanzania during the visit of Emperor (then crown Prince) Akihit to Tanzania in August 1983. The President made particular reference to Japan's food aid to Tanzania during the drought period and to the construction of Selander bridge.[22]

Japan was also interested in establishing cordial relations with Tanzania because of Tanzania's importance in the international community during the cold war period. As Ampiah writes 'Interestingly Japanese politics share with 'African Politics' the culture of placing importance on individuals: there is a Japanese obsession with identifying someone who is dependable. President Nyerere was not only the International figure and has outspoken leader in the non-aligned movement but also respected leader with long political career in Tanzania. Japan wanted support from leaders like him to have some kind of recognition among the third world countries and from a anti-apartheid state in Africa in all those crucial years of international politics. Nyerere was also perceived as a man of peace, who fervently believed in negotiation rather than restoring to force. As Harace Campbell in his article points out "the formation of the Frontline States...showed the ability of Tanzania to bring together states of differing ideological postures in the cause of liberations, a fact which contributed to the Japanese interest in Nyerere.[23]

Subsequently after dismantlement of apartheid in 1990s, the importance of Tanzania was less crucial for Japan. During this period, Japan renewed its focus on Africa. By 1995 Japan disbursed aid to all 47 sub-Saharan African states worth U.S. $ 1.33 billion. Sub-Saharan Africa was also the largest receipants of Japan's total grant assistance in 1996. Zambia and Zaire assumed the leading positions. Zambia replaced it as the second largest receipant of technical assistance. Over the four year period Zambia as the leading receipant of this aid, received Yen 105 mn compared to the Yen45mn that Tanzania received over the same period.

However, Japan has not given much attention to trade and investment. Its major trading partner in Africa, is South Africa which accounts for approximately two-thirds of all Japanese trade with sub-Saharan Africa. Japan's export to South Africa was 185.2 billion Yen which include general machinery, electric machinery automobiles, auto parts etc. in 1999. And its imports from South Africa was approximately 257.8 billion Yen which includes food products, gold, crude metal, coal and metal products. During 1999 Japanese ODA loan to South Africa was 20.1 billion Yen and ODA grants was 3.7 billion Yen.[24] This is because South Africa is seen by Japanese analyst as the only African country with economic and technological base in the whole of Africa. President Mandela's visit to Japan also have given a new boost between those two countries relations resulted in launching of the financial co-operation package amounting to U.S. $ 1.6 billion by Japan to South Africa.

Another important development in bilateral relationship began in 1998 when then Vice-President Thabo Mbeki visited Japan. It was the first time in the official documents both government used the term "Partnership". It was since Thabo Mbeki became President of South Africa. one notices a very intense relationship developed between the two countries. Subsequently President Mbeki was invited to the North-South dialogues with G-B leaders held in Tokyo. On the inauguration ceremony Japan's foreign minister announced substantial development assistant grant for South Africa in its programme to alleviate poverty.

Japanese Ambassador, Yasukumi Enoki explained this relationship in the speech organised by South African Institute of International Affairs that 'for South Africa, one foot is in Africa, while the other is in the western global world. While Japan stands more on the G-8 side and South Africa stands more on the OAU or Non-alignment side. Japan and South Africa share the same role to bridge the North and the South.

It was during the G-8 Summit that which allowed the first international deliberation on Millenium Africa Recovery Programme/ New African Initiative (MAP/NAI). Japan hosted the first international seminar on the MAP/NAI where President Obasago of Nigeria delivered keynote address. Both the countries re-affirmed the conviction that African development should recognise the Principles of Africa's 'ownership of solutions' and 'partnership with the international community'. Both the government welcomed the fact that the Millenium Africa Recovery Programme/New Partnership Initiative, adopted by the OAU Summit Meeting in 2001, emphasised the principle of democracy, good governance and sustainable development. Japan expressed its intention to actively support this initiative through the TICAD (Tokyo International Conference on African Development).

The TICAD enterprise epitomises the Japanese government "New Africa Thrust'. The initiative to hold TICAD in October 1993 was taken by the Japanese Government and was co-organised by the United Nations Development Programme (UNDP) and a non-governmental organisations, the Global Coalition for Africa (GCA). It was attended by the heads and ministers of states of sub-Saharan African countries officials from the World Bank and the IMF, the ECA and OAU alongwith representatives of EU and DAC donor countries. The purpose of the conference was two fold : First to encourage sub-Saharan African states to adopt and advance economic and political reforms, and second to restore international consciousness in Africa.[25]

It was also an attempt to arrest, the growing sense of donor fatigue and 'Afro-pessimism' of the early 1990's. In reference to TICAD, Thabo Mbeki during his visit to Japan remarked that the "Japanese commitment to the development of Africa is further demonstrated by the important initiative through TICAD, which started in 1993 and continues to be a valuable platform for engaging developmental issues". It is because of these and many other reasons' he said, 'we are confident that this country will be amongst one strongest partners in our initiative of putting Africa on a sustainable development path'. Following TICAD-I, the Japanese government had boosted its bilateral ODA programme to sub-Saharan Africa. These aid were mainly disburse to assist economic reforms in and towards democratisation in several SSA states. It also contributed U.S. $ 100 million to the promotion of education in Africa. In the multilateral from TICAD process helped to organise many inter-regional follow-up sessions under the sponsorship of Japan, the UNDP and the GCA. In this the process had evolved two divergent ends — one which sought to reverse declining aid disbursal to sub-Saharan Africa by formulating a more market-oriented system of aid giving, one more palatable to aid donor, another which sought to transplant Asian development experience to Africa, to promote the idea of 'adopting Asian models to the African setting'.[26]

Infact, TICAD's main thrust was to make Asia's development experience relevant to Africa through enhanced Asia-Africa co-operation both political and economic. As the late Prime Minister Keize Obuchi while inaugurating the TICAD-II in 1998 explained that " Many countries in Asia, including Japan are in the grip of severe economic crises. However, as the people saying that friend in need is a friend indeed. This is the spirit with which the approach the challenges of the times and which indeed underlay TICAD-II, and for that reason I believe the holding of conference is significant."[27]

The TICAD initiative is indicative that Japan would like to play an active role in promoting Afro-Asian co-operation. Through TICAD It will try to determine or influence the policies of multilateral organisations like IMF and World Bank on sub-Saharan Africa. However in its TICAD efforts it could include the other Asian states like India, China and those of South and South-East Asian countries with which African countries have long association. It is time to find out whether there is a scope for African countries to reorient its development pattern in order to get rid of their critically dependent structures inherited as a colonial legacy.

11

Accounting for Religious Terrorism

*Dr. Aswini K. Mohapatra**

Etiologically, terrorism as an organized phenomenon originated in the second half of the 19th century Europe in the backdrop of the Enlightenment, which challenged many fundamental assumptions of political authority, rooted in the theological doctrines of the medieval period. The methods of challenge to the traditional authority of the Kings and the Church varied among the radical nationalist groups. While the Germans and Italians were successful in establishing unified nation-states, others like the Irish, Serbs, Macedonians and Armenians adopted terrorist methods in their struggle for national independence or political autonomy.[1] Again in the aftermath of the World War II, terrorism came to be closely associated with national and anti-colonial movements in Asia and Africa. During this period religion proved to be a potent technique of mass mobilisation for the liberation efforts of the secular-nationalist leadership.[2] By evoking historical and sacred themes, employing religious slogans and symbols, nationalists sought to whip up revolutionary favour among the unlettered masses. In brief, religion was used functionally to reach certain goals, which were not immediately derived from it. Instead, religion itself became an expression of protest against imperialism, and protection against grave forms of injustice.

*Dr. Aswini K. Mohapatra, Faculty, School of International Studies, JNU, New Delhi.

Evolution

At the end of the Cold War, what was traditionally considered as "ideological" terrorism-the phenomenon that brought terrorism to the global stage via hijacking and bombings-perpetrated by such groups as the *Shinning Path* and *Tupac Amaru* in Peru, Italian *Red Brigades* and *Red Army* in Japan lost its support and *raison d'etre*. In the early 1990s, the world came to witness an entirely new phase in the evolution of terrorism. A series of spectacular terrorist violence including the 1993 WTC bombing in New York, the 1995 Aum Shinrikyo attack of the Tokyo subway through sarin nerve gas, the 1995 Okalahoma city bombing, the 1998 simultaneous bombings of U.S. embassies in Nairobi and Dar-el-Salaam marked the beginning of what is now popularly known as New Terrorism or the post-modern terrorism. Unlike the earlier period when most of the terrorist groups had secular nationalist/separatist goals or revolutionary ideals, many deriving their inspiration from the ideas of Marx and Lenin, the predominant motivation behind this new terrorism have been the religious zeal tinged with messianic fervour.[3] The call for jihad (holy war), for instance, has become the battle cry for the soldiers of Islam in their struggle to end the era of *Jahiliyya* (pagan ignorance of the pre-Islamic Arabia), and the killing of uninvolved bystanders is justified in defence of their faith.[4]

The religious motivation is not confined to Islam alone, though the pan-Islamic Jihadi movement represents an enduring source of global security challenge. Timothy McVeigh who bombed the federal building in Oklahoma City was motivated by the Christian patriot movement; Yigal Amir, the assassin of the late Israeli Premier Yitzhak Rabin in 1995 was guided by Jewish messianic ideals; Aum Shinrikyo (The Supreme Truth), which carried out the Tokyo subway attack, was inspired by similar worldview to destroy the "corrupt world".[5] So did America's Christian anti-abortion activists who justified the bombing of abortion clinics in Alabama and Georgia in 1997 as defensive actions on behalf of the unborn.[6] By the mid-1990s, the proportion of terrorist groups motivated by religious considerations increased manifold.

Thirty years ago there was not a single religious cult or terrorist groups animated by religious beliefs. Even as recently as 1980, only two out of the world's 64 terrorist groups were religiously motivated. It was mostly the *Shi'ite* Muslim groups active in West Asia since the 1979 Iranian revolution that accounted for a quarter of all terrorist-related deaths.[7] By contrast, there has been a virtual explosion of identifiable religious terrorist groups from none in 1968 to today's level, where over half of all terrorist groups active throughout the world are predominantly motivated by religious concerns. It is worth mentioning that in the year 1968 the hijacking of an Israeli Airliner in July to Algiers by the Marxist-Leninist Palestinian factions marked the beginning of modern global terrorism. In fact, approximately 20 per cent of all international terrorist incidents during 1970-73 periods were related to the Palestinian cause.[8]

Despite an unprecedented growth in terrorist acts in the name of religion, attention of the international community was not sufficiently focused on combating this menace until the events of the 11 September 2001. The airborne terrorist assaults on the American cities demonstrated not just the scale of violence or lethality of attacks, but also the operational reach of new terrorism. As the subsequent investigations reveal, Osama bin-Laden's Al-Qaeda (the base) is truly global in terms of its networking, recruitment patterns and operational areas.[9] The movement's cells are found at one time in 60 countries and its activists drawn from a host of nations. The assassins responsible for the death of the Afghan warlord Ahmed Shah Masood were Algerians with Belgian passports, whose visas to enter Pakistan had been issued in London. Of the 19 hijackers involved in the 11 September suicide mission led by Muhammad Atta, an Egyptian architect trained in Germany, and 15 were Saudi citizens from the mountainous province of Asir. Likewise, over a quarter of the Kashmiri *fedayeen* (those who sacrifice their lives for a cause) are recruited from various Muslim countries ranging from Chechnya, Sudan and Algeria to Pakistan.

In sum, the distinction between state and non-state terrorism is no longer valid. Instead, what appears in the current phase of global terrorism is an amorphous network that defies labels. It consists of dispersed organisations, small groups and individuals who communicate, co-ordinate and conduct their campaign in an internetted manner, often without a central command.[10] The Al-Qaeda, for example, presents a united front of Islamist factions transcending their regional divisions and other particularistic properties in pursuit of establishing the *nizam al-Islami* (Islamic order) in the world modelled on the *Medinian Caliphate.*[11] Over the years, it had brought together under the banner of the International Islamic Front for Jihad a diverse range of terrorist groups active worldwide, notably the Egyptian *Islamic Jihad, al Gama Al-Islamiyya,* the Pakistan-based *Harkat ul-Mujhahideen* and *Jamiat ul-Mujahideen,* the *Ittihad al-Islami* of Somalia, Algeria's Armed Islamic Group or the *GIA,* Abu Sayyaf of the Philippines, and the *mujahideen* of Chechnya and Dagestan.

For these terrorist organisations, martyrdom is a compelling lure, and self-sacrifice valued above many other virtues including mercy and pity. Dehumanisation of the enemy is dominant theme in their belief system; elimination, not its defeat, is their prime objective. Nowhere has this been more glaring than in the 1988 charter of the Islamic Resistance Movement, popularly known as *Hamas.* It describes the Jewish state on Palestinian territory as utter absurdity and hence, its destruction is the pre-condition of liberating Palestine. This is to be accomplished by spreading the spirit of Jihad through which it aspires to raise the banner of Allah on every inch of the Palestinian territory.[12] For Hamas, the war is not simply with the Israeli government but with the whole of Israeli society. The enemy is seen in depersonalised and monolithic terms, and the young men in its cadres who carry out suicide missions striking terror at the heart of the Zionist state are called *istishhadis* (self-chosen martyrs). Unlike the Hamas, the Islamic International Brigade of bin Laden symbolises the cult of borderless terrorism, less interested in promoting a political cause than eradication of what its members define as evil. For them weapons of mass destruction, if available, are more efficient means to achieve the end.

Causation

The recent upsurge of religious terrorism, particularly the growth of pan-Islamic jihadi movement is indicative of a fundamental change in the post-Cold War global politics. Analysts, in attempting to explain the phenomenon, have either attributed it to the non-religious factors such as the failures of secular-nationalist state-building experiments, crisis of legitimacy,[13] decline of the developmental, service-oriented state, marginalising and coercive processes of globalisation, or to the theological sources of political extremism. The process of globalisation carries implicit homogenisation tendencies and messages, which, in turn, contributes to the strengthening of the particularalist (religio-ethnic) identities. "The rejection of these globalisation tendencies" according to an analyst, "in its purest form is associated with and expressed by the resurgence of religious and ethnic politics in various extremist configurations."[14]

As a dialectical process, globalisation fosters interconnectiveness and at the same time, stimulates conflicts with those who are alienated from it. Some of these groups with their proud cultural traditions find it difficult to reconcile themselves with their status on the margins of the world system they did not create and cannot control.[15] Overwhelmed by the feelings of political impotence in a world where force and potential for force dominate the agenda, they turn towards religion, which gives them *expressive* instrument such as suicide bombings. The *expressive violence* (ritualistic, symbolic and communicative) of the World Trade Centre attack had meaning both for the victims (anxiety and humiliation) and for the perpetrators (status, prestige and reputation in the Muslim world).[16]

True, the process of globalisation together with the Western cultural hegemony has propelled religious terrorism to the forefront in the post-bipolar world. But, it has drawn strength and sustenance from the all-encompassing phenomenon of religious fundamentalism. It provides the concepts of cosmic war accompanied by strong claims of moral justifications and an enduring absolutism, which transform the worldly struggles into sacred battles. In spiritualising violence, religion gives terrorism a remarkable staying power. Those, for example, carried out the 11 September suicide mission and the December attack on the Indian Parliament were not a bunch of clinical psychopaths or zombies. They were instead the products of an ideology, which could be aptly described as the radical Islamic fundamentalism.[17] It is more than simply a rejection of modernity or a revolt against the West; it seeks to establish an alternative global order.

Central to the contemporary Islamist discourse is the belief in the superiority of the Self (Islam) and demise of the Other (West). The superiority of Islam is presented as a given or as an element of the religious truth, which bestows on the faith a higher duty of leading the humanity since the collapse of the fragmented and decadent Other is inevitable.[18] In pursuit of this fundamentalist utopia, which entails the risk of confrontation with the Christian West, acts of violence acquire legitimacy. Unlike the process of decolonisation of the past decades, radical Islamist movement is not purely political; it is instead a cultural iceberg with the revolutionary violence only at the tip. The doctrinal vision of the world and revolutionary rhetoric of some radical Muslim thinkers and activists, namely Maulana Abul Ala Maududi of Pakistan, Sayyid Qutb and Abd al-Salam Faraj of Egypt have over the years contributed to the moulding of the Muslim mindset to the idea that they are under constant threat from the West and from their *jahiliyya* rulers.[19]

In the fundamentalist theoretical constructs, jihad becomes a struggle in pursuit of "God's just order in the world"; it is a struggle between believers and non-believers in which the use of techniques of terror in combating the latter is morally sanctioned. Its enemies become *satanised*, so much so that it forecloses the options for negotiations and compromises.[20] The roots of contemporary terrorism lie in such radical interpretation of theology promoted by and circulated through educational networks supervised by the clergy. Over thirty thousand Islamic *madrassas* (seminaries) in Pakistan continue to preach a narrow and violent version of Islam, and many of them in the course of a protracted intra-Afghan war became the supply-line for a pan-Islamic jihadi movement. Thus, what guarantees potency to the fundamentalist Islam is the way it has been used either as a regime-challenging instrument or as regime-legitimising ideology in the dysfunctional or authoritarian states. In many Muslim countries, Islam is simply the vehicle and coinage of the struggle between the state and its challengers. In countries ruled by military junta such as Pakistan under Zia Ul-Haq and Bangladesh under Zia ur-Rehman in the mid-1980s, Islam serves the instrumental function as the purveyor of legitimacy, while in the oil-rich Arab countries it represents the higher idea of State or the constitutive element of state identity.

The oil boom of the 1970s was more than simply a politically pacifying factor (through distribution of revenues to appease larger sections of population) for the conservative Gulf monarchies; it provided the ground for constructing a new ideology to counteract the intrusive Pan-Arabism. Labelled as "petro-islam", it derives from the premise that "it is not merely an accident that oil is concentrated on the thinly populated Arabian countries rather than in the densely populated Nile Valley or Fertile Crescent, and that this apparent irony of fate is indeed a grace and a blessing from God that should be solemnly acknowledged and lived up to."[21] An important ideological function of petro-Islam was to promote Muslim universalism, a safer doctrine than the geographically more limited but politically more troublesome idea of Pan-Arabism.[22] It was in pursuit of this ideal that the leading Gulf States directed a substantial portion of their bilateral and multilateral aid towards the non-Arab states with large Muslim population through internal charity organisations, notably the *Rabita-e-Alam-e-Islami*, and trans-national bodies like the Organisation of Islamic Conference (OIC). Various such Muslim extremist groups active in India today as the *Jamait-e-Islami-e-Hind*, *Jamait-Ahle-Hadis*, *Students' Islamic Movement of India*, *Tabligh-e-Jamait*, and *Darul Hida* receive funds from the Gulf-based Islamic trustees like the *Rabita* set up by the Saudis for propagation of Islam.

Externally, religious fundamentalism derives legitimacy either through alliance with global great powers in their zero-sum game to contain each other, or functioning as regional proxies in the inter-state conflicts. Pakistan's Army of Islam comprising a host of Islamist terrorist outfits such as the *Harkatul Mujahideen* (HuM), *Lashkar-e-Tayyaba* (LeT), and *Jaish-e-Mohammad* (JeM) employed against India to settle old scores appropriately fits into the second category. So does the formation of *Hizb'allah*, a predominantly *Shi'ite* organisation, which has emerged as the ideological Trojan horse of the Iranian Islamic revolution in Lebanon. Since the mid-1980s, its cadres have turned the fury of their jihad against the Jewish state of Israel.[23] These states rely on such fanatic elements not because they are committed to a particular brand of Islamic idealism, but to carry out a low-intensity war that has sufficient debilitating potential to the targeted state.

In the mid-1990s, if the U.S. tacitly acquiesced to the creation of Taliban by Pakistan, it was because Washington viewed the latter as anti-Iran, anti-Shia and pro-Western. Likewise, a decade earlier President Ronald Reagan had attempted to use the Sunni Islamists as an instrument against the Kremlin following the Soviet invasion of Afghanistan. Thus, began what Oliver Roy has aptly characterised it as "a joint venture"[24] between the US, Saudi *Wahabbis*, the Muslim Brethren and the Pakistani *Jamaat-i-Islami*, which in the next decade and half turned a local conflict into the pan-Islamic jihad to fight the Soviet Union. While Washington wished to demonstrate that the war in Afghanistan involved the entire Muslim world against the Soviet occupation, Saudi Arabia sought to take advantage of the "frontier of anarchy" to distract the domestic political opposition,[25] and Pakistan aimed at levering itself into a dominant position in the Islamic world and securing the so called "strategic depth" against India.

In West Asia, the Brethren and the Saudi-based World Muslim League organized "Islamic" humanitarian aid for the Afghan resistance, and established an "Islamic legion" made up of Arab volunteers who would be received by the Pakistani intelligence service, the ISI and *Jamaat-i-Islami* in Peshawar before sending them to join the *mujahidin* groups.[26] Even after the withdrawal of the Soviet forces in 1989, Arabs continued to drift to Afghanistan for military training and introduction to a new ideology based on a deadly mixture of *Salafism* and puritanical *Deobandism*. Salafism is a minoritarian tendency within Islam, whose central features were crystallized in the teachings of a 14th century scholar, Taqi al-Din Ahmad Ibn Taymiyya. The essence of the *Salafi* ideology is to reform the religion by emulating the generation of the Prophet Muhammad and his companions who are referred to as *al-salaf al-salih*, (the pious ancestors), whence the name *Salafi*. Another salient feature of Salafism is that war against the Muslim rulers is permissible if they fail in their primary duty to rule according to the *shari`a* (Islamic law), as its absence conduces to the pollution of Islam by idolatry. This stance is a significant departure from Sunni political traditions, which prohibit the right to rebel against a Muslim ruler howsoever bad he may be.[27] Historically, however, the mainstream *Salafiyya* has been much more concerned with the state of Muslim themselves than with relations between Islam and the outside world.

A branch of Sunni Hanafi Islam, Deobandis arose in India during the last quarter of the 19th century as a reform movement with twin objectives of training religious scholars to safeguard the traditional Islamic values and to resist the colonial state ruled by non-Muslims.[28] What was, however, taught to the Afghan refugees in hundreds of *madrassas* set up along Pakistan's Pushtun belt was an extreme form of Deobandism, which was much closer to the Wahhabi creed[29] than the reformist agenda of the original Deoband seminary. The new generation of jihad volunteers known as the Arab Afghans became a major security issue in the countries of their origin, as many of them formed clandestine guerrilla cells modelled on Afghan lines in the Arab countries, while others had their bases inside Afghanistan to conduct campaign elsewhere.[30] Although the outside world became aware of the menace of "Arab Afghanis" in November 1991 when the name of the leader of a group that had made an armed attack on a police station in eastern Algeria was given as Tayib al-Afghani,[31] the Americans woke up to the danger only after the August 1998 bombing of the U.S. embassies in Kenya and Tanzania.

Needless to mention, those who carry out acts of terror in the name of God are neither representatives of their religion nor approved by it. Nor can the phenomena be adequately explained by materialist explanations like the human misery, the terrible poverty or gross inequalities. Africa, for example, tops the list in terms of low per-capita income and weak human resources, mal-distribution of political power and culture of corruption, but remains largely free from the terrorist activity. So is the case with Latin America, especially Central America where the involvement of America has spawned social inequality and chronic political instability, and yet has not turned into a breeding ground for holy terror. If the religion-oriented violence is on the rise today, it is not due to what an analyst calls a "cluster of absences" of political institutions such as popular participation and vibrant civil society[32] or, the debilitation of the state engendered by the forces of "Mcworld".[33] It has as much to do with the absence of theological defences against the spread of political extremism as the pervasive sense of powerlessness or inability to make the choice between "Mecca and mechanisation".[34]

No wonder, it is the Muslim World that has experienced the higher proportion of intra-and inter-state violence in the past decades, as evident in a recent study of the post-Cold War civilisational conflicts. Islamic groups, according to its assessment, were involved in 109 ethnic conflicts between the period of 1990-98, 38 as the minority group, 33 as the majority group, and 38 in which both groups are Islamic.[35] Notwithstanding the apparent variations in the nature of the polity (theocratic, autocratic or illiberal democratic), there is hardly any member states of the OIC that have been free of major political violence in the last two decades. The fact that Islam is a political religion *per excellence* may in part account for the recurrent violence in societies wherever there is a sizeable Muslim population.

In comparison with other major religions of the world, Islam from the very beginning has united and governed the community of believers as a political religion. In fact, Muhammad was as much of a political leader as a Prophet, and his new "religious association had long been conceived of as a community organised on political lines, not as a church within a secular state."[36] The Christian era, for instance, begins with Christ's birth, whereas the Muslim era starts with the year when Muhammad and his followers achieved political power by establishing the Muslim community in Medina.[37] Historically, from the famous War of Camels at Khoraiba in southern Iraq through the killing of Ali by the fanatic *Kharijites* (seceders) near Kufa[38] to the rise of ultra-conservative Wahhabism in the 19th century and Bin-Laden's *fatwas*, it is the political component of Islam that has rendered it violence prone. Consequently, Jihad raised to the level of a "sixth pillar" of the faith[39] has become an instrument to confront the Other (Christian West) in a bid to establish the *hakimiyya*, or divine sovereignty over all creation. The concept of jihad, which otherwise refers to inner struggle of moral discipline or spiritual striving is currently portrayed in fundamentalist literature as a form of political struggle through direct action to combat the Muslim backslider.

Two years after the rout of Osama-Taliban axis of terror, the war in Afghanistan is far from over. As the reports emanating from Kabul suggest, remnants of Taliban regime are regrouping inside north-western Pakistan to wrest control from Mullah Omar in an attempt to put up an alternative to Afghanistan's interim political arrangement hammered out in Bonn in 2001.[40] No matter what the Pakistani President Parvez Musarraf pontificates to the world about his commitment to combat terrorism, Islamabad persists in its jihadi politics so as to preserve its option of resurrecting the Taliban-Osama brand of radicals should Pakistan lose the strategic leverage in the aftermath of the June 2004 national elections. Just as Pakistan quietly nurtures the neo-Taliban option, the absence of responsive and inclusive political dispensation in much of greater West Asia fuels the danger of revival of Islamic terror.

Conclusion

In explaining the causation of religious terrorism, this essay argues that the phenomenon is a function of several interrelated variables, which need to be addressed in a holistic manner. The use of raw power alone is no antidote to the scourge of terrorism; it has to be complemented by efforts to redress "aspirational deprivation" of the socially mobilised segments[41] and reduce marginalisation in Muslim societies through state policy of co-optation and incremental democratisation. Interestingly, however, democracy as such does not guarantee a terrorist-free society. The phenomenon of terrorism may have its origin in dysfunctional states, but it is the stable democracies of the world that suffer the whiplash. This is indeed one of the paradoxes of liberal democracy. Among the factors that render democratic polity vulnerable to frequent terrorist assaults include: first, the existence of an array of civil societal institutions and Non-governmental Organisations (NGOs) occupying an autonomous space between state and citizens and second, the cumbersome process involved in reaching consensual decisions. The latter arguably makes pluralist democracies "weak states"[42] particularly in dealing with the terrorist menace, whereas the expansion of civil society at times becomes a threat to democratic institutions in a bid to protect human rights and individual liberty from arbitrary and capricious state power.

In the past decade and half, the civil society associations have been more concerned with empowerment and values of human rights than serving as vehicle for social change. In the process, many of them have allowed themselves to be used purposely or otherwise by anti-systemic forces and movements — such as the Naxalites and separatist groups in India, and fundamentalists in Muslim countries — to undermine state capacity to function as the provider of security to its citizens. In pursuit of safeguarding human rights, they harp on the excesses committed by the state in its efforts to curb political extremism rather than seeking out ways to defend rights of those who disagree with terrorists politically or resist them physically. Consequently, the civil society groups end up in defending minority rights withholders as against the majority rights holders.

Terrorism is thus not simply the product of the deficit of democracy; it grows in strength because of democracy and even, in spit of it. For not only does it allow disparate political and social formations to inhabit their space uncoerced by fear of repression, but also brings in juridical-institutional constraints on state that benefit the nihilist outlaws. Given these inherent contradictions and structural barriers to act effectively in combating terrorism, there is an urgency to forge solidarity among countries with liberal-democratic forms of governance, which would provide a robust basis for a successful war on terrorism.

NOTES

1. See Walter Laqueur, *The Age of Terrorism* (London: Little, Brown, 1987), pp. 11-17; Bruce Hoffman, *Inside Terrorism* (New York: Columbia University

Press, 1998), pp. 13-44. Laqueur in his seminal work also contends that terrorists' targets up to the 1970s included the kings, ministers, head of states, generals, and other political figures but never the innocent bystanders. The famous guerrilla leader Che Guevara was in principle opposed to military operations in urban centres to avoid large-scale casualties.

2. Instances abound: Mustafa Kemal Ataturk in Turkey at the end of the World War I; Indonesian President Sukerno; PLO leader Yasser Arafat in the early 1970s and a galaxy of Indian nationalists in the early days of freedom struggle, particularly the Khilafat movement led by Gandhiji.
3. Steven Simon and Daniel Benjamin, "America and the New Terrorism", *Survival,* Vol. 42, No. 1 (Summer 2000), pp. 59-74.
4. See the text of Osama bin Laden's *fatwa* in Bernard Lewis, "License to Kill: Usama bin Laden's Declaration of Jihad", *Foreign Affairs,* vol. 77, no. 6 (November/December 1998), pp. 14-19.
5. For a comprehensive discussion on religious terrorist movements, see Magnus Ranstorp, "Terrorism in the Name of Religion", *Journal of International Affairs,* Vol. 50, No. 1 (Summer 1996), pp. 40-62.
6. Mark Juergensmeyer, *Terror in the Mind of God: The Global Rise of Religious Violence* (Berkeley: University of California Press, 2000) p. 9.
7. The phrase "Islamic terrorism" was coined after the 1979 Islamic Revolution when a group of Iranian students claiming themselves as followers of the Imam Khomeini occupied American embassy compound and kept fifty-two diplomats as hostage for 444 days. Throughout the 1980s, Iran and Syria headed a new Comintern of subversive movement in West Asia with Beqa Valley in Lebanon as the headquarters of international terrorism. See Daniel Pipes, "Terrorism: The Syrian Connection", *The National Interest* (Spring 1989), pp. 20-28.
8. Edger O'Ballance, *Terrorism in the 1980s* (London: Sterling, 1989), pp. 3-4; also see Bansidhar Pradhan, "Terrorism as an Instrument of Armed Struggle and Diplomacy: The Changing Face of the PLO", *International Studies,* Vol. 38, No. 4 (2001), pp. 396-425.
9. Gilles Kepel, *Jihad: Expansion and Decline of the Islamist Movement* (Cambrideg: Belknap Press, 2002).
10. On the changing nature of global terrorism, see Therese Delpech, " The Imbalance of Terror", *The Washington Quarterly,* Vol. 25, No. 1 (Winter 2002), pp. 31-40; Philip B. Heymann, " Dealing with Terrorism", *International Security,* Vol. 26, No. 3 (Winter 2001/02), pp. 24-38.
11. For a discussion of the struggle between the West and Islam over who will provide the definition to the post-Cold War world order, see John Kelsay, *Islam and War: The Gulf War and Beyond* (Louisville: John Knox Press, 1993), Chap. 5; also see Bassam Tibi, *The Challenge of Fundamentalism: Political Islam and the New World Order* (Berkeley: University of California Press, 1998), pp. 54-55.

12. See Meir Litvak, "The Islamization of the Palestinian-Israel Conflict: The Case of Hamas", *Middle Eastern Studies*, Vol. 34, No. 1 (January 1998), pp. 148-163..
13. Simon Bromley, *Rethinking Middle East Politics: State Formation and Development* (Cambridge: Polity Press, 1994), pp. 153-184.
14. Richard Falk, "State of Siege: Will Globalization Win Out?" *International Affairs*, Vol. 73, No. 1(1997), p. 131.
15. Bruce Lawrence, *Shattering the Myth: Islam Beyond Violence* (Princeton: Princeton University Press, 1998), pp. 34-51.
16. Christopher Coker, *Globalisation and Insecurity in the Twenty-first Century: NATO and the Management of Risk* (Adelhi Paper No. 345), (Oxford University Press: IISS, 2002), p. 40.
17. Mark Huband, *Warriors of the Prophet: The Struggle for Islam* (Boulder, Colorado: Westview Press, 1998), pp.2-22; also see Joel Beinin and Joe Stork (eds.), *Political Islam: Essays from Middle East Report* (New York: I. B. Tauris, 1997).
18. For an evaluation of Islamist discourse in West Asia, see Salwa Ismail, "Confronting the Other: Identity, Culture, Politics, and Conservative Islamism in Egypt", *International Journal of Middle East Studies*, Vol. 3o (1998), pp. 199-225.
19. See Aswini K. Mohapatra, "Radical Islam: Ideology Behind Global Terrorism", *India Quarterly*, Vol. 58, No.2 (April-June 2002), pp. 93-112.
20. Mark Juergensmeyer, "Terror in the Name of God", *Current History*, (November 2001), p. 28.
21. Nazhi N. Ayubi, *Over-stating the Arab State: Politics and Society in the Middle East* (London: I. B. Tauris, 1995), p. 232.
22. Fouad Ajami, "The End of Pan-Arabism", *Foreign Affairs*, Vol. 57, No.2, (Winter 1978-79), p. 365
23. On Iranian connection to Hezbollah, see Edgar O'balance, *Islamic Fundamentalist Terrorism, 1979-95: The Iranian Connection* (London: Macmillan, 1997).
24. Oliver Roy, *The Failure of Political Islam* (London: I.B. Tauris Publishers, 1994), p. 109.
25. See, Madawi Al-Rasheed, "Saudi Arabia's Islamic Opposition", *Current History*, vol. 95, no.1 (January 1996), pp. 16-22
26. On the link between the West Asian Islamic militants and Pakistan, see Samina Ahmed, "The (Un) holy Nexus?", *Newsline* (Karachi)), Vol. 10, no. 3 (September 1998), pp. 31-34
27. The right to rebel against a ruler who compromises with Islam is justified by the Shiite traditional teachings, partly due to the injustice done to the House of Ali, the fourth Caliph, and partly, the spiritual –political status of the Ulama. See Emmanuel Sivan, "Islamic Radicalism: Sunni and Shiite" in E. Sivan and

M. Friedman (eds.), *Religious Radicalism and Politics in Middle East* (New York State University, 1990), pp. 39-46.

28. Fazlur Rahman, *Islam* (London: Weidenfeld & Nicolson, 1966), pp. 204-205.
29. *Wahhabis* of the early19th century Arabia raised jihad against the "apostates" from within the Community and destroyed everything that appeared to them to represent a deviation from authentic Islam, including the tombs in Medina. For details, see Aziz Al-Azmeh, *Islams and Modernities* (London: Verso, 1993), pp.104-120.
30. James Bruce, "Arab Volunteers of the Afghan War", *Jane's Intelligence Review*, Vol. 7, No. 4 (April 1995), pp. 175-179.
31. Godfrey Jansen, "The Afghans- an Islamic Time Bomb", *Middle East International*, 20 November 1992, p. 16.
32. See Leonard Binder, *Islamic Liberalism: A Critique of Development Ideologies* (Chicago: University of Chicago Press, 1988), p. 225.
33. Mcworld, according to Barber, represents the forces sweeping the world into a uniform, west-centered world economy and culture. Islamists try to harness Jihad to defend the autonomy allowing them to come to terms with "Mcworld". Benjamin Barber, "Jihad vs. Mcworld", *The Atlantic Monthly*, (March 19912), pp. 53-63.
34. This theme was popularized by Daniel Lerner in his seminal work on modernization in West Asia in the late 1950s.D. Lerner, *The passing of Tradition Society: Modernizing the Middle East* (New York: Free Press, 1958), p. 40.
35. Jonathan Fox, "Two Civilizations and Ethnic Conflict: Islam and the West", *Journal of Peace Research*, Vol. 38, No. 4 (2001), p. 463.
36. H.A.R. Gibb, *Mohammedanism* (London: Oxford University Press, 1962), p. 27.
37. Wilfred Cantwell Smith makes this interesting comparison in his *Islam in Modern History* (New York: The New American Library, 1957), p. 23.
38. Will Durant, *The Story of Civilization: The Age of Faith* (New York, 1950), pp. 191-192.
39. Rahman, *Islam*, p. 37.
40. Carlotta Gall, "Taliban Gather Openly in Pakistan and Talk of Return", *International Herald Tribune*, (May 7, 2003), p. 8.
41. Aspirational deprivation refers to a perceived discrepancy between individuals' aspirations arising from contact with process of modernisation and technological revolutions and the inability of the state to fulfil them. For the state capability to deliver, particularly those underdeveloped ones are progressively undermined by the forces of globalisation. For details, see Ted Robert Gurr, *Why Men Rebel* (Princeton, New Jersey: Princeton University Press, 1970), Chap. 2.

42. The distinction between weak and strong states should not be confused with overall power capabilities as stressed by the realists in theoretical literature dealing with IR. It is rather based on the domestic political structure which mainly refers to relationship between the organization of the state and societal groups. For details, see Stephen Krasner, *Defending the National Interest* (Princeton University Press, 1978), Chap. 3.

12

Trends in Trading Patterns of Asia-Pacific

Prof. B. Satyanarayan

Asia Pacific includes the below mentioned groups and countries: (1) Japan, (2) The Newly Industrialised Countries (NICS)-Hong Kong, Korea, Singapore and Taiwan; (3) ASEAN, (4) Indonesia, Malaysia, Philippines, Thailand; and (4) People's. Republic of China. Asia-Pacific region is twice as large as Europe and USA. The changing pattern of production, trade and investment in accordance with the changing comparative advantage in the region has seen one tier of countries fuelling the economies of another tier, thereby resulting in deeper integration. Japan is the epicenter of the region. The next stage, where the manufacturing activity was relocated was the NICs-Hong Kong, Korea, Singapore and Taiwan. Next came the ASEAN-4 — Indonesia, Malaysia, Philippines and Thailand and then China. These diverse and expanding production, trade and investment linkages have been important ingredients in the growth of the Asia-Pacific as a dynamic region. Asia-Pacific, now the driving force of the global economy must have vision of what its role in the new global order should be, so that it is realised in the years to come.

Most of the Asia Pacific countries have chosen an exported growth model and therefore trade has an important role to play in each of the country's economic development processes. Besides, the trade amongst these countries has also been significant and has promoted the development of the region as a whole. Therefore, an in-depth analysis of the trading patterns in the region would help us to understand the growth pattern in the region. It would also give us an insight into the 'economic relationship between countries in the region and the scope for a more proactive region trading arrangement.

Asia-Pacific Total Trade

The spectacular growth of Asia Pacific region during the last two decades has been the focus of global attention and admiration. Because of this growth. the region had achieved such economic resilience that, in spite of the slowing down in global economic output in some years, it had continued to maintain a remarkable rate of economic growth, almost twice as high as the global average. In fact it was expected that the dynamism of Asia-Pacific was to provide a stimulus to the growth of the world economy. The increasingly open market and big emerging economies such as China, India and Indonesia, are arousing the interest of the world business community has the markets of the future for trade and investment. The East-Asian crisis of 1997 and its spectacular recovery have added another dimension to the already increasing interest in the region. Developing economies are looking towards East Asia for several lessons to be learnt so as to emulate the 'miracle' and avoid the 'crisis'. It is in this context, a review of the growth trends in trade of Asia Pacific countries is undertaken. This paper analyses three main aspects of Asia Pacific total trade:

- Asia Pacific trade and share in World trade
- Country/group wise share in Asia Pacific
- Asia Pacific trade by broad regions

(i) Asia Pacific Trade and Share in World Trade

The merchandise trade of Asia Pacific (the ten economies together)increased more than four times from an average annual of US$ 608 billion between 1980-84 to US$ 2568 billion between 1995-99. This phenomenal growth in the region's external trade, far above the world average, has resulted in the region's rising 24% during 1995/2000 (Table 1). While Asia Pacific trade experienced an average annual growth of 11% between 1985-89 over the 1980-84 periods, the growth was still higher at 16.5% between 1990-94 over the 1985-89 period. A look at Table 2 shows that growth rates in both these periods are much higher than the average World growth in trade. In spite of the East Asian crisis in 1997, the growth rates in 1995-99 over the 1990-94 periods are also slightly higher than the growth rates in world trade. It is noteworthy that the region's developing economies have achieved much higher growth than the Asia Pacific average. The four NICs have achieved the fastest rates of growth in the 1980s and have maintained the momentum in the 1990s. Among the ASEAN-4, Malaysia and Thailand have witnessed high growth rates, while the performance of Indonesia and Philippines has been relatively sluggish. China has been the star performer of Asia Pacific with its exports growing nearly twelve times in this period. All countries showed fall in trade in 1998 and negative growth due to the adverse impact of the 1997 economic crisis in East Asia.

Looking at the country shares in world trade, we see that although Japan's share in world trade has declined from an annual average of nearly 8% between 1980-84 to 6.8% in 1995-99, yet it. Continues to be the leader in Asia with the largest individual share. Its share in world exports has fallen from a high of 9.5% in 1985-89 to 7.7 in 1980-84 to 6% in 1994-99. After the Plaza accord in September 1985, the value of the Yen began to rise rapidly, adversely affecting those sectors of the manufacturing heavily dependent on exports. Fluctuations in the exchange rate of yen have had a major impact on Japanese trade performance and on corporate balance sheets with

Table 1: Asia-Pacific Trade and Share in World Trade

(a= Average annual; Fig. In US$ million; percentage)

	1980-1984	*1985-1989*	*1990-1994*	*1995-1999*	*2000*
I Japan					
Total	283137(7)	393000(8)	584125(8)	739714(7)	858760(7)
Exports	147475(8)	231759(10)	340034(9)	416500(8)	479249(8)
Imports	135662(7)	161240(6)	244091(6)	323214(6)	379511(6)
II NICs					
Total	189123(5)	343555(7)	698575(9)	1089321(10)	1308166(10)
Exports	90854(5)	178577(7)	345387(9)	542852(10)	660324(10)
Imports	98269(5)	164978(7)	353187(9)	546469(10)	647842(10)
(i) Hong Kong					
Total	47173(1)	99992(2)	238641(3)	368345(3)	414665(3)
Exports	22538(1)	50078(2)	117330(3)	176016(3)	201860(3)
Imports	24635(1)	49915(2)	121310(3)	192330(3)	212805(3)
(ii) Korea					
Total	48761(1)	89879(2)	162115(2)	259262(2)	332749(3)
Exports	22860(1)	46711(2)	78262(2)	132198(2)	172268(3)
Imports	25900(1)	43168(2)	83852(2)	127064(2)	160481(2)
(iii) Singapore					
Total	48734(1)	67207(1)	146845(2)	238906(2)	272420(2)
Exports	21414(1)	31619(1)	69360(1)	118645(2)	137875(2)
Imports	27320(1)	35588(1)	77485(2)	120261(2)	134545(2)
(iv) Taiwan					
Total	44454(1)	86476(2)	150974(2)	222809(2)	288332(2)
Exports	24041(1)	50169(2)	80435(2)	115994(2)	148321(2)
Imports	20413(1)	36307(1)	70539(2)	106815(2)	140011(2)
III ASEAN 4					
Total	92457(2)	106422(2)	246198(3)	417041(4)	472189(4)
Exports	48214(3)	55779(2)	118609(3)	211835(4)	263296(4)
Imports	44242(2)	50643(2)	127589(3)	205207(4)	208893(3)
(i) Indonesia					
Total	92457(1)	106422(1)	246198(1)	417041(1)	472189(1)
Exports	21906(1)	18378(1)	32777(1)	51345(1)	56321(1)
Imports	14240(1)	12761(1)	26759(1)	37060(1)	30962(0.5)
(ii) Malaysia					
Total	25915(1)	33690(1)	84286(1)	149769(1)	180334(1.5)
Exports	13494(1)	18693(1)	42082(1)	77748(1)	98135(2)
Imports	12422(1)	14997(1)	42203(1)	72022(1)	82199(1)
(iii) Philippines					
Total	13193(0.3)	13447(0.3)	26443(0.4)	61355(0.8)	73591(0.8)
Exports	5361(0.3)	5981(0.2)	10309(0.3)	25909(0.5)	39783(1)
Imports	7832(0.4)	7466(0.3)	16134(0.4)	35447(1)	33808(0.5)

(*Contd.*)

(iv)Thailand					
Total	17203(0.5)	28146(0.8)	75933(1)	117512(1)	130981(1)
Exports	7454(0.4)	12727(0.5)	33441(1)	56834(1)	69057(1)
Imports	9749(0.5)	15419(1)	42492(1)	60678(1)	61924(1)
IV China					
Total	43144(1)	88436(2)	170739(2)	322301(3)	455429(4)
Exports	21680(1)	39747(2)	86873(2)	176778(3)	249297(4)
Imports	21464(1)	48688(2)	83866(2)	145523(3)	206132(3)
Asia Pacific					
Total	607861(16)	931412(19)	1699636(22)	2568377(24)	3094544(24)
Exports	308223(17)	505863(21)	890903(24)	1347965(25)	1652166(26)
Imports	299638(16)	425549(17)	808733(21)	1220412(22)	1442378(22)
World Trade					
Total	3793300	4959400	7598200	10923800	12822900
Exports	1863400	2436100	3754800	5410700	6310100
Imports	1929900	2523400	3843400	5513100	6512800

Table 2: Growth Trends in Asia-Pacific Total Trade

(*average annual growth*)

Countries	*1985-89/1980-84*	*1990-94/1985-89*	*1995-99/1990-94*
I. JAPAN	7.6	9.7	5.4
II. NICs	16.3	20.6	11.2
III. ASEAN-4	3.0	26.2	13.8
IV. CHINA	21.0	18.6	17.7
ASIA PACIFIC	11.2	16.5	10.2
WORLD TRADE	6.2	10.6	8.7

large trade component. In 1997, export (merchandise) volume rose 9.5% but the dollar value of merchandise exports rose only 2.5% due to fall in the value of yen. In 1998, export volume is estimated to have risen by 4.5% but the dollar value is estimated to have declined. In the same year import volume has risen only modestly but imports in value terms have declined significantly. In 1999 a needed impetus for the recovery of the economies hit by the crisis in Asia, but the yen's appreciation against the dollar significantly eroded such export competitiveness. In 2000, as most of the crisis hit economies are showing sharp signs of upswing. Japan' s total trade has grown rapidly by 17.6% with growing demand from these Asian Countries. Its share in world trade now is between 7-8%.

The NICs have shown an upward trend in their share in world trade, both as a group as well as individually. The NICs share in world merchandise trade has doubled from an average of 5% in 1980-84 to 10% between 1995-99. Both, the share of exports and imports in world exports and imports have also doubled from 5% to 10% in that period. In 1998, however there has been a slight decline in NICs share in world trade to 8.2% due to the negative growth in trade but the 1999/2000 trade figures show positive growth in trade and the gradually increasing share in world trade, thereby implying that the countries have recovered from crises.

The growth trends in trade have been phenomenal between 1980 and almost up to 1995. The NICs total trade experienced an average annual growth rate of 16.3% between 1980-84 and 1985-89, 21% between 1985-89, 21% between 1985-89 and 1990-94 and 11% between 1990-94 and 1995-99. Most of the initial growth from 1980 onwards is mainly due to the NICs becoming the platform for the Japanese manufacturing industries. While Japan found it no longer profitable to carry on production in labour intensive manufacturing due to. Rising labour costs and low value addition and moved to high technology and products with greater value addition, most of the low technology, labour intensive manufacturing shifted location to the NICs where labour and raw materials were cheaper. This resulted in the spurt of trading and investment activities in the region and especially between Japan and NICs.

While Japan pumped in vestment to set up manufacturing bases in the NICs, the NICs in turn exported low-end parts, components and labour intensive products from these manufacturing bases, back to Japan to feed their high-technology industries. This resulted in the rising foreign trade of the NICs, not only interregional but also as a part of world trade. It helped the NICs get the required investment and know how for setting up the manufacturing infrastructure and developing the NICs block. In 1998, the growth in foreign trade has been negative for Asia Pacific. (World trade also experienced a slight slump in 1998). This is due to the adverse impact of the East-Asian crisis that hit most of the countries in the region. In fact all countries in the region experienced a negative growth trend in trade in 1998 because the Asia-Pacific economies have strong backward and forward linkages and a trickle down effect is inevitable. From 1999, positive growth trends show sure signs of recovery. Individually in the NICs, all countries show a slight, more or less doubling of share in world trade between 1980 and 1999. Only Hong Kong's share has nearly tripled from an average annual of 1.2% om 1980-84 to 3.4% in 1995-99.

The next group, the ASEAN region is rich in resource but low in technology. The ASEAN region has also had a similar experience as the NICs with most countries following the flying geese model. With rising costs of labour and material in the NICs, the manufacturing locations have now moved to the ASEAN countries. Besides possessing cheap labour, they are also rich in natural resources. Japan and the NICs have funded many projects in the region for resource extraction and labour intensive manufacturing. Most of the textile and other low technology manufacturing bases are now relocated in ASEAN countries. Infrastructural investment in oil extraction, road and transportation etc., have resulted in the flow of investment into the region and helped in expanding the trade in the region. The ASEAN-4, i.e., Indonesia, Malaysia, Philippines and Thailand together show an increase in world trade from an average annual of 2.4% in 1980-84 to 4% in 1995-99. Individually also their shares in world trade seems to have doubled between 1980 and 1997 (except Indonesia). While Indonesia's share in world trade has remained around 1 %. Malaysia's share has doubled from 0.7% to 1.4%, Philippines from 0.3% to 0.6%, while Thailand's share increased from 0.5% to 1.1%. the ASEAN region was most badly hit by the Asian crisis. While all the countries showed high growth rate in trade between 1985-95, there has been a sharp decline in trade growth in 1996-and 1997 (except for Philippines). For one, the competition from China where costs are still lower, has posed an obstacle in ASEAN's expanding foreign trade. Second, the global trade reversionary trend seems to have started showing up right from mid 1996. All growth rates in trade showed negative trend in 1998, the ASEAN region being the worst hit. In 1999, however signs of recovery were being felt with positive growth in trade in Malaysia and Thailand and a fall in the negative trend in Indonesia and Philippines.

China the sleeping tiger seems to have awakened with its share in world trade tripling from an average annual of 1% in 1980-84 to around 3% in 1995-99. China seems to have tapped a high share of the low technology, labour intensive manufacturing in the region and is posing a major threat to the ASEAN foreign trade. China has the advantage of low labour costs, a controlled and planned production system, and an all-pervading Confucius environment, all of which together have resulted in the expanding production and foreign trade. It's trade within the Asia-Pacific region and outside with USA and EU is steadily expanding, China is being perceived as the next giant of the region. Although the Asian crisis did effect China but it was minimal with a slight negative growth of less than 1%. In 1999 growth in trade has picked up to 10%.

Overall the Asia-Pacific share in world trade has grown from an average annual of 16% in 1980-84 to 24% in 1995-99. This increase in total trade is experienced both in exports and imports of goods where exports increased from 16% to 26% while imports increased from 15% to 22%. Although the growth trends in trade have been influenced with the world-trading environment, yet the region has reached a stage where it can easily overcome the global fluctuations in trade. The financial crisis of 1997 that hit the Asian economies has caused a temporary downswing in the economic activity of the region, but recent trends show that the countries are on the recovery path.

(ii) Country/group wise Share in Asia Pacific

Table 3 gives us a picture of country/group-wise shares in the total trade of Asia Pacific region. Japan, as is obvious, has the highest share in Asia Pacific trade, but the share seems to be gradually falling. While in 1980-84 Japan's trade on an average constituted 47% of the region' s trade, its share has fallen to 29% during 1995-99. This is because although Japan's trade has fallen due to the increasing shares of the other three entities, i.e., the NICs, the ASEAN-4 and China. As was seen in the earlier section, the rapid growth in trade in the NICs, ASEAN-4 and China has lead to the spectacular increase in the relative shares of these countries/groups not only in the Asia Pacific trade but also in world trade.

Table 3: Country Share In Asia Pacific Trade

(Percentage)

	1980-1984	*1985-1989*	*1990-1994*	*1995-1999*	*2000*
I Japan					
Total	47	42	34	29	28
Exports	48	46	38	31	29
Imports	45	38	30	26	26
II NICs					
Total	31	37	41	42	42
Exports	29	35	39	40	40
Imports	33	39	44	45	45
(i) Hong Kong					
Total	8	11	14	14	13
Exports	7	10	13	13	12
Imports	8	12	15	16	15
(ii) Korea					
Total	8	10	10	10	11
Exports	7	9	9	10	10
Imports	9	10	10	10	11
(iii) Singapore					
Total	8	7	9	9	9
Exports	7	6	8	9	8
Imports	9	8	10	10	9
(iv) Taiwan					
Total	7	9	9	9	9
Exports	8	10	9	9	9
Imports	7	9	9	9	10
III ASEAN-4					
Total	15	11	14	16	15
Exports	16	11	13	16	16
Imports	15	12	16	17	14

(Contd.)

(i) Indonesia					
Total	6	3	4	3	3
Exports	7	4	4	4	3
Imports	5	3	3	3	2
(ii) Malaysia					
Total	4	4	5	6	6
Exports	4	4	5	6	6
Imports	4	4	5	6	6
(iii) Philippines					
Total	2	1	2	2	2
Exports	2	1	1	2	2
Imports	3	2	2	3	2
(iv) Thailand					
Total	3	3	4	5	4
Exports	2	3	4	4	4
Imports	3	4	5	5	4
IV China					
Total	7	9	10	13	15
Exports	7	8	10	13	15
Imports	7	11	10	12	14

The NICs group share in Asia-Pacific trade has gone up from an average annual of 31% in 1980-84 to 42% in 1995-2000. The NICs initially formed the production base for Japanese lowed technology inputs and components but are now themselves the producers of high technology products, including sophisticated machinery and equipment. Among the NICs; Hong Kong is the largest contributor to Asia Pacific trade, with its share increasing from 7.7% in 1980-84, has increased to 10% of total Asia-Pacific trade in 1995-99. Taiwan's share in Asia-Pacific total trade has risen from 7% in 1980-84 to 9% in 1995-99.

The next group ASEAN-4 still seems to have a relatively small share in Asia Pacific trade, though it has a large potential. The relocation of production and outsourcing of parts, components and intermediate products in the ASEAN by major companies, especially from Japan has contributed phenomenally to the growth and diversification of manufactured exports from these countries. For instance intra-firm trade plays a significant role in the manufactured exports from these countries. For instance intra-firm trade plays a significant role in the manufactured exports of Malaysia and Thailand. In ASEAN-4, Malaysia has the highest share (5.8) followed by Thailand (4.2) in the Asia-Pacific trade in 2000. Indonesia's share has fallen from 5.8% in 1980 to 2.8% in 2000, while Philippines share has remained the same (2.5%).

The growing integration of China in the global market place is evident from its trade exposure during the 1980s measured by the share of its trade in GDP. For China, its trade exposure has increased three times from 12% in 1980 to 36% in 2000. China's integration with the Asia-Pacific can be seen by its share in the total Asia trade, which has nearly doubled from around 7% in 1980 to 13% in 1994-99 and further to 15% in 2000.

The Asia-Pacific region has not only shown dynamism in world trade, but has also achieved significant and sustained growth in intra-regional trade. While the Asia-Pacific intra-regional trade will be discussed in the latter section, it would be worthwhile to see the broad regional distribution of Asia-Pacific trade to know its main partner countries/groups in world trade. The next section shows the direction of Asia-Pacific trade by broad regions and share of both inter and intra-regional trade.

(iii) Asia Pacific Trade by Broad Regions

The Asia Pacific trade with the rest of the world still constitutes 50-55% of their total world trade. The broad breakdown of the regional destination of merchandise trade of Asia Pacific is given in Table 4. While intra-regional trade was only 31% in 1980 and extra regional trade was as high as 69%,' this share has increased with intra-regional trade constituting 41% in 1990 and nearly 49% in 2000. Extra-regional trade on the other hand has declined from 69% in 1980 to 51% in 2000. In the pattern of intra-regional trade, North America (N.A.) and Western Europe (W.E.) constitute the predominant markets for the exports of almost all the economies of the region. For many countries of the region, the USA is the single largest trading partner. For the region as a whole, North America (of which USA is the main trading country) absorbed nearly 24% of its exports in 1980,29% in 1990 and 26% in 2000. Similarly, Western Europe (of which European Union is the major block) accounted 16% of the region's exports in 1980, 19% in 1990 and a decline back to 16% in the post-crisis period in 2000. More importantly, the United States and the European Union are the main markets for the manufactured exports of Asia Pacific countries, both for the high technology products of Japan and the NICs and for the labour-intensive manufacturers of the ASEAN and China. As for imports, the share of North America has declined from 20% to 16% while that of Western Europe has marginally increased from 10% to 12% in the period. Overall there is not much change in the total trade shares of North America which constituted 22% of total Asia Pacific trade in 1980, went up to 25% in 1990 and declined to 22% in 2000. Similarly, the region's trade with Western Europe was14% in 1980 increased to 17% in 1990 and declined to 14% in 2000.

Table 4: Asia Pacific Trade By Broad Regions

Part-I

Regions		*1980*	
	Exp	*Imp*	*Total*
North America	63270	54575	114696
	(24.3)	(20.4)	(21.7)
Western Europe	42248	28633	71454
	(16.2)	(10.4)	(13.5)
Latin America	5963	5423	11386
	(2.3)	(2.0)	(2.2)
Africa	11656	5825	17481
	(4.5)	(2.2)	(3.3)
Others	56304	92050	150930
	(21.7)	(34.3)	(28.6)
Extra-Regional Trade	179441	186506	365947
	(69.0)	(69.6)	(69.3)
Intra-Regional Trade	80563	81598	162161
	(31.0)	(30.4)	(30.7)
Total Asia-Pacific Trade	260004	268104	528108

(*Contd.*)

Part-II

Regions	*1990*			*2000*		
	Exp	*Imp*	*Total*	*Exp*	*Imp*	*Total*
North America	185986 (29.12)	123922 (21.0)	309908 (25.8)	402687 (26.8)	208772 (16.0)	611459 (21.8)
Western Europe	118555 (18.56)	94246 (15.9)	2128801 (17.3)	235199 (15.5)	164409 (12.6)	399608 (14.2)
Latin America	4692 (0.73)	12352 (2.1)	17044 (1.4)	16323 (1.1)	67531 (5.2)	83854 (3.0)
Africa	11920 (1.87)	6614 (1.1)	18534 (1.5)	20023 (1.3)	16720 (1.3)	36743 (1.3)
Others	64208 (10.05)	97957 (16.6)	162165 (13.2)	147588 (9.8)	157615 (12.1)	305203 (10.9)
Extra-Regional Trade	385361 (60.00)	335091 (56.7)	720452 (58.6)	821820 (54.6)	615047 (47.2)	1436867 (51.2)
Intra-Regional Trade	253180 (40.00)	255871 (43.3)	509051 (41.4)	682025 (45.4)	687320 (52.8)	1369345 (48.8)
Total Asia-Pacific Trade	638541	590962	1229503	1503845	1302367	2806212

The shares of the other regions are relatively small with Latin America having a share of 3% and Africa's share declining from 3% in 1980 to 1.3% in 2000. All other regions/countries (for e.g. Eastern Europe, Middle East, Oceania etc.) together constituted 28% of Asia Pacific trade in 1980, but this share has declined to 11% in 2000. This clearly shows that North America dominated by U.S. and Western Europe mainly European Union, continue to remain important as trading partners for Asia Pacific while the trade with other regions seems' to have declined. Therefore, the share of overall extra-regional or inter-regional trade has declined in the total trade of Asia Pacific, while the share of intra-regional trade has increased.

Although the markets of the Asia Pacific countries have grown in importance, thereby enhancing intra-regional trade, the markets of North America and Western Europe continue to remain vital for exports of Asia Pacific countries. In fact, Asia Pacific gets a major part of its dynamism due to its trade with these two regions. Therefore, the promotion of intra-regional trade must be consistent with and complementary to enhancing the securing access to the markets of mainly U.S. and European Union. In other words, intra-regional and inter-regional trade will have to go hand in hand to maintain the momentum and growth of Asia Pacific's external trade.

REFERENCES

1. John Naisbitt: (1996), "Megatrends Asia", Simon & Schuster, Rockefeller Centre, New York.
2. John Naisbitt & Patricia Aburdence (1991), "Megatrends-2000" Simon & Schuster, New York.
3. M.R. Agarwal (1979), "*Regional Economic Cooperation in South-Asia*", Sultan Chand & Co., New Delhi.
4. David Aikman, (1986), "*Pacific Rim: Area of Changes, Area of opportunities*", Little Brown & Co., Boston.
5. Asian Development Bank (1997), "Emerging Asia", ADB Publication.
6. Colin Bradford (Ed) (1987), "*Trade and Structural Change in Pacific Asia*", UCP, Chicago.
7. K. Dilip Das (1996), "*The Asia-Pacific Economy*", Macmillan Press Ltd., New Delhi.
8. Peter Drysdale (1988), "*International Economic Pluralism: Policy in East Asia and the Pacific*", Allen & Unwin, Sydney.
9. IIFT, (1995), "*Studies in Trade and Investment: Review and Analysis of Intra-regional Trade Flows in Asia and the Pacific*", New Delhi.
10. V.R. Panchamukhi, (1989) "*Growth, Trade and Structural Change in the Asian Region*", RIS, New Delhi.
11. V.R. Pancharnukhi and Rehman Sobhan (Ed) (1955), "*Towards an Asian Economic Area*", RIS, New Delhi.
12. Gautam Mathur, (1965), "*Planning for Steady Growth*", Basil Blockwell, Oxford.
13. B. Satyanarayan, (1986), "*India's Trade with Asia and the Far East Countries*", B.R. Publishing Corporation, New Delhi 52.
14. B. Satyanarayan (Ed) (1996), "*A Comparative Study of Foreign Direct Investment in India and China: Problems and Prospects*", HPH, BOMBAY.

13

Transnational Networks of Indian Diaspora in Australia

Ajaya Kumar Sahoo

Indian Diaspora

Although Indian migration has been taking place for centuries, but never before in history, India witnessed such massive movements of people from India to other parts of the world as in the 19th and early 20th centuries. Among the immigrants of diverse nationalities, overseas Indians constitute a sizable segment. In terms of sheer numbers, they make the third largest group, next only to the British and the Chinese. The people of Indian origin with more than 20 million population settled in 120 countries, constitutes more than 40 per cent of the population in Fiji, Mauritius, Trinidad, Guyana and Surinam. They are smaller minorities in Malaysia, South Africa, Sri Lanka, Uganda, UK, USA, Canada and Australia (Bhat 2003). There were four broad patterns of overseas migration observed from the literature on Indian diaspora: (*a*) pre-colonial migration; (*b*) colonial migration that began in the 1830s to the British, French and Dutch colonies; (*c*) post-colonial migration to the industrially developed countries; and (d) recent migration to West Asia

Transnational Perspective

The concept transnationalism has wider connotation today within the interdisciplinary study such as anthropology, sociology, geography and international migration. Though number of scholars have addressed the concept of transnationalism (see Portes 1997; Guarnizo 1996; Basch *et al.* 1994; Vertovec & Cohen 1999; Foner 1997), I used in this paper one significant definition for effective understanding of what exactly transnationalism means. Linda Basch *et al.* (1994: 4) for instance, defined transnationalism as the processes by which "…immigrants forge and sustain multi-standard social relations that link together their societies of origin and settlement". Through constant mobility of people, labour, money and resources, immigrants now actively construct transnational social field that extends beyond the single location, forming a distinct kind of 'social field' in which they maintain familial, economic, political and cultural ties. Although it is true that transnational migration has a long history, and it is also true that earlier migrants also maintained linkages to their homelands, yet there is an element of truth in the debate surrounding contemporary migrants, as compared to earlier migrants when we talk about their networks and their imagined or virtual community.

Transnational communities generally refer to the migrant communities, living in the host societies but maintain economic, political, social and emotional ties with their homeland and with other diasporic communities of the same origin. The establishment of this transnational community is related to more general processes of globalisation, deterritorialisation in the contemporary world (Wahlbeck 1998: 3). For example, modern means of cheaper and more efficient modes of communication and transportation technology today have allowed immigrants to maintain transnational relations with their homeland as well as their land of settlement.

Transnational community emerges on the basis of solidarity ties, which goes beyond narrow kinship systems. Robin Cohen (cited in Schnapper 1999) has examined three general preconditions for the emergence of transnational communities. They are such as: (1) the number and activity of non-governmental organisations; (2) the action of international associations such as Amnesty International and Green Peace; and (3) membership in supra national organisations and the number of populations they are directly involved with.

To call a community transnational, it should have certain qualities and characteristics. These qualities are include the community's presence in different parts of the world, population percentage and the transactions and transnational networks they have with their kith and kin, and also with their home country (see Bhat and Sahoo 2003). Of course, the present day transnational networks differ from the earlier diasporic networks, but there is still a striking balance between the two. In the sense, in diasporic network the immigrants are involve in a two-way process i.e., with the countries of their origin and their present location through 'dwelling' and 'attachment', whereas in the transnational network this reciprocity goes beyond these two-way process, involving two or more nation states along with other diasporic community at the same time. The diasporic and transnational networks are given below in the Figures 1 and 2.

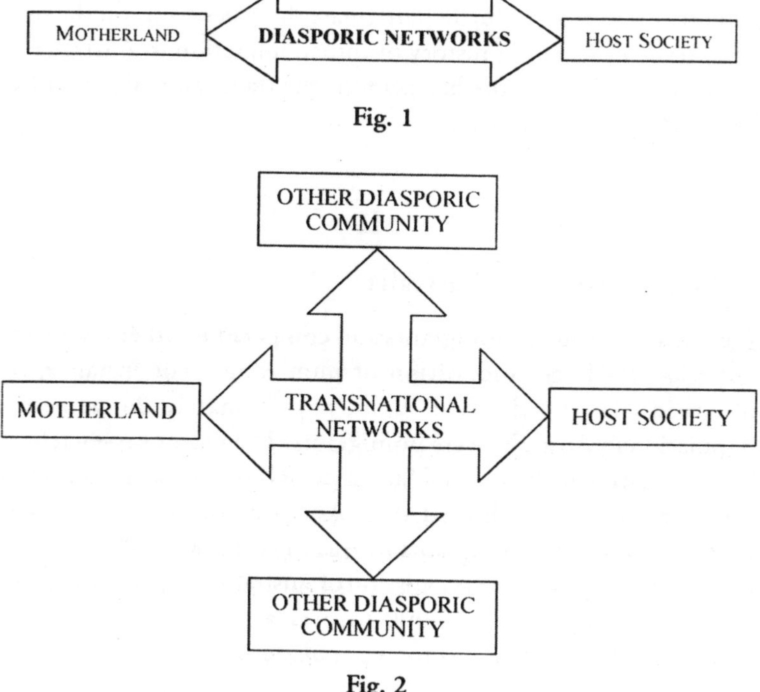

Fig. 1

Fig. 2

Recognising this significance the present study focuses on Indians, as an archetype of transnational communities, unlike Jews, Chinese, Armenians, Mexicans, and Salvadorans in the present context. As the networks between Indian immigrants — permanent, return and temporary[1] — all over the world have today span across the borders and resulted in the formation of global Indian community. The Indians by their cultural, religious and linguistic differences identified as one of the distinctive ethnic groups around the world. They maintain group cohesiveness and build networks in order to capitalise the socio-economic positions in the host society which is manifested in the formation of world associations and organisations such as Global Organisation of People of Indian Origin (GOPIO), World Punjabi Associations (WPA), and World Telugu Federation (WTF) etc. The dynamics and undercurrents of this associations is to create pan Indian identity on the one hand, and mobilise capital, labour and other resources to further articulate these networks on the other. After presenting a brief history of Indian migration to Australia, the following section will further examine the transnational networks of Indian diaspora in Australia.

II

Indian Diaspora in Australia

Australia is a land of immigrants and compared to other countries it has relatively larger proportion of immigrants. For instance, it is observed that, by the year 2000, approximately 24 percent of population in Australia were immigrants. The recent survey released by the Australian Bureau of Statistics (ABS) — Australia's official statistical agency — showed that, Asians constitute an important part among all the immigrants to Australia. Between the year 1981 and 2000 the Asian-born population of Australia remarkable increased from a population of 276,000 to over a million, and now they constitute 6% of Australia's total population.[2]

The Context

The history of Indian emigration to Australia dates back to 19th Century. It was observed from the literatures that, the Indians those who initially entered into Australia were mainly Sikhs and Muslims from the Punjab region in north-western India. Before the development of new transportation and communication technology, most of the Indians migrated to Australia *especially* to run the Camel trains. They were called 'Afghans' in the sense that they kept the communication and supply line open between Melbourne and the Centre of Australia.[3] Between 1860 and 1901, more Indians arrived and engaged in works such as agricultural labourers, hawkers and domestic assistants.

There are three broad waves of migration found in the literatures about the history of Indian migration to Australia. The first wave of migration started during the early part of 20th century when both Australia and India were under the British colonial rule, and most of them were belong to the Sikh community. The Sikhs mainly moved to Australia to work on the banana plantations in Southern Queensland. However, as the immigration of Indians and others Asians started progressing, Australian government implemented various regulations to restrict the entry of these immigrants. The Immigration Act of 1901 restricted the entry of Indians to Australia (see Scott 1968; Lasker 1945), as a result, the Indian population slowly dwindled and remained at around 6,500 to 7,000 until after the end of World War II. This form of migration comes under the category of *old diaspora*.[4] The single largest inflow of Indian immigration to Australia occurred in the 1930s from Jalandhar district of Punjab. They went to work as labourers in the sugar plantations in Woolgoolga — which is half way between Sydney and Brisbane (MEA 2001).

The second wave of migration of Indians started after 1947 when India got independence, and, in this migratory flow large number of British and Anglo Indians[5] joined. The relaxation of the restrictive immigration policy by the Australian authorities in 1966 led to a marked rise in migration to Australia. According to some estimates, the Indian population rose from 7,500 in 1947 to 14,167 in 1961 and to 29,212 in 1971. Further the declaration of the Whitlam Labour Government in 1972 — that Australian immigration policy would be completely free from any discrimination on grounds of race, skin, colour or nationality — resulted in the marked rise in Asia-Pacific immigration (Laxminarayan 1998: 29). This period saw a see change in the nature of the Indian immigrants. Earlier majority of Indians were railway and dockworkers from the Anglo-Indian community, while from the 1970s onward they were largely professionals (MEA 2001).

The third wave of Indian migration to Australia occurred about 25 years ago, after Australia abandoned its Whites policy.[6] When the policy was abolished, many white-collar workers and professionals came to settle in Australia and they mostly originated from Punjab and Gujarat. They use their skills in government services, private enterprises, large corporations, and generally hold white-collar jobs (Helweg 1992). The big influx of Indians began with the revolution in communication technology (IT Boom), where large number of computer software professionals started migrating to Australia from 1976 onwards. This new pattern of migration designated as *new diaspora*[7] for want of a better term. Another great influx of Indians migrated to Australia during this period from the former British, French and other colonies of Africa. After the Africanisation policy[8] in various parts of the African countries, many Indians were prosecuted there, and majority of them went to Australia instead of coming back to India, as Australia and New Zealand during this time were the most favourite countries because they provided refuge to these Indians. Today large numbers of Indians *especially* 'twice migrants'[9] regarded Australia as their homeland. These twice migrants are differ significantly from the earlier Indian immigrants in the sense that, the earlier Indian immigrants who came directly to Australia were basically educated professionals, while the twice migrants on the other hand, were more dynamic and business oriented professionals. Today one can find in every IT shop in Australia a few Indians working there.

The current waves of Indian immigration constituted mostly by engineers, toolmakers, doctors and students. It may be mentioned here that the Gujarati business families from Africa and the second-generation relatives of Indians are also in this flow. A new wave of Indian immigrants started recently which has significant implication for the history of Indian migration to Australia. As a result of the government funding, Australian educational institutions recruited 'full fee paying' overseas students, and, not to surprise, during this time many universities in India had permanent representatives, which helped further to recruit these students from India.[10] In 1998, it was seen that the bright and attentive Indian students replaced the counter staff and chefs at McDonalds and other places. Apart from different socio-economic and religious background of Indian students, there are also thousands of Punjabi-speaking students migrated to Australia from India and Pakistan for higher education. The Punjabi community living in Australia today is the most young and self-supporting community. According to the Australian Bureau of Statistics, 87% of Punjabis residing in Australia are aged below 50 and over 83% of the population are proficient in English.[11]

The High Level Committee on Indian Diaspora constituted by the Ministry of External Affairs, Government of India, surveyed and brought out its report on 2001, which estimated that there are 190,000 Indians living in Australia including 160,000 PIOs. These include about 50,000 PIOs who had arrived in Australia on secondary and tertiary migration from other countries like Fiji[12] (about 40,000); and from Uganda, Kenya, Tanzania, South Africa, the UK, Malaysia, etc. (about 10,000) and 30,000 NRIs who overall constitute 1.02% of the total Australian population of 18,700,000. Western Australia has the highest proportion of the Indian population followed by

Victoria and the Australian Capital Territory, New South Wales, Northern Territory, South Australia, Western Australia and Tasmania (MEA 2001: 277-279).

Transnational Networks

Transnational networks among immigrant communities are not a new phenomenon, as immigrants have always been involved themselves in the affairs of their home countries even in the past. But what is new today is that, it has heightened the intensity and durability of transnational ties. For instance, today the immigrant's are simultaneously involved with socio-cultural and political life of the communities of origin and destination. The transnational networks among Indians can be discernible through the recent developments in communication technology. For example, the transnational TV Channels such as '*Reminiscent Television*', one of the most useful channels for Indians in Australia, has several sub channels to connect Indians across the world. These sub-channels are such as: Lashkara Channel for Punjabi people; Gurjari Channel for Gujarati people; Anjuman Channel an Urdu Channel for Urdu people; Bengla Channel for Bengalis; Asia Channel for all Asians in Australia; CCITV Channel for Tamil people; RAAG Channel especially for South Asians. The transnational networks of Indians in Australia further can be discernible through their involvement in socio-cultural, religious and economic activities.

Social Networks

Aldrich and Zimmer (1989) have provided two models to discuss the social networks of immigrants i.e., *role-set* and *action-set*. The *role-set* depends on the factors like the existence of ethnic immigrant community that have the experience of chain migration, and have wider connection to their homeland and other immigrants. The *action-set* is depending on the formal and informal organisations that the ethnic minority communities have maintained. Advancement in technologies of travel and communication and the process of globalisation has made a profound impact on the social relations of Indians in the contemporary world. In past these kinship networks were maintained through sending remittances, letters and occasional home visits whereas today, it is further strengthened with the development of instant communication networks such as cheaper and faster travel, telephone, telegraph and Internet etc.

Family is the main source through which Indians in diaspora maintain their cultural identity through nurturing ideas and values, and, they also pass on this to their next generations. They create and recreate the identity through practicing food habits, speaking mother tongues in homes, through marriage patterns, celebrating festivals etc.

Indians in Australia maintain their close networks with the homeland through involvement in economic transactions such as sending significant part of their savings back home in the form of remittances in order to invest on real estate, industrial establishment, small business, educational institutions and to contribute towards welfare activities such as charities, old age homes, famine/flood victims and so on.

The basis of any family is marriage and in India it is the most important aspect of cultural symbol. Indians in Australia have remained close-knit and arranged their son/daughter's marriage as much similar as performed in India.[13] During the last few decades as a result of revolution in communication and information technology, it is observed that marriages are performed on a transnational context. For instance, the matrimonial ads on the Internet today have made it easier for searching suitable brides/grooms from different caste, regional, linguistic, religious and ethnic backgrounds. In one of the matrimonial sites in the Internet [www.123-matrimonials.com], which carries the ads of Australian Indians, twice migrants, divorce as well as non-Indians and connect to the global Indians reads as follows:

We are looking for a suitable match for our educated, attractive niece, who is 32 years old. We are Hindu Punjabi Khatris and seeking similar. Our niece is attractive, sophisticated, educated and respectful. She has been brought up in Pune, Maharashtra and has also completed her education in Pune. We have settled in Australia from the past 19 years. We have two daughters, both happily settled in Sydney, NSW. Our daughters have been educated in Australia. Our younger daughter is a doctor (in research) with a hospital in Sydney and the elder is employed in a senior position in the Public Service.

Cultural Networks

Festivals are the cultural symbols of India, which is celebrated among Indians all over the world. It provides Indians the platform to bind them together in a tight-knit community. The Indian communities in Australia celebrate innumerable national, regional, local, and religious festivals. The major festivals of Indians, which is celebrated with much fanfare in Australia, are such as Holi, Diwali, Dasahara, Id, Rakhee, Baisakhi, Bhddha Jayanti etc. Besides these festivals it is observed that Indians also celebrate the 'Ganesh Visarjana' festival with the help of local associations.[14] During these festivities Indians invite their kith and kin settled in different parts of the world to celebrate on a grand manner. As a result of easy and cheaper communication travel they also fly down to India — the homeland to celebrate these festivals with the families back home.

Another significant aspect of cultural assimilation of Indians in Australia is the celebration of 'Independence Day' where Indians [in Melbourne especially, as this is the largest concentration of Indians in Australia] from all parts congregated together. The purpose of organising these cultural programmes is to provide forum to promote different aspects of Indian culture to Australians and other non-Indians. Besides fostering Indian culture, these cultural events further promote solidarity of the diaspora to both Indo-Australians and the wider community.

Like all ethnic groups, Indians in Australia define themselves partly by their cuisine. They remain emotionally attach to the Indian food, cloth, music and language. They wear Indian dresses on important occasions and participate in all Indian cultural events. Further they continue to attach with the homeland through construction of Indian restaurants, spice shops, movie stores, and other such relics in the urban areas wherever a sizeable Indians live.

Religious Networks

Religion has served as the major symbolic resources in building community and professing ethnic identity. Indians in Australia have retained their religious identity what they carried with them during the time of their immigration. Religious groups like Hindus, Sikhs, Christians, Muslims and Buddhist etc., have made success in transplanting their religious traditions and customs in Australia. Often maintenance of religious identity in the host society refers to as ethnicity. Ethnicity is the cultural characteristics that connect a particular group or groups of people to each other.[15] Hindus for instance, have made tremendous effort to construct and reconstruct their ethnic identity through building large temples across Australia.[16] There are hundreds of Hindu temples can be found in Australia especially in major metropolitan areas likes Melbourne, Canberra, Sydney NSW, Queensland and Perth, which have wider networks with their counterparts not only in Australia but also with other temples in different parts of the world.

Often religious organisations plays important role in retaining the ethnic identity among immigrants, while binding them through caste, creed and regional affiliations. For instance, the establishment of *Hindu Heritage Society* (HHS) in Australia during 1998 has provided platform for Hindus of different castes, creeds, regions and individual beliefs to share their ideas and practices. During the initial stage of establishment, the HHS was known as Kalaa Mandir. Today the HHS organized several unique cultural, religious and educational programs besides making charitable contributions in India and abroad. The HHS is also the member of FAIA (Federation of Australian Indian Associations).[17]

Another feature of religious practice of Indians aboard is their faith in Gurus/spiritual teachers.[18] During the last few decades it is observed that several spiritual leaders/gurus have made their presence in Australia. The important spiritual leaders who have extended their spiritual teachings across Australia through establishment of Centres/ Mandirs are such as Swaminarayan, Sathya Sai Baba, Mata Amritanandamayi, Sachidananda Swami, Meher Baba, Swami Murugananda Saraswati, Maharishi Mahesh Yogi, Maheshyogi, Swami Prabhupada (ISKON), Swami Chinmayananada (Chinmaya Mission), Swami Ranganamananda (Ramakrishna Mission), Leaders of Arya Samaj and VHP, and OSHO (Rajneesh). They have made it possible further to maintain transnational networks among Indians across the world through the arrangement of seminars, discourses, symposia, workshops and charitable works.

Communication Networks

Information and communication technology plays important role in connecting and bridging the gap between communities staying across the world. It is the most crucial mode of transnational network to promote linkages and sharing information between homeland and the diaspora communities. The diasporic community engages in on-line services like the Internet, Usenet, and the World Wide Web to interact or communicate with their friends and relatives world over. For instance, the ethnic Indian radio channels in Australia, which provides information to Indians, are such as: SBS Radio — provides

Hindi and Punjabi programmes; Radio 2000 — provides information specifically for Punjabi communities. Besides these two there are other channels such as Radio Preetlari, Radio Satrang and Radio Darpan have also provides popular programmes to the Indian communities in Australia.

As a result of the revolution in transportation and communication technology, it is now easier for Indians to know the daily affairs happening at both the ends. The best collections of Indian newspapers and magazines, which have circulated among Indians in Australia and reaches to all Indians settled in different parts of the world are such as: Business Line — the first Indian business newspaper available in Australia; Goa Herald Newspaper — the paper includes the news and views about Goa; India Abroad — the weekly Indian newspaper featuring news, politics, economics and matrimonial classifieds. Similarly, there are several ethnic Indian newspapers which have dominant in Australia are such as: The Indian Down Under, The Indian Post, India Voice, The Indian Link, Bharat Times, Bharatiys Samachar, The Indian Observer etc.

Indians abroad have formed associations, which reflect their diversities in religious, regional, linguistic, and caste affiliations (Bhat 1992: 210). There are several associations/organisations found in Australia which have inter-linked with other associations in Australia simultaneously links with the global associations in the world. These associations organise seminars, workshops, and cultural programmes at different periods of time (especially on special occasions) to engage Indians in Australia and other parts of the world.[19]

Conclusion

Given the opportunity of Australia's National Policy on Multiculturalism,[20] Indians have successfully retains their cultural identity and simultaneously maintains transnational networks with their kith and kin around the world. They have successful in venturing out every field of profession, business and politics. Today, Indians in Australia are well known and respected in the Australian Cyber world. They compete and excel with the Australian national levels of income, education and employment. As Jupp (1988 in Faria, 2001: 143) points out, the multicultural policy of Australia are culturally relativist to some degree in that, they favour the dominant strand. He also states that, the core of Australian life and institutions remain essentially British. With the ethnic minorities remaining small and peripheral, there is little public policy that can contribute to fostering the maintenance of ethnicity, even though it might acknowledge the existence of minority cultures.

REFERENCE

1. Permanent migrants are those who migrated during 19th and early 20th century as indentured labour, whereas return migrants who went after independence especially during 1960's and 70's as professionals' skilled labourers [also called new migrants] and the temporary migrants include students and business personnel etc.
2. According to 2001 census, there are 19,485,300 people living in Australia. Of the 22% of the population born overseas, 11.2% were born in Europe, while 5.2% were born in Asia. See more detail about the statistics of Australia from the Australian Bureau of Statistics, Australian Social Trends 2001, Population Composition: Asian-born Australians: http://www.abs.gov.au
3. See the arrival of Indians to Australia: http://www.sikh.com.au
4. Old diaspora refers to migration of Indians during the indentured period between the end of the 18th century and the beginning of the 19th century to various British, French and Dutch colonies as plantation and coolie labourers.
5. The term Anglo-Indian is defined by the Indian constitution as follows: "An Anglo-Indian means a person whose father or any of whose other male progenitors in the male line is or was of European descent but who is domiciled within the territory of India and is or was born within such territory of parents habitually resident therein and not established there for temporary purposes only" (The Constitution of India, paragraph 366). There is a sizeable Anglo-Indian community in Australia. Although their largest settlement is in Perth, their numbers are significant in Sydney and Melbourne. Today, they are still counted as 'Indian Nationals' in the Australian Census.

6. The White Australia Policy, embedded in the *Immigration (Restriction) Act 1901*, remained a guiding principle of Australian immigration until its gradual abolition between 1966 and 1973.
7. A distinction between the 'Old' and 'New' Indian Diaspora in Australia as Helweg points out can be categorized under several grounds such as migration process, resident patterns, relations with the wider Australian society, concept of identity, social networks, political behaviour, economic processes, and the situation of the second generation (See Helweg, 1992).
8. Africanisation Policy was regulated during the 1950's and 60's where Indians in particular and other migrants in general was abandoned to settle in these countries and they are bound to leave these countries.
9. See Parminder Bhachu. 1985. *Twice Migrants*. London: Tavsitock Publication.
10. It is estimated that Canberra University recruiting about 500 students every year. Many regional universities such as University of Ballarratt have opened campus in Sydney to cater to these foreign students.
11. See http://www.sikh.com.au
12. Today there is a large Fiji Indian population in Australia who call Australia there home. These Fiji Indians have changed the face of Indian Australia. While earlier Indian migration was that of educated professionals, these new Fiji Indians were more dynamic and business going. Their arrival has increased the services enjoyed by all Indians (http://www.sikh.com.au/).
13. About the attitude of Indian immigrants towards Marriage, sex roles and traditions see (Callan, 1983).
14. he 'Ganesh Visarjana' festival is regarded as the biggest festival in Australia among Indians. Over 5,000 Indians attended it every year and one can find there are food stalls, shops, and cultural displays from all states in India available at that time. It is true that the religious rituals are also observed in these festivals. For example, last year over thirty cultural, spiritual and religious organisations gathered together in order to celebrate the Ganesh Visarjan.
15. Ethnicity is also sometimes used as a euphemism for race, or as a synonym for minority group. While ethnicity and race are related concepts, the concept of ethnicity is rooted in the idea of societal groups, marked by shared nationality, tribal affiliation, whereas race is rooted in the idea of biological classification of homo sapiens to subspecies according to morphological features such as skin color or facial characteristics.
16. Sri Mandir is considered as the first Hindu temple in Australia, which is situated at Auburn in Sydney. The temple was established during the year 1977, and it has the distinction of being the oldest Hindu temple in Australia. The main objective of Sri Mandir is to promote the Hindu culture and philosophy to the wider Indian community simultaneously to the non-Indians in Australia.
17. See the detail objectives and activities of HHS from the following sites <www.hinduheritage.org.au>

18. A guru is a Hindu religious teacher. It is based on a long line of Hindu philosophical understandings of the importance of knowledge and that the teacher, guru, is the sacred conduit to self-realization. Till today in India and among people of Hindu or Sikh persuasion, the title retains its significant hallowed space (Wikipedia Encycloperdia 2004).
19. See the list of Indian associations in Australia: http://www.indiaoz.com.au/Associations/index.php
20. The multicultural policy of Australia was first extensively implemented by Prime Minister Malcolm Fraser's Liberal National Country Party coalition government of 1976-1983.

SUGGESTED READINGS

Aldrich, H.E., & Zimmer, C. (1986), "Entrepreneurship through Social Networks", in D. L. Sexton & R.W. Smilor (eds.) *The Art and Science of Entrepreneurship*. Chicago: Upstart, pp. 3-20.

Basch, L., Glick Schiller, N. and Szanton Blanc, C. (1994), Nations Unbound: Transitional Projects, Postcolonial Predicaments and Deterritorialised Nation-States. Basel: Gordon & Breach.

Bhat, C.S. (1992), "Indian Ethnic Associations in London: Search for Unity in Diversity", in C.S. Bhat *et al.*, (eds.) *Sociology of Development and Change*. New Delhi: Orient Longman, pp. 210-228.

Bhat, C.S., and Sahoo, A.K. (2003), "Diaspora to Transnational Networks: The Case of Indians in Canada", in Sushma J. Verma and Radhika Seshan (eds.), *Fractured Identity: The Indian Diaspora in Canada*. New Delhi: Rawat Publication, pp. 141-167.

Bhat, C.S. (2003), "India and the Indian Diaspora: A Policy Issues", in Ajay Dubey (ed.), *Indian Diaspora: Global Perspective*. Kalinga Publication: New Delhi, pp.11-24.

Callan, Victor J. (1983), "The attitude of Indian Immigrants in Australia to Marriage, Sex Roles and Traditions", in George Kurian and Ram P. Srivastava (eds.), *Overseas Indians: A Study in Adaptation*. New Delhi: Vikas Publishing House, pp. 294-306.

Faria, Ana Ivete. (2001), "The future of Indian ethnicity in Australia – An educational and cultural perspective", *International Education Journal*, Vol. 2 (4), pp. 134-143.

Foner, Nancy. (1997), "What's New About Transnationalism? New York Immigrants Today and Turn of the Century", *Diaspora: A Journal of Transitional Studies*, Vol. 6 (3).

Guarnizo, Luis E. (1996), The Rise of Transitional Social Formations: Mexico and the Dominican Republic. Unpublished paper.

Helweg, Arthur. (1992), "Indians in Australia: Theory and Methodology of the New Immigration", in Mahin Gosine (ed.), *The Coolie Connection.* New York: Windsor Press, pp.41-64.

Jupp, J. (1988), The Australian People: An Encyclopaedia of the Nation, Its people and their Origins. Sydney: Angus and Robertson.

Lasker, Bruno. (1945), Asian on the Move: Population Pressure, Migration, and Resettlement in Eastern Asia under the influence of want and war. New York: Henry Holt and Company.

Laxminarayan, K. (1998), "Indian Diaspora: A Demographic Perspective". Occasional Paper No-3, Centre for the Study of Indian Diaspora: University of Hyderabad.

Ministry of External Affairs (MEA). (2001), Report of the High Level Committee on Indian Diaspora. New Delhi: Indian Council of World Affairs.

Portes, Alejandro. (1997), "Immigration theory for a new century: Some problems and opportunities", *International Migration Review,* 31: 799-825.

Schnapper, Dominique. (1999), "From Nation States to the Transitional World: On the Meaning and Usefulness of Diaspora as a Concept", *Diaspora: A Journal of Transnational Studies,* 8 (3): 225-54.

Scott, Franklin D. (ed.) (1968), World Migration in Modern Times. New Jersey: Prentice Hall, Inc.

The Constitution of India. (1958), Paragraph 366, New Delhi: Government of India Press.

Vertovec, S., and Robin Cohen. (eds.) (1999), Migration, Diasporas and Transnationalism. Cheltenham: U.K.: Edward Elgar Publishing Ltd.

Wahlbeck, Osten. (1998), Transnationalism and Diasporas: The Kurdish Example. Paper presented at the International Sociological Association XIV World Congress of Sociology, July 26 - August 1, Montreal: Canada.

Wikipedia Encyclopedia. (2004), Guru and its Definitions. See Web Page <http://en.wikipedia.org/wiki/Guru> [viewed as on 1st September 2004].

14

Security Concerns and Refugees in South Asia

Ms. Yachana

Poverty, famine, civil war and ecological imbalance have contributed to the continuous increase in the number of refugees in the world. Among these the refugees in the Asian and the African continents far surpass the others. Even in the Asian continent the countries, lying in the Indian subcontinent, present a very grim picture of the problem of refugees. Continuous increase in the number of refugees in the subcontinent is bound to cause economic, social and political conflicts; and further it may create such conflicts as would endanger the very existence of this region. We must keep in mind Norman Mayairs' for warning that "Till to-day the refugees are being deemed as superficial means to say an aberration in a general system but soon they may become an important section of the society in global system."

Behind the refugee problem in South Asia lie the inter-state conflicts occurring among the countries of this region. In South Asian region there exists a situation of continuous racial conflict, religious fanaticism and armed hostility for many decades. The refugee problem of South Asian region is the consequence of these conflicts. The refugee problem of South Asian region has its own unique sociology. One would find inter-relationship between refugee problem of South

Asian region and its causative factors like internal conflict, under development, ecological imbalance and feeling of insecurity. In order to comprehend these inter-relationships, it is of imperative necessity to understand those social and political conditions which lie at the very root of these conflicts and are the causes of prevalent insecurity.

The increasing burden of refugees on the countries of South Asian region would not only lead to social, political and economic instability but destroy ecological balance also which would endanger the very existence of this continent because ecological imbalance does not remain confined to displacement of population: it far extends to it and creates new tensions among the states of this region.

Sense of insecurity is the cause that lies behind the refugee problem. Therefore, it would be wise to understand those conflicts which exists in this region and to investigate why these conflicts exist, why does there exist such contradictions in inter-state relations of this region? Why a regional out look is not, evolving? What is the form of various conflicts of the region? All these questions are the aspects of sociological investigation to explain the social fabric of this region. What political structures this region has inherited, how have they evolved'. For comprehending the refugee problem fully the study of social and political structures of South Asian countries is indispensable. With this study we would be able to answer who the refugees are, how are they! What is the form of refugee problem have? What is its nature? Which factors are responsible for refugee problem in this region? How the big number of refugees is influencing this region? What can be the sociological suggestions to understand and solve the refugee problem?

South Asia has its own socio-political structure. There have been specific and diverse trends of social and political development of this sub-continent. The social structure of this sub-continent has been textured with uniqueness. The society here is formed of different religions, races and communities. It is the most densely populated area of the world and equally backward and poor. Social diversity, poverty and under development are the causes of conflicts in this region. There is. strong contradiction in inter-state relations of this region. The roots of this contradiction lie in those historical social, political and economic conflicts which existed in the region from the very beginning. All the states of this region had been under the colonial rule and their mutual conflicts and differences have been the legacy of ideological garbage of those colonial powers who had sown the seeds of divide and rule policy in this region. The mind set so inherited is the greatest impediment in evolving a regional approach in this area. So far the questions of conflicts arising in South Asia is concerned, most of them are internal and the reason behind these conflicts is the existence of inherited social and political systems which could be understood by explaining the long historical process of these systems. What is the structure of the socio political system which South Asia has inherited? How have they evolved? These questions have to enquired upon to understand the problems of this region. It is of imperative necessity to comprehend the social structure and its texture before any study of this reason. There are three major religions have and seven countries India, Pakistan, Bangladesh, Nepal, Bhutan, Sri Lanka and Maldives located in this, subcontinent. Among these countries Bhutan and Sri Lanka have Buddhists in majority (about 70 percent), India and Nepal have Hindu religion in Majority (82 and 90 percent respectively), Pakistan, Bangladesh and Maldives have Muslims in majority (97, 86 and 100 percent respectively). (Oommen) Thus this region has three major religions. Owing to the diversity of races, tribes and lingual multiplicity I this region is proving to be the breeding ground of conflicts. It has always been the battle ground of racial violence and religious fanaticism of course, the diverse social structure is responsible for social conflicts but the political structure of this region has been for more responsible than the social one. Political development of the region has hither to, been the development of democratic system but it has never been uniform and neither has if been free from the attack of opposite forces. Religion always has been the most influential factor in socio political life of the people of this region, irrespective of the presence of secular groups.

Racial violence, religious fanaticism, separatist activities an have their roots in the history of this region. The present refugee problem also emanates from this perspective. The colonial powers not only exploited the resources of this region but destroyed the social harmony also. All the problems of this region are the creations of the colonial powers. Piling of dangerous arms in this region is again the result of colonial policy which is intending to transform this region into the land of homeless refugees. Even after so many decades of political independence there has been little change in politic economic structure of this region — In spite of the end of cold war and beginning of the process of globalisation, scarcity, hunger, famine and poverty remain which confront us to day in the form of Refugee Problem.

To understand the refugee problem in South Asia it would be necessary to distinguish between the refugee problem of this region and that of the world at large. Who are the refugees in world context, what is their condition and what are the national and international concepts in reference to refugees? Who according to UNHCR are refugees? And how far the refugees of South Asia related to this concept? For the first time In 1969 'Africa Unity Convention' defined the term refugee. According to it, "Any person who takes refuge in a foreign country due to subjugation of his homeland, foreign rule or due to complete break down of public peace and order is a refugee."

Can this definition cover all types of refugees? If South Asian refugees are measured with this definition, their number will be negligible because here communities are farced to be refugees due to internal turmoil. The majority of refugees in South Asia are due to environmental factors which the definition does not mention at all. Today the majority of refugees is constituted of those who can not be covered under such standards, concepts or definitions but are forced to lead an inhuman life. In the last decade the number of unidentified refugees has increased. Environmentalist Alther Vosting opened that as much as the number of refugees is so much is the number of environmental refugees. According to experts the number of unidentified refugees is more than that of identified refugees in the world. Those who are refugees with in their own national boundaries due to hunger, poverty, indebtedness and ecological imbalance are quite big in number in South Asia. If an in-depth study of refugee problem is carried out, the refugees would appear to be of many categories e.g., Internal refugee, Economic refugee and Environmental refugee. It has been discovered by the studies of refugee problem that the root cause of this problem is, unmistakably the sense of insecurity. It can be social, religious, political economic or environmental factors. Here environmental refugees are big in number. The cause of this problem is ecological imbalance which is the consequence of destruction, soil erosion, water and air pollution destruction of organic species, destruction of ocean resources and natural calamities.

The word 'Environmental Refugee' was used for the first time by Hinnave' In the UNEP report. According to him, "The environmental refugees are those who were forced to leave their traditional habitat temporarily or permanently and whose existence and quality of life got disturbed due to this destruction. Its cause may lie in environment or on the people living there."

According to data available from the UN office only 15 million refugees are registered with the office of UNHCR while there exist 35 million refugees in the world. The number of unidentified refugees far exceeds this number. In South Asia million of refugees are compelled to live under the open sky and bare earth. Very recently, on the occasion of World Refugee Day, an official of the UNHCR said that there is need for enacting a law for refugees on national and international level and equally was the need to frame a comprehensive policy to create a balance between Humane assistance and national interests. The fresh UNHCR data reveals that till the last of December 2000 nearly 35 million refugees have been covered under UNHCR.

Refugee problem in South Asia is becoming grim day by day. Ecological balance is being disturbed whid1 certainly would increase the number of environmental refugees in near future. L' Clarke writes In his book (Internal Refugee' that "It Is replete with many Instances where the capacity of life support systems has decreased to the level of complete break down. Where these channels have broken down people have no option except to lead a life of scarcity or run away from their roots." The swelling crowed of refugees in South Asia might create many dangers in this region and its consequence to India might be even more alarming as it has large size and better socio-economic conditions to attract these refugees. Only balanced economic development can bridle the refugee problem in South Asia. A regional approach to the economic development is of imperative necessity. To-day, India has become a haven for millions of Tibetan, Sri Lanka, Afghani, Bangladeshi, Nepali, Bhutanese and Burmese refugees. Environmental degradation has further accentuated this problem. Internal dissentions, conflicts and violence in India's neighbouring countries have direct affected India. Therefore, refugee problem in South Asia has direct leaning on India.

The form of refugee problem that exists in South Asia can explain, to a greater extent, the nature of the problem and its uniqueness vis-à-vis the world problem. The studies conducted to investigate the refugee problem establish that sense of insecurity has been the principal reason behind this problem. The sense of insecurity may be different in different locales and its nature may also vary from state to state. In South Asia as sum, the feeling of insecurity is the, consequence of internal factors as this region is the most fertile ground internal conflicts. In order to overcame the feeling of insecurity, the South Asian states adopted those alternatives which have proved ineffective and dangerous as militarisation and armament, to over come feeling of insecurity I resulted in stockpiling of arms in this region which have further aggravated the already grim situation. *Secondly*, the states of this region have made unsuccessful efforts to strengthen themselves by coercion and terror. *Thirdly*, some states have used the strategy of attention diversion which implies engaging external dangers to divert them from internal problems. South Asia, to-day faces many problems. Many possible invasions have kept it engaged. Political leadership and policy division/transfer has continuously initialed the structural weaknesses of the state system of this region. *Secondly*, there exist those flash points which sprout from minimal national integration, state building problems. *Thirdly*, difference between economic backwardness and regional development creates such flash points. The regional-development in this region is not uniform. Half of the population lives in object poverty which, undoubtedly, is the destabilizing factor in politics of this area. Historical experiences prove that social and political expectations of poor and backward masses make the state aggressive and coercive against political opposition and revolt. Poverty and economic backwardness has given rise to religious fanaticism, alienation and racial violence, Civil war in Sri Lanka, Separatist movements in Kashmir and North Eastern States of India, demand for free Baluchistan and Sindh Pradesh in Pakistan, Chakma revolt in Bangladesh and terrorism in Nepal and Bhutan are deeply rooted in economic backwardness. Such a situation creates a feeling of insecurity and produces refugees. Further, the disturbed environmental balance (ecological balance) is move alarming. It is made worse by soil erosion, deforestation, water, soil and air pollution and global warming. Ecological imbalance may prove to be more alarming to this region as its economy is totally based on agriculture. Therefore, the refugee problem of this region is as much as political and economic as it is ecological.

Like the geographical diversity of this region the refugee problem is also unique. While on one side of this region small states like Bhutan, Maldives and Sri Lanka exist, on the other side we would find in India an enormous country with better socio-political conditions apt to attract the refugees from other states. Though most of the conflicts in South Asian countries are internal but the number of environmental refugees is not less. The refugee from smaller states like Nepal, Bangladesh, Sri Lanka, Myamar, Tibet, Afghanistan tend to migrate into India. The nature of refugee problem in this region is peculiar. In Sri Lanka it is the consequence of racial violence, in Bangladesh it is the Bihari Muslims who wish to migrate to Pakistan but are not allowed and have become refugee in their own homeland. In India and Nepal the problem of Tibetan refugees is more complex as the UNHCR report mentions that there exists no hope or them to return to their homeland. The number of Bihari Muslims in Bangladesh has reached more then a million who are living in 66 refugee camp set with the assistance of the Red Cross in inhuman conditions. The same is the condition of Bangladeshi refugees settled in Bihar. To-day, they are being evicted from their settlements, and sometimes persecuted and murdered.

The atmosphere of continuous tension in South Asian States would never allow normalisations of civic life. Unless, exodus, immigration, tension and Violence are curbed the refugee problem can not be solved and since the sense of insecurity prevails in these societies conflicts can not be resolved.

South Asian region has always been in flux. May be, the external aggressions had been less in number but internal dissentions have been the order of the day. So far the refugee problem of this region is concerned, it as already has been said, is due to socio political conflicts and ecological conflicts. According to immigration specialist Saniay Hajarika, "From 1851 to 1981 about 6 million people became immigrants and the number is even on the increase. Construction of dams, mines, factories, sanctuaries, road, railway tracks and other development projects have forced the people to migrate."

South Asia presents a spectacle of geographical economic and political diversities. Geographical and ecological conditions, unequal resources, unequal regional development, lingual and religious diversities have generated conflicts. The South Asian countries are diverse in size and type. While India comprises of 73.2 percent of the total area the smaller states have only 26.8 percentage of the area obviously, the geo-political, social and economic structure of this region has been solely responsible for minor and major conflicts.

The factors that have caused social and political turmoil in this region on mostly internal as Ram S. Melkote observed. "*Political processes in this region are again an way to tribalisation. The forces like racial, religions and cultural have again challenged the dormant social forces and are demanding the restructuring of social and political institutions.*" Behind the political conflicts in this sub-continent mutual suspicions are the main cause. The smaller states of this region fear that India may impose its preponderance and India equally fears that its smaller neighbours may form a group opposed to its interests by entering into political alignment with some external super power. There is absence of mutual confidence in this region. Social and political conditions in this region are fast changing and in political instability, social and economic turmoil the conflicts are be coming more pronounced. Violent "Struggles have increased and environmental balance is disturbed. Consequently, sense of insecurity has increased many fold which has further aggravated refugee problem. Environmental imbalance may blacken the future of this region as Prof. Shaukat Hasan has said, "*The demand on natural environment would determine whether the South Asian region is worth living or not This would give form to the security concerns of these societies.*" Therefore, it is obvious that the environmental factors are more responsible for the refugee problem in this reason than social and political factors.

According to a comment of the UNICEF. "Among the poor in the twenty first century women and children far exceed in numbers than the male members, Even among those dying in war, women and children are in majority. War and environmental degradation have rendered 40 million people homeless and among these most are women and children. In the last decade in the war ravaged areas women and children have been systematically raped and every year 2 million girls of 5 to 15 year of age group have been forced into prostitution."

Continuous increase in the number of refugees in the world has created an international problem; especially, to the developing nations it has become a I curse which are already grappling with their domestic problems. The large number of refugees is a big burden to the developing nations because their economic structure is two profile to bear this burden. The refugees need food, water and land. This has disbalanced the environment. The multitude of refugees interferes in the employment market, as a result labour becomes cheap and unemployment increases. Their demand for basic utility items leads to price rise which induces communal tensions, suicides, crimes etc. Extra demand on energy, water, medicine, food etc breads down the domestic structure and destroys social fabric. It causes many social and political problem and leads to social disintegration. A study conducted in India reveals that the Bangladeshi infiltrators determine the results of 52 assemble seats in West Bengal and effectively influence another 100 Assembly segments in elections. According to the report of a work group of Home Ministry on border management in 2000, there are nearly 15 million Bangladeshi infiltrators in India and their number increase by three lakhs every year. These infiltrators are destroying the social fabric of Assam, West Bengal, Tripura and North Eastern states. This is a dangerous development to the security of the state. These infiltrators have disturbed the social balance in many states. In Tripura, their infiltration has reduced the Tripurans into minority. This trend has been responsible for the emergence of the separatist terrorist groups in these states. In North Eastern states these infiltrators have established a firm grip on political system which is obviously, an ominous signal to the security of the nation. If the infiltration continues unabated the aborigines would be reduced to minority and their cultural heritage will be destroyed. It may deprive them of political power, employment and means of livelihood etc. Behind these silent invasions lies the refugee problem which needs an early solutions. India suffers most in South Asian region.

Observations and investigations of South Asia's refugee problem explains its sociology and extends some sociological suggestions for its solutions. Like endless problems of the world this problem too demands some tough measures as the problem is not superficial. The study of refugee problem at world level is very new. As the problem exists in South Asia, it needs to investigate the multiple factors sociologically. It needs to identify those factors which have turned this regions into a conflict Zone. Only then we would be able to recognize some theoretical and practical aspects. It requires to develop a regional approach. Most of the conflicts in this region spring from communal conflicts. Therefore, while investigating racial-national conflicts, two things have to be dept in mind. *First*, the state, here, has failed in adjusting the forces related with races and communities. *Second*, politicisation of communal nationalism, religions fundamentalism and basic loyalties has reemerged.

Behind the conflicts in South Asia region lies the under developments. I Therefore, the challenge is to bong this region in the world main stream. Equally challenging is to bring the neo social groups in the national main stream. It is of imperative necessity that the old conservative institutional frame work has to be replaced with new and dynamic system and a proper understanding of the political aspirations of the social groups should be there. Equally necessary is to strengthen democratic processes, include racial and social group in national decisions, adjustment between the interests of racial groups and the nation, and evolving a regional approad1. The challenge before the region is how to accommodate racial aspirations. Without disturbing or destroying the existing regional systems. Only in this equilibrium, the solutions of refugee problem can be perceived because there is dose inter-relationship between racial conflicts poverty and refugee problem.

A political leadership with strong will power and broad out look is necessary to face this grave challenge. The leadership must be capable of adopting regional approach, Is the political machinery ready to go beyond the security concern? Is the political leadership of this region ready to adopt abroad out look respecting the racial feelings of the social groups? Is the social leadership ready to accept new social commitments to create more democratic environment with the support of social groups, labour arid capital? These are the important questions which need to be answered before any steps is taken to resolve refugee problem. The South Asian leadership needs an extensive exercise at non-political level and a sincere effort at political level. Only then an agenda with regional out look and inter-regional aspirations can be prepared.

A linkage between individual and individual facilitated and prepared by coordination among education, health, regional tourism and business groups in this region is a decisive factor for regional cooperation and approach. International tourism is as important as other factors for economic growth of the region. Such non-political and constructive approach lessens dead locks. Therefore, a regional problems like degradation of resources, disturbed ecological balance, backward economy, insecurity, poverty and impoverishment. To-day the solutions of South Asian refugee problem lies in the resolutions of these challenges. For this, it is expected from the organisation like SAARC that they would prepare and encourage governmental and non governmental leadership to think seriously on these issues. Educationists, researchers, voluntary organisations and communication media must prepare an atmosphere of regional thinking and approach only then the grave problem like refugee problem would be resolved.

REFERENCES

Black, Richard 2001, *Fifty Years of Refueee Studies*, International Migration Review, Vol. XXXV No. 1, New York.

Chengappa, Raj 2001, *Kabul ki Aur Kooch*. Indian Today, Oct. 2001.

Clark, L. 1988, Internal Refugee. The Hidden Half in the U.S. Committee for Refugee, World Refugee Survey, Washington.

Crips. J: 1990, Human Rights and Refugee, Refugee, Nov. 1990.

Datta, Shyamlal 2001, Mismanaging Migrations. The Sunday Statesman 2 Oct 2001.

El-Hinnavi, E. 1985, Environmental Refugee. U.N.E.P, Nairobi Report.

Good-Gill, Guy S. 2001, Refugees Challenges to Protection, International Migration Review, Vol. XXXV, No. 1.

Hajarika, S. 1993, Bangladesh and Assam: Land Pressures, Migration and Ethnic Conflict. A Research Paper.

Khobung, Lal T.: 2001, Geography and Politics of Refugee in South Asia, Thesis, School of International Studies, J.N.U., New Delhi.

Kiravela, Gamini 1996, Political Structure of Regional Cooperation and Conflict in Post cold war South Asia. A Research Paper present in a workshop, Organized by "Society for Peace and Security Development Studies".

Lama, M.P. 2002, The Afghan Refugee. The Hindu, 5 Feb., 2002.

Mayars, N. 1986, Environmental Dimensions to Security issues. Environmentalist Vol. 6, 1986.

Namboth, Suresh 2002, Their Homeland, The Hindu, 17 March, 2002

Oommen, T.K. 2002, New Direction for South Asia. The Hindu 4 Feb. 2002.

Ram S. Melkote 1993, Reconceptualising Peace in Indian Ocean. A Research Paper in Seminar at the university of Hyderabad.

Ray, Shantanu 2001, Coming Home to Banishment Outlook, Dec. 2001.

SAARCLAW 1997, Seminar Report on Refugee: SAARC Region Building a Legal Framework, 2 and 3 May, 1997.

Sharma Nilotpal 2002, Migration and its Impact on Society, Employment News, 25-31 May, 2001.

Shaukat, Hasan 1991, Environmental Issues and Security in South Asia. A Research Paper.

Shashidhar 2001, yisv Ki Anthin Sharnarthee Samasya. Dainik Hindustan, 28 July, 2001.

Tomar, Alok 1999, Sharnarthio Ka Samajshartra. Dainik Jagran, 1 Oct, 1999.

Index